ESSAYS

IN

ENGLISH LITERATURE

1780–1860

ESSAYS

IN

ENGLISH LITERATURE

1780—1860

BY

GEORGE SAINTSBURY

First Series

Essay Index Reprint Series

BOOKS FOR LIBRARIES PRESS

FREEPORT, NEW YORK

First Published 1891
Reprinted 1972

Library of Congress Cataloging in Publication Data

Saintsbury, George Edward Bateman, 1845-1933.
Essays in English literature, 1780-1860.

(Essay index reprint series)
Reprint of the 1891 ed.
1. English literature--18th century--Addresses, essays, lectures. 2. English literature--19th century--Addresses, essays, lectures. I. Title.
PR453.S3 1972b 820'.9 72-5800
ISBN 0-8369-7292-9

PRINTED IN THE UNITED STATES OF AMERICA

CONTENTS

INTRODUCTION

THE KINDS OF CRITICISM

THE KINDS OF CRITICISM.

It is probably unnecessary, and might possibly be impertinent, to renew here at any length the old debate between reviewers as reviewers, and reviewers as authors—the debate whether the reissue of work contributed to periodicals is desirable or not. The plea that half the best prose literature of this century would be inaccessible if the practice had been forbidden, and the retort that anything which can pretend to keep company with the best literature of the century will be readily relieved from the objection, at once sum up the whole quarrel, and leave it undecided. For my own part, I think that there is a sufficient connection of subject in the following chapters, and I hope that there is a sufficient uniformity of treatment. The former point, as the least important, may be dismissed first. All the literature here discussed is—with the exception of Crabbe's earliest poems, and the late aftermath of Peacock and Borrow—work of one and the same period, the first half of the present century. The authors criticised were all contemporaries ; with only one exception, if with one, they were all writing more or less busily within a single decade, that of 1820 to 1830. And they possess the further connection (which has at least the reality of having been present to my mind in selecting them), that while every one of them was a man of great literary power, hardly one has been by general consent, or except by private crotchet would be, put among the very greatest. They stand not far below, but distinctly below, Scott, Byron, Wordsworth, Shelley, Coleridge, and Keats. Yet again, they agree in the fact that hardly one of them has yet been securely set in the literary niche which is his due, all having been at some time either unduly valued or unduly neglected, and one or two never having yet received even due appreciation. The greatest of all critics was accused, unjustly, of having a certain dislike of clear, undoubted supremacy. It would be far more fair to say that Sainte-Beuve had eminently, what perhaps all critics who are not mere carpers on the one hand, or mere splashers of superlatives on the other, have more or less—an affection for subjects possessing but qualified merit, and so giving to criticism a certain additional interest in the task of placing and appraising them.

THE KINDS OF CRITICISM.

This last sentence may not meet with universal assent, but it will bring me conveniently to the second part of my subject. I should not have republished these essays if I had not thought that, whatever may be their faults (and a man who does not see the faults of his own writing on revising it a second time for the press after an interval, must be either a great genius or an intolerable fool), they possess a certain unity of critical method. Nor should I have republished them if it had seemed to me that this method was exactly identical with that of any other critic of the present day in England. I have at least endeavoured to wear my rue with a difference, and that not merely for the sake of differing.

THE KINDS OF CRITICISM.

Mr. Goldwin Smith, whose work is not likely to be impeached for defect either in form or in substance, wrote but a few months ago, in melancholy mood, that the province of criticism appeared to be now limited to the saying of fine things. I agree with him that this is one vicious extreme of the popular conception of the art; but in order to define correctly, we cannot be contented with one only. The other, as it seems to me, is fixed by the notion, now warmly championed by some younger critics both at home and abroad, that criticism must be of all things "scientific." For my own part, I have gravely and strenuously endeavoured to ascertain from the writings both of foreign critics (the chief of whom was the late M. Hennequin in France), and of their disciples at home, what "scientific" criticism means. In no case have

I been able to obtain any clear conception of its connotation in the mouths or minds of those who use the phrase. The new heaven and the new earth which they promise are no doubt to be very different from our own old earth and heaven; of that they are sure, and their sureness does not fail to make itself plain. But what the flora and fauna, the biology and geology of the new heaven and earth are to be, I have never succeeded in ascertaining. The country would appear to be like that Land of Ignorance which, as Lord Brooke says, "none can describe until he be past it." Only I have perceived that when this "scientific" criticism sticks closest to its own formulas and ways, it appears to me to be very bad criticism; and that when, as sometimes happens, it is good criticism, its ways and formulas are not perceptibly distinguishable from those of criticism which is not "scientific." For the rest, it is all but demonstrable that "scientific" literary criticism is impossible, unless the word "scientific" is to have its meaning very illegitimately altered. For the essential qualities of literature, as of all art, are communicated by the individual, they depend upon idiosyncrasy: and this makes science in any proper sense powerless. *She* can deal only with classes, only with general laws; and so long as these classes are constantly reduced to "species of one," and these laws are set at nought by incalculable and singular influences, she must be constantly baffled and find all her

THE KINDS OF CRITICISM.

elaborate plant of formulas and generalisations useless. Of course, there are generalisations possible in literature, and to such I may return presently; but scientific criticism of literature must always be a contradiction in terms. You may to some considerable extent ascertain the general laws of language, of metre, of music, as applied to verbal rhythm and cadence; you may classify the subjects which appeal to the general, and further classify their particular manners of appeal; you may arrange the most ingenious "product-of-the-circumstances" theories about race, climate, religion. But always sooner or later, and much more often sooner than later, the mocking demon of the individual, or, if a different phrase be preferred, the great and splendid mystery of the idiosyncrasy of the artist, will meet and baffle you. You will find that on the showing of this science falsely so called, there is no reason why Chapelain should not be a poet, and none why Shakespeare is. You will ask science in vain to tell you why some dozen or sixteen of the simplest words in language arranged by one man or in one fashion, why a certain number of dabs of colour arranged by another man or in another fashion, make a permanent addition to the delight of the world, while other words and other dabs of colour, differently arranged by others, do not. To put the matter yet otherwise, the whole end, aim, and object of literature and the criticism of literature, as of all art, and

THE KINDS OF CRITICISM.

the criticism of all art, is beauty and the enjoyment of beauty. With beauty science has absolutely nothing to do.

THE KINDS OF CRITICISM.

It is no doubt the sense, conscious or unconscious, of this that has inclined men to that other conception of criticism as a saying of fine things, of which Mr. Goldwin Smith complains, and which certainly has many votaries, in most countries at the present day. These votaries have their various kinds. There is the critic who simply uses his subject as a sort of springboard or platform, on and from which to display his natural grace and agility, his urbane learning, his faculty of pleasant wit. This is perhaps the most popular of all critics, and no age has ever had better examples of him than this age. There is a more serious kind who founds on his subject (if indeed founding be not too solemn a term) elaborate descants, makes it the theme of complicated variations. There is a third, closely allied to him, who seeks in it apparently first of all, and sometimes with no further aim, an opportunity for the display of style. And lastly (though as usual all these kinds pervade and melt into one another, so that, while in any individual one may prevail, it is rare to find an individual in whom that one is alone present) there is the purely impressionist critic who endeavours in his own way to show the impression which the subject has, or which he chooses to represent that it has, produced on him. This last is in a better case than the others; but still he, as it seems to me, misses the full and proper office of the critic, though he may have an agreeable and even useful function of his own.

THE KINDS OF CRITICISM.

For the full and proper office of the critic (again as it seems to me) can never be discharged except by those who remember that "critic" means "judge." Expressions of personal liking, though they can hardly be kept out of criticism, are not by themselves judgment. The famous "J'aime mieux Alfred de Musset," though it came from a man of extraordinary mental power and no small specially critical ability, is not criticism. Mere *obiter dicta* of any kind, though they may be most agreeable and even most legitimate sets-off to critical conversation, are not criticism. The most admirable discourses from the merely literary point of view on taste, Shakespeare, and the musical glasses, with some parenthetic reference to the matter in hand, are not criticism. There must be at least some attempt to take in and render the whole virtue of the subjects considered, some effort to compare them with their likes in other as well as the same languages, some endeavour to class and value them. And as a condition preliminary to this process, there must, I think, be a not inconsiderable study of widely differing periods, forms, manners, of literature itself. The test question, as I should put it, of the value of criticism is "What idea of the original would this critic give to a tolerably instructed person who did not know that original?" And again, "How far has this critic seen steadily and seen whole, the subject which he has set himself to consider? How far has he referred the main peculiarities of that subject to their proximate causes and effects? How far has he attempted to place, and succeeded in placing, the subject in the general history of literature, in the particular history of its own language, in the collection of authors of its own department?" How far, in short, has he applied what I may perhaps be excused for calling the comparative method in literature to the particular instance? I have read very famous and in their way very accomplished examples of literature ostensibly critical, in which few if any of these questions seem to have been even considered by the critic. He may have said many pretty things; he may have shown what a clever fellow he is; he may have in his own person contributed good literature to swell the literary sum. But has he done anything to aid the general grasp of that literary sum, to place his man under certain lights and in certain aspects, with due allowance for the possibility of other aspects and other lights? Very often, I think, it must be admitted that he has not. I should be the first to admit that my own attempts to do this are unsuccessful and faulty; and I only plead for them that they are such attempts, and that they have been made on the basis of tolerably wide and tolerably careful reading.

THE KINDS OF CRITICISM.

THE KINDS OF CRITICISM.

For, after all, it is this reading which is the main and principal thing. It will not of course by itself make a critic; but few are the critics that will ever be made without it. We have at this moment an awful example of an exceedingly clever writer who has commenced critic, disdaining this preparation. Some of my friends jeer or comminate at Mr. Howells; for my part I only shudder and echo the celebrated "There, but for the grace of God." Here is a clever man, a very clever man, an excellent though of late years slightly depraved practitioner in one branch of art, who, suddenly and without preparation, takes to another, and becomes a spectacle to men and angels. I hope that we shall one day have a collection of Mr. Howells's critical *dicta* on novels and other things; they will be one of the most valuable, one of the most terrible of books as showing what happens when a man speaks without knowledge. To read what Mr. Howells says of Mr. Thackeray is almost an illiberal education. The reason of the error is quite obvious. It is simply that the clever American does not know; he has not sufficient range of comparison. For my own part, I should not dare to continue criticising so much as a circulating library novel, if I did not perpetually pay my respects to the classics of many literatures: and I am not sure that I do not appreciate the classics of many literatures all the better from my not infrequent reading of circulating library novels.

THE KINDS OF CRITICISM.

The only objection of validity that I have ever seen taken to what I have ventured to call comparative criticism, is that it proceeds too much, as the most learned of living French critics once observed of an English writer, *par cases et par compartiments*, that is to say, as I understand M. Brunetière, with a rather too methodical classification. This, however, was written some seven or eight years ago, and since then I have found M. Brunetière speaking about critical method as distinguished from the science of criticism, and insisting on the necessity of comparison, not less positively, and no doubt with far more authority, than I have done myself. Yet I half think that M. Brunetière, like most of us, does not practise quite up to the level of his preaching; and I should say that on mediæval literature, on Romantic literature, and on some other things, his own excellent censorship might be further improved by a still more catholic sympathy, and a still more constant habit of looking at everything and every writer in conjunction with their analogues and their opposites in the same and other literatures. This constant reference of comparison may indeed stand in the way of those flowing deliverances of personal opinion, in more or less agreeable language, which are perhaps, or rather certainly, what is most popular in criticism; I do not think that they will ever stand in the way of criticism proper. As I understand that long and difficult art, its end, as far as the individual is concerned, is to provide the mind with a sort of conspectus of literature, as a good atlas thoroughly conned provides a man with a conspectus of the *orbis terrarum.* To the man with a geographical head, the mention of a place at once suggests its bearings to other places, its history, its products, all its relations in short; to the man with a critical head, the mention of a book or an author should call up a similar mental picture. The picture, indeed, will never be as complete in the one instance as in the other, because the intellect and the artistic faculty of man are far vaster than this planet, far more diverse, far more intricately and perplexingly arranged than all its abundant material dispositions and products. The life of Methuselah and the mind of Shakespeare together could hardly take the whole of critical knowledge to be their joint province. But the area of survey may be constantly increased; the particularity of knowledge constantly made more minute.

THE KINDS OF CRITICISM.

Another objection, more fantastic in appearance but rather attractive in its way, is that the comparative critic becomes too much of a universal lover, and too little of an enthusiast, that he has an irritating and ungentlemanly habit of seeing blemishes in the greatest, a pottering and peddling fancy for discovering beauties in the most insignificant; that he lacks the exclusiveness and the fastidiousness of intellectual aristocracy, the fervour and rapture of æsthetic passion. To this, one can answer little more than, "It may be so." Certainly the critic of this kind will very rarely be able to indulge in the *engouement* which is the apparent delight of some of his class. He will deal very cautiously in superlatives, and his commendations, when he gives them, will sometimes have, to more gushing persons, the slightly ludicrous air which attached to the modest boast of somebody that he was "the third best authority in England on gray shirtings." On the other hand, the critic of this kind will not be able to neglect the uninteresting with the serene nonchalance of some of his fellows. He will sometimes have to look back on days and months and years of laborious reading and say to himself, "Were it not well for us, as others use, to take all this for granted?" But to say this is to say no more than that the thorough-going practice of any art and mystery involves a great deal of tedious, thankless, and even positively fruitless work, brushes away a good many illusions, and interferes a good deal with personal comfort. Cockaigne is a delightful country, and the Cockaigne of criticism is as agreeable as the other provinces. But none of these provinces has usually been accounted a wise man's paradise.

THE KINDS OF CRITICISM.

It may be asked, "What is the end which you propose for this comparative reading? A method must lead somewhere; whither does this method lead? or does it lead only to statistics and classifications?" Certainly it does not, or at

THE KINDS OF CRITICISM.

least should not. It leads, like all method, to generalisations which, though as I have said I do not believe that they have attained or ever will attain the character of science, at least throw no small light and interest on the study of literature as a whole, and of its examples as particulars. It gives, I think (speaking as a fool), a constantly greater power of distinguishing good work from bad work, by giving constantly nearer approach (though perhaps it may never wholly and finally attain) to the knowledge of the exact characteristics which distinguish the two. And the way in which it does this is by a constant process of weakening or strengthening, as the case may be, the less or more correct generalisations with which the critic starts, or which he forms in the early days of his reading. There has often been brought against some great critics the charge that their critical standards have altered at different times of their career. This simply means that they have been constantly applying the comparative method, and profiting by the application. After all, there are few, though there are some, absolute truths in criticism ; and a man will often be relatively right in condemning, from certain aspects and in certain combinations, work which, under other aspects and in other combinations, he has been relatively quite as right in admiring. Occasionally, no doubt, there will be an apparent exception to the rule of critical development, as in the case of Hazlitt :

but that remarkable exception does not fail to justify the rule. For in truth, Hazlitt's critical range was not so wide as his penetration was deep; and he avows, almost exultingly, that after a comparatively early time of life, he practically left off reading. That is to say, he carefully avoided renewing his plant, and he usually eschewed new material—conditions which, no doubt, conduce to the uniformity, and, within obvious limits, are not prejudicial to the excellence of the product.

THE KINDS OF CRITICISM.

It is possible that the title "The Kinds of Criticism" may have excited in some readers expectations of the discussion of a subject which has not yet been handled. We have recently seen revived the sempiternal argument between authors and critics—an argument in which it may be as well to say that the present writer has not yet taken part either anonymously or otherwise. The authors, or some of them, have remarked that they have never personally benefited by criticism; and the critics, after their disagreeable way, have retorted that this was obvious. A critic of great ingenuity, my friend Mr. Andrew Lang, has, with his usual humour, suggested that critics and reviewers are two different kinds, and have nothing to do with each other essentially, though accidentally, and in the imperfect arrangements of the world, the discharge of their functions may happen to be combined in the same person. As a matter of practice, this is no doubt too often the case; as a matter

THE KINDS OF CRITICISM.

of theory, nothing ought much less to be the case. I think that if I were dictator, one of the first non-political things that I should do, would be to make the order of reviewers as close a one, at least, as the bench of judges, or the staff of the Mint, or of any public establishment of a similar character. That any large amount of reviewing is determined by fear or favour is a general idea which has little more basis than a good many other general ideas. But that a very large amount of reviewing is determined by doubtless well-meaning incompetence, there is no doubt whatever. It is on the whole the most difficult kind of newspaper writing, and it is on the whole the most lightly assigned and the most irresponsibly performed. I have heard of newspapers where the reviews depended almost wholly on the accident of some of the staff taking a holiday, or being laid for a time on the shelf, or being considered not up to other work ; of others, though this I own is scarcely credible, where the whole reviewing was farmed out to a manager, to be allotted to devils as good to him seemed ; of many where the reviews were a sort of exercising-ground on which novices were trained, broken-down hacks turned out to grass, and invalids allowed a little gentle exercise. And I know of not a few papers and not a few reviewers in which and by whom, errors and accidents excepted, the best work possible is given to one of the most important kinds of work. Of common mistakes on the subject, which are not merely silly crazes, such as the log-rolling craze and the five-pound note craze and the like, the worst known to me, though it is shared by some who should know better, is that a specialist is the best reviewer. I do not say that he is always the worst; but that is about as far as my charity, informed by much experience, can go. Even if he has no special craze or megrim, and does not decide offhand that a man is hopeless because he calls Charles the Great Charlemagne, or *vice versâ*, he is constantly out of focus. The perfect reviewer would be (and the only reviewer whose reviews are worth reading is he who more or less approximates to this ideal) the Platonic or pseudo-Platonic philosopher who is "second best in everything," who has enough special knowledge not to miss merits or defects, and enough general knowledge to estimate the particular subject at, and not above, its relative value to the whole. There have been good critics who were unable to bring themselves down to the mere reading of ephemeral work, but I do not think they were the better for this; I am sure that there never was a good reviewer, even of the lowest trash, who was not *in posse* or *in esse* a good critic of the highest and most enduring literature. The writer of funny articles, and the "slater," and the intelligent *compte-rendu* man, and the person who writes six columns on the general theory of poetry when he professes to review Mr. Apollo's last book, may do all these things well and

THE KINDS OF CRITICISM.

not be good critics; but then all these things may be done, and done well, and yet not be good reviews.

THE KINDS OF CRITICISM.

Whether the reviewer and the critic are valuable members of society or useless encumbrances, must be questions left to the decision of the world at large, which apparently is not in a hurry to decide either way. There are, no doubt, certain things that the critic, whether he be critic major or critic minor, Sainte-Beuve or Mr. Gall, cannot do. He cannot certainly, and for the present, sell or prevent the sale of a book. "You slated this and it has gone through twenty editions" is not a more uncommon remark than the other, "They slated that and you extol it to the skies." Both, as generally urged, rest on fallacy. In the first case, nothing was probably farther from the critic's intention than to say "this book is not popular"; the most that he intended was "this book is not good." In the second case, it has been discovered of late (it is one of the few things that we have discovered) that very rarely has any really good thing, even in the most famous or infamous attacks on it, been attacked, even with a shadow of success, for its goodness. The critics were severe on Byron's faults, on Keats's faults, and on the present Laureate's faults; they were seldom severe on their goodness, though they often failed to appreciate it fully.

This, however, is in one sense a digression, for there is no criticism of contemporary work in this volume. I think, however, as I have just endeavoured to point out, that criticism of contemporary work and criticism of classics should proceed on the same lines, and I think that both require the same qualities and the same outfit. Nor am I certain that if narrow inquiry were made, some of the best criticism in all times and in all languages would not be found in the merest casual reviewing. That in all cases the critic must start from a wide comparative study of different languages and literatures, is the first position to be laid down. In the next place he must, I think, constantly refer back his sensations of agreement and disagreement, of liking and disliking, in the same comparative fashion. "Why do I like the *Agamemnon* and dislike Mr. Dash's five-act tragedy?" is a question to be constantly put, and to be answered only by a pretty close personal inquiry as to what "I" really do like in the *Agamemnon* and do dislike in Mr. Dash. And in answering it, it will hardly be possible to consider too large a number of instances of all degrees of merit, from Aeschylus himself to Mr. Dash himself, of all languages, of all times. Let Englishmen be compared with Englishmen of other times to bring out this set of differences, with foreigners of modern times to bring out that, with Greeks and Romans to bring out the other. Let poets of old days be compared with poets of new, classics with romantics, rhymed with unrhymed. Let the straitest doctrin-

THE KINDS OF CRITICISM.

aire criticism of men of talent like Boileau and simpletons like Rymer be compared with the fullest appreciations of Coleridge and Hazlitt, of Sainte-Beuve and Mr. Arnold. "Compare, always compare" is the first axiom of criticism.[1]

THE KINDS OF CRITICISM.

The second, I think, is "Always make sure, as far as you possibly can, that what you like and dislike is the literary and not the extra-literary character of the matter under examination." Make sure, that is to say, that admiration for the author is not due to his having taken care that the Whig dogs or the Tory dogs shall not have the best of it, to his having written as a gentleman for gentlemen, or as an uneasy anti-aristocrat for uneasy anti-aristocrats, as a believer (fervent or acquiescent) in the supernatural, or as a person

[1] Only by dint of this constant comparison, can the critic save himself from the besetting error which makes men believe that there is some absolute progress in life and art, instead of, for the most part, mere eddyings-round in the same circle. I am tempted to glance at this, because of a passage which I read while this Essay was a-writing, a passage signed by a person whom I name altogether for the sake of honour, Mr. James Sully. "If we compare," says Mr. Sully, "Fielding for example with Balzac, Thackeray, or one of the great Russian novelists, we see at once what a simple toylike structure used to serve art for a human world. A mind versed in life as contemporary fiction depicts it, feels, on turning to the already antiquated forms of the eighteenth century, that it has to divest itself for the nonce of more than half its equipment of habitual thought and emotion." This might serve as text for a long sermon, I only cite it in passing as an interesting example of the *idola specus* which beset a clever man who loses the power of comparative vision, and sees *Tom Jones* as a toylike structure with the *Kreutzer Sonata* beside it as a human world.

who lays it down that miracles do not happen, as an Englishman or a Frenchman, a classic or a romantic. Very difficult indeed is the chase and discovery of these enemies: for extra-literary prejudices are as cunning as winter hares or leaf-insects, in disguising themselves by simulating literary forms.

THE KINDS OF CRITICISM.

Lastly, never be content without at least endeavouring to connect cause and effect in some way, without giving something like a reason for the faith that is in you. No doubt the critic will often be tempted, will sometimes be actually forced to say, "'J'aime mieux Alfred de Musset,' and there's an end of it." All the imperfect kinds, as they seem to me, of criticism are recommended by the fact that they are, unlike some other literary matter, not only easier writing but also easier reading. The agreeable exercises of style where adjectives meet substantives to whom they never thought they could possibly be introduced (as a certain naughty wit has it), the pleasant chatter about personal reminiscences, the flowers of rhetoric, the fruits of wit, may not be easy, but they are at any rate easier than fashioning some intelligent and intelligible response to the perpetual "Why?" the *quare stans* of criticism.

In the following pages, I shall no doubt be found, like other people, to have come very far short of my own ideal, and my own precepts. I may even say that I have knowingly and intentionally come short of them to some extent. Biographical

THE KINDS OF CRITICISM.

and anecdotic detail has, I believe, much less to do with the real appreciation of the literary value of an author than is generally thought. In rare instances, it throws a light, but the examples in which we know practically nothing at all, as in that of Shakespeare, or only a few leading facts as in that of Dante, are not those in which criticism is least useful or least satisfactory. At the same time biographical and anecdotic details please most people, and if they are not allowed to shoulder out criticism altogether, there can be no harm in them. For myself, I should like to have the whole works of every author of merit, and I should care little to know anything whatever about his life; but that is a mere private opinion and possibly a private crotchet. Accordingly some space has been given in most of these Essays to a sketch of the life of the subject. Nor has it seemed advisable (except as a matter of necessary, but very occasional, digression) to argue at length upon abstract and general questions such as the definition of poetry, or the kinds and limits of the novel. Large as is the body of criticism so-called which the last hundred years have seen, it may be doubted whether there is even yet accumulated a sufficient *corpus* of really critical discussion of individuals. If I have in these Essays contributed even a very little to such an accumulation, I shall have done that which I purposed.

I

CRABBE

CRABBE.

THERE is a certain small class of persons in the history of literature the members of which possess, at least for literary students, an interest peculiar to themselves. They are the writers who having attained, not merely popular vogue, but fame as solid as fame can ever be, in their own day, having been praised by the praised, and having as far as can be seen owed this praise to none of the merely external and irrelevant causes—politics, religion, fashion or what not—from which it sometimes arises, experience in a more or less short time after their death the fate of being, not exactly cast down from their high place, but left respectfully alone in it, unvisited, unincensed, unread. Among these writers, over the gate of whose division of the literary Elysium the famous, "Who now reads Bolingbroke?" might serve as motto, the author of "The Village" and "Tales of the Hall" is one of the most remarkable. As for

Crabbe's popularity in his own day there is no mistake about that. It was extraordinarily long, it was extremely wide, it included the select few as well as the vulgar, it was felt and more or less fully acquiesced in by persons of the most diverse tastes, habits, and literary standards. His was not the case, which occurs now and then, of a man who makes a great reputation in early life and long afterwards preserves it because, either by accident or prudence, he does not enter the lists with his younger rivals, and therefore these rivals can afford to show him a reverence which is at once graceful and cheap. Crabbe won his spurs in full eighteenth century, and might have boasted, altering Landor's words, that he had dined early and in the best of company, or have parodied Goldsmith, and said, "I have Johnson and Burke: all the wits have been here." But when his studious though barren manhood was passed, and he again began, as almost an old man, to write poetry, he entered into full competition with the giants of the new school, whose ideals and whose education were utterly different from his. While "The Library" and "The Village" came to a public which still had Johnson, which had but just lost Goldsmith, and which had no other poetical novelty before it than Cowper, "The Borough" and the later Tales entered the lists with "Marmion" and "Childe Harold," with "Christabel" and "The Excursion," even with "Endymion" and "The

CRABBE.

Revolt of Islam." Yet these later works of Crabbe met with the fullest recognition both from readers and from critics of the most opposite tendencies. Scott, the most generous, and Wordsworth,[1] the most grudging, of all the poets of the day towards their fellows, united in praising Crabbe; and unromantic as the poet of "The Village" seems to us he was perhaps Sir Walter's favourite English bard. Scott read him constantly, he quotes him incessantly; and no one who has read it can ever forget how Crabbe figures in the most pathetic biographical pages ever written — Lockhart's account of the death at Abbotsford. Byron's criticism was as weak as his verse was powerful, but still Byron had no doubt about Crabbe. The utmost flight of memory or even of imagination can hardly get together three contemporary critics whose standards, tempers, and verdicts, were more different than those of Gifford, Jeffrey, and Wilson. Yet it is scarcely too much to say that they are all in a tale about Crabbe.

CRABBE.

[1] In 1834, after Crabbe's death, Wordsworth wrote to his son: "Your father's works . . . will last, from their combined merit as poetry and truth, full as long as anything that has been expressed in verse since the date of their first appearance." A very different estimate by Wordsworth of Crabbe has been published in Mr. Clayden's *Rogers and his Contemporaries*. Here he argues at great length that "Crabbe's verses can in no sense be called poetry," and that "nineteen out of twenty of his pictures are mere matter of fact." It is fair to say that this was in 1808, before the appearance of "The Borough" and of almost all Crabbe's best work.

CRABBE.

In this unexampled chorus of eulogy there rose (for some others who can hardly have admired him much were simply silent) one single note, so far as I know, or rather one single rattling peal of thunder on the other side. It is true that this was significant enough, for it came from William Hazlitt.

Yet against this chorus, which was not, as has sometimes happened, the mere utterance of a loud-voiced few, but was echoed by a great multitude who eagerly bought and read Crabbe, must be set the almost total forgetfulness of his work which has followed. It is true that of living or lately living persons in the first rank of literature some great names can be cited on his side ; and what is more, that these great names show the same curious diversity in agreement which has been already noticed as one of Crabbe's triumphs. The translator of Omar Khayyám, his friend the present Laureate, and the author of "The Dream of Gerontius," are men whose literary ideals are known to be different enough ; yet they add a third trinity as remarkable as those others of Gifford, Jeffrey, and Wilson, of Wordsworth, Byron, and Scott. Much more recently Mr. Courthope has used Crabbe as a weapon in that battle of his with literary Liberalism which he has waged not always quite to the comprehension of his fellow-critics ; Mr. Leslie Stephen has discussed him as one who knows and loves his eighteenth century. But who reads him ? Who quotes him ? Who likes him? I think I can venture to say, with all proper humility, that I know Crabbe pretty well; I think I may say with neither humility nor pride, but simply as a person whose business it has been for some years to read books, and articles, and debates, that I know what has been written and said in England lately. You will find hardly a note of Crabbe in these writings and sayings. He does not even survive, as "Matthew Green, who wrote 'The Spleen,'" and others survive, by quotations which formerly made their mark, and are retained without a knowledge of their original. If anything is known about Crabbe to the general reader, it is the parody in "Rejected Addresses," an extraordinarily happy parody no doubt, in fact rather better Crabbe in Crabbe's weakest moments than Crabbe himself. But naturally there is nothing of his best there; and it is by his best things, let it be repeated over and over in face of all opposition, that a poet must be judged.

CRABBE.

Although Crabbe's life, save for one dramatic revolution, was one of the least eventful in our literary history, it is by no means one of the least interesting. Mr. Kebbel's book[1] gives a very fair summary of it; but the Life by Crabbe's son which is prefixed to the collected editions of the poems, and on which Mr. Kebbel's own is avowedly based, is perhaps the more interesting of the two. It is written with a curious mixture of the old

[1] *Great Writers; Crabbe:* by T. E. Kebbel. London, 1888.

CRABBE.

literary state and formality, and of a feeling on the writer's part that he is not a literary man himself, and that not only his father, but Mr. Lockhart, Mr. Moore, Mr. Bowles and the other high literary persons who assisted him were august beings of another sphere. This is all the more agreeable, in that Crabbe's sons had advantages of education and otherwise which were denied to their father, and might in the ordinary course of things have been expected to show towards him a lofty patronage rather than any filial reverence. The poet himself was born at Aldborough, a now tolerably well-known watering-place (the fortune of which was made by Mr. Wilkie Collins in *No Name*) on Christmas Eve, 1754. That not uncommon infirmity of noble minds which seeks to prove distinguished ancestry seems to have had no hold on the plain common sense of the Crabbe family, who maintained themselves to be at the best Norfolk yeomen, and though they possessed a coat-of-arms, avowed with much frankness that they did not know how they got it. A hundred and forty years ago they had apparently lost even the dignity of yeomanhood, and occupied stations quite in the lower rank of the middle class as tradesmen, non-commissioned officers in the navy or the merchant service, and so forth. George Crabbe, the grandfather, was collector of customs at Aldborough, but his son, also a George, was a parish schoolmaster and a parish clerk before he

CRABBE.

returned to the Suffolk port as deputy collector and then as salt-master, or collector of the salt duties. He seems to have had no kind of polish, and late in life was a mere rough drinking exciseman; but his education, especially in mathematics, appears to have been considerable, and his ability in business not small. The third George, his eldest son, was also fairly though very irregularly educated for a time, and his father, perceiving that he was "a fool about a boat," had the rather unusual common sense to destine him to a learned profession. Unluckily his will was better than his means, and while the profession which Crabbe chose or which was chosen for him—that of medicine—was not the best suited to his tastes or talents, the resources of the family were not equal to giving him a full education, even in that. He was still at intervals employed in the Customs warehouses at "piling up butter and cheese" even after he was apprenticed at fourteen to a country surgeon. The twelve years which he spent in this apprenticeship, in an abhorred return for a short time to the cheese and butter, in a brief visit to London, where he had no means to walk the hospitals, and in an attempt to practise with little or no qualification at Aldborough itself, present a rather dismal history of apprenticeship which taught nothing. But Love was, for once, most truly and literally Crabbe's solace and his salvation, his master and his patron. When he was barely eighteen, still an apprentice, and possessed, as far as can be made out, of neither manners nor prospects, he met a certain Miss Sarah Elmy. She was three or four years older than himself and much better connected, being the niece and eventual co-heiress of a wealthy yeoman squire. She was, it is said, pretty; she was evidently accomplished, and she seems to have had access to the country society of those days. But Mira, as Crabbe called her, perhaps merely in the fashion of the eighteenth century, perhaps in remembrance of Fulke Greville's heroine (for he knew his Elizabethans rather well for a man of those days), and no doubt also with a secret joy to think that the last syllables of her Christian name and surname in a way spelt the appellation, fell in love with the boy and made his fortune. But for her Crabbe would probably have subsided, not contentedly but stolidly, into the lot of a Doctor Slop of the time, consoling himself with snuff (which he always loved) and schnaps (to which we have hints that in his youth he was not averse). Mira was at once unalterably faithful to him and unalterably determined not to marry unless he could give her something like a position. Their long engagement (they were not married till he was twenty-nine and she was thirty-three) may, as we shall see, have carried with it some of the penalties of long engagements. But it is as certain as any such thing can be that but for it English literature would have lacked the name of Crabbe.

There is no space here to go through the sufferings of the novitiate. At last, at the extreme end of 1779, Crabbe made up his mind once more to seek his fortune, this time by aid of literature only, in London. His son has printed too rare scraps of a very interesting Journal to Mira which he kept during at least a part of the terrible year of struggle which he passed there. He saw the riots of '80; he canvassed, always more or less in vain, the booksellers and the peers; he spent three-and-sixpence of his last ten shillings on a copy of Dryden; he was much less disturbed about imminent starvation than by the delay of a letter from Mira ("my dearest Sally" she becomes with a pathetic lapse from convention, when the pinch is sorest) or by the doubt whether he had enough left to pay the postage of one. He writes prayers (but not for the public eye), abstracts of sermons for Mira, addresses (rather adulatory) to Lord Shelburne, which received no answer. All this has the most genuine note that ever man of letters put into his work, for whatever Crabbe was or was not, now or at any time, he was utterly sincere; and his sincerity makes his not very abundant letters and journals unusually interesting. At last, after a year, during which his means of subsistence are for the most part absolutely unknown, he, as he says himself, fixed "by some propitious influence, in some happy moment" on Edmund Burke as the subject of a last appeal.

CRABBE.

Nothing in all literary history is, in a modest way and without pearls and gold, quite so like a fairy tale as the difference in Crabbe's fortunes which this propitious influence brought about. On the day when he wrote to Burke he was, as he said in the letter, "an outcast, without friends, without employment, without bread." In some twenty-four hours (the night-term of which he passed in ceaselessly pacing Westminster Bridge to cheat the agony of expectation) he was a made man. It was not merely that, directly or indirectly, Burke procured him a solid and an increasing income. He did much more than that. Crabbe, like most self-educated men, was quite uncritical of his own work: Burke took him into his own house for months, encouraged him to submit his poems, criticised them at once without mercy and with judgment, found him publishers, found him a public, turned him from a raw country boy into a man who at least had met society of the best kind. It is a platitude to say that for a hundred persons who will give money or patronage there is scarcely one who will take trouble of this kind; and if any devil's advocate objects the delight of producing a "lion," it may be answered that for Burke at least this delight would not have been delightful at all.

CRABBE.

The immediate form which the patronage of Burke and that, soon added, of Thurlow took, is one which rather shocks the present day. They made Crabbe turn to the Church, and got a complaisant bishop to ordain him. They sent him (a rather dangerous experiment) to be curate in his own native place, and finally Burke procured him the chaplaincy at Belvoir. The young Duke of Rutland, who had been made a strong Tory by Pitt, was fond of letters, and his Duchess Isabel, who was,—like her elder kinswoman, Dryden's Duchess of Ormond—

CRABBE.

> A daughter of the rose, whose cheeks unite
> The varying beauties of the red and white,

in other words, a Somerset, was one of the most beautiful and gracious women in England. Crabbe, whose strictly literary fortunes I postpone for the present, was apparently treated with the greatest possible kindness by both; but he was not quite happy,[1] and his ever-prudent Mira still would not marry him. At last Thurlow's patronage took the practical form (it had already taken that, equally practical, of a hundred pounds) of two small Chancellor's livings in Dorsetshire, residence at which was dispensed with by the easy fashions of the day. The Duke of Rutland, when he was appointed Lord Lieutenant of Ireland, did not

[1] Although constantly patronised by the Rutland family in successive generations, and honoured by the attentions of "Old Q." and others, his poems are full of growls at patrons. These cannot be mere echoes of Oldham and Johnson, but their exact reason is unknown. His son's reference to it is so extremely cautious that it has been read as a confession that Crabbe was prone to his cups, and quarrelsome in them—a signal instance of the unwisdom of not speaking out.

take Crabbe with him, a circumstance which has excited some unnecessary discussion; but he gave him free quarters at Belvoir, where he and his wife lived for a time before they migrated to a neighbouring curacy—his wife, for even Mira's prudence had yielded at last to the Dorsetshire livings, and they were married in December 1783. They lived together for nearly thirty years, in, as it would seem, unbroken mutual devotion, but Mrs. Crabbe's health seems very early to have broken down, and a remarkable endorsement of Crabbe's on a letter of hers has been preserved. I do not think Mr. Kebbel quotes it; it ends, "And yet happiness was denied"—a sentence fully encouraging to Mr. Browning and other good men who have denounced long engagements.[1] The story of Crabbe's life after his marriage may be told very shortly. His first patron died in Ireland, but the duchess with some difficulty prevailed on Thurlow to exchange his former gifts for more convenient and rather

CRABBE.

[1] Rogers told Ticknor in 1838 that "Crabbe was nearly ruined by grief and vexation at the conduct of his wife for above seven years, at the end of which time she proved to be insane." But this was long after her death and Crabbe's, and it is not clear that while she was alive Rogers knew Crabbe at all. Nor is there the slightest reason for attaching to the phrase "vexation at the conduct" the sense which it would usually have. A quatrain found after Crabbe's death wrapped round his wife's wedding-ring is touching, and graceful in its old-fashioned way.

The ring so worn, as you behold,
So thin, so pale, is yet of gold:
The passion such it was to prove;
Worn with life's cares, love yet was love.

better livings in the neighbourhood of Belvoir, at the chief of which, Muston, Crabbe long resided. The death of his wife's uncle made him leave his living and take up his abode for many years at Glemham, in Suffolk, only to find, when he returned, that (not unnaturally, though to his own great indignation) dissent had taken bodily possession of the parish. His wife died in 1813, and the continued kindness, after nearly a generation, of the house of Rutland, gave him the living of Trowbridge, in Wiltshire, with a small Leicestershire incumbency near Belvoir added, instead of Muston. At Trowbridge he lived nearly twenty years, revisiting London society, making the acquaintance personally (he had already known him by letter) of Sir Walter, paying a memorable visit to Edinburgh, flirting in an elderly and simple fashion with many ladies, writing much and being even more of a lion in the society of George the Fourth's reign than he had been in the days of George the Third. He died on 3rd February 1832.

CRABBE.

Crabbe's character is not at all enigmatical, and emerges as clearly in those letters and diaries of his which have been published, as in anecdotes of him by others. Perhaps the famous story of his politely endeavouring to talk French to divers Highlanders, during George the Fourth's visit to Edinburgh, is slightly embroidered—Lockhart, who tells it, was a mystifier without peer. If he did gently but firmly extinguish a candle-snuff while

Wordsworth and Sir George Beaumont were indulging in poetic ecstasies over the beautiful undulations of the smoke, there may have been something to say for him as Anne Scott, to whom Wordsworth told the story, is said to have hinted, from the side of one of the senses. His life, no less than his work, speaks him a man of amiable though by no means wholly sweet temper, of more common sense than romance, and of more simplicity than common sense. His nature and his early trials made him not exactly sour, but shy, till age and prosperity mellowed him ; but simplicity was his chief characteristic in age and youth alike.

CRABBE.

The mere facts of his strictly literary career are chiefly remarkable for the enormous gap between his two periods of productiveness. In early youth he published some verses in the magazines and a poem called "Inebriety," which appeared at Ipswich in 1775. His year of struggle in London saw the publication of another short piece "The Candidate," but with the ill-luck which then pursued him, the bookseller who brought it out became bankrupt. His despairing resort to Burke ushered in "The Library," 1781, followed by "The Village," 1783, which Johnson revised and improved not a little. Two years later again came "The Newspaper," and then twenty-two years passed without anything appearing from Crabbe's pen. It was not that he was otherwise occupied, for he had little or nothing to do, and for the greater part of the time, lived away from his parish. It was not that he was idle, for we have his son's testimony that he was perpetually writing, and that holocausts of manuscripts in prose and verse used from time to time to be offered up in the open air, for fear of setting the house on fire by their mass. At last, in 1807, "The Parish Register" appeared, and three years later "The Borough"—perhaps the strongest division of his work. The miscellaneous Tales came in 1812, the "Tales of the Hall" in 1819. Meanwhile and afterwards, various collected editions appeared, the last and most complete being in 1829—a very comely little book in eight volumes. His death led to the issue of some "Posthumous Tales" and to the inclusion by his son of divers fragments both in the Life and in the Works. It is understood, however, that there are still considerable remains in manuscript; perhaps they might be published with less harm to the author's fame and with less fear of incurring a famous curse than in the case of almost any other poet.

CRABBE.

For Crabbe, though by no means always at his best, is one of the most curiously equal of verse-writers. "Inebriety" and such other very youthful things are not to be counted; but between "The Village" of 1783 and the "Posthumous Tales" of more than fifty years later, the difference is surprisingly small. Such as it is, it rather reverses ordinary experience, for the later poems exhibit the greater play of fancy, the earlier the exacter graces of form and expression. Yet there is nothing really wonderful in this, for Crabbe's earliest poems were published under severe surveillance of himself and others, and at a time which still thought nothing of such value in literature as correctness, while his later were written under no particular censorship, and when the Romantic revival had already, for better or worse, emancipated the world. The change was in Crabbe's case not wholly for the better. He does not in his later verse become more prosaic, but he becomes considerably less intelligible. There is a passage in "The Old Bachelor," too long to quote but worth referring to, which, though it may be easy enough to understand it with a little goodwill, I defy anybody to understand in its literal and grammatical meaning. Such welters of words are very common in Crabbe, and Johnson saved him from one of them in the very first lines of "The Village." Yet Johnson could never have written the passages which earned Crabbe his fame. The great lexicographer knew man in general much better than Crabbe did; but he nowhere shows anything like Crabbe's power of seizing and reproducing man in particular. Crabbe is one of the first and certainly one of the greatest of the "realists" who, exactly reversing the old philosophical signification of the word, devote themselves to the particular only. Yet of the three small volumes by which he, after

CRABBE.

his introduction to Burke, made his reputation, and on which he lived for a quarter of a century, the first and the last display comparatively little of this peculiar quality. "The Library" and "The Newspaper" are characteristic pieces of the school of Pope, but not characteristic of their author. The first catalogues books as folio, quarto, octavo, and so forth, and then cross-catalogues them as law, physic, divinity, and the rest, but is otherwise written very much in the air. "The Newspaper" suited Crabbe a little better, because he pretty obviously took a particular newspaper and went through its contents — scandal, news, reviews, advertisements—in his own special fashion: but still the subject did not appeal to him. In "The Village," on the other hand, contemporaries and successors alike have agreed to recognise Crabbe in his true vein. The two famous passages which attracted the suffrages of judges so different as Scott and Wordsworth, are still, after more than a hundred years, fresh, distinct, and striking. Here they are once more:—

CRABBE.

Theirs is yon House that holds the parish poor,
Whose walls of mud scarce bear the broken door;
There, where the putrid vapours, flagging, play,
And the dull wheel hums doleful through the day;—
There children dwell who know no parents' care;
Parents who know no children's love dwell there!
Heart-broken matrons on their joyless bed,
Forsaken wives, and mothers never wed;

Dejected widows, with unheeded tears,
And crippled age with more than childhood fears;
The lame, the blind, and, far the happiest they!
The moping idiot and the madman gay.

Anon, a figure enters, quaintly neat,
All pride and business, bustle and conceit;
With looks unaltered by these scenes of woe,
With speed that, entering, speaks his haste to go,
He bids the gazing throng around him fly,
And carries fate and physic in his eye:
A potent quack, long versed in human ills,
Who first insults the victim whom he kills;
Whose murderous hand a drowsy Bench protect,
And whose most tender mercy is neglect.
Paid by the parish for attendance here,
He wears contempt upon his sapient sneer;
In haste he seeks the bed where Misery lies,
Impatience marked in his averted eyes;
And some habitual queries hurried o'er,
Without reply he rushes on the door:
His drooping patient, long inured to pain,
And long unheeded, knows remonstrance vain,
He ceases now the feeble help to crave
Of man; and silent, sinks into the grave.

The poet executed endless variations on this class of theme, but he never quite succeeded in discovering a new one, though in process of time he brought his narrow study of the Aldborough fishermen and townsfolk down still more narrowly to individuals. His landscape is always marvellously exact, the strokes selected with extraordinary skill *ad hoc* so as to show autumn rather than spring, failure rather than hope, the riddle of the painful earth rather than any joy of living.

CRABBE.

Attempts have been made to vindicate Crabbe from the charge of being a gloomy poet, but I cannot think them successful; I can hardly think that they have been quite serious. Crabbe, our chief realist poet, has an altogether astonishing likeness to the chief prose realist of France, Gustave Flaubert, so far as his manner of view goes, for in point of style the two have small resemblance. One of the most striking things in Crabbe's biography is his remembrance of the gradual disillusion of a day of pleasure which, as a child, he enjoyed in a new boat of his father's. We all of us, except those who are gifted or cursed with the proverbial duck's back, have these experiences and these remembrances of them. But most men either simply grin and bear it, or carrying the grin a little farther, console themselves by regarding their own disappointments from the ironic and humorous point of view. Crabbe, though not destitute of humour, does not seem to have been able or disposed to employ it in this way. Perhaps he never quite got over the terrible and, for the most part unrecorded, year in London: perhaps the difference between the Mira of promise and the Mira of possession—the "happiness denied"—had something to do with it: perhaps it was a question of natural disposition with him. But when, years afterwards, as a prosperous middle-aged man, he began his series of published poems once more with "The Parish Register," the same manner of seeing is evident, though the minute elaboration of the views themselves is almost infinitely greater. Nor did he ever succeed in altering this manner, if he ever tried to do so.

CRABBE.

With the exception of his few Lyrics, the most important of which, "Sir Eustace Grey" (one of his very best things), is itself a tale in different metre, and a few other occasional pieces of little importance, the entire work of Crabbe, voluminous as it is, is framed upon a single pattern, the vignettes of "The Village" being merely enlarged in size and altered in frame in the later books. The three parts of "The Parish Register" the twenty-four Letters of "The Borough," some of which have single and others grouped subjects, and the sixty or seventy pieces which make up the three divisions of Tales, consist almost exclusively of heroic couplets, shorter measures very rarely intervening. They are also almost wholly devoted to narratives, partly satirical, partly pathetic, of the lives of individuals of the lower and middle class chiefly. Jeffrey, who was a great champion of Crabbe and allotted several essays to him, takes delight in analysing the plots or stories of these tales; but it is a little amusing to notice that he does it for the most part exactly as if he were criticising a novelist or a dramatist. "The object," says he, in one place, "is to show that a man's fluency of speech depends very much upon his confidence in the approbation of his auditors": "In Squire Thomas we have the history of a mean, domineering spirit," and so forth. Gifford in one place actually discusses Crabbe as a novelist. I shall make some further reference to this curious attitude of Crabbe's admiring critics. For the moment I shall only remark that the singularly mean character of so much of Crabbe's style, the "style of drab stucco," as it has been unkindly called, which is familiar from the wicked wit that told how the youth at the theatre

CRABBE.

> Regained the felt and felt what he regained,

is by no means universal. The most powerful of all his pieces, the history of Peter Grimes, the tyrant of apprentices, is almost entirely free from it, and so are a few others. But it is common enough to be a very serious stumbling-block. In nine tales out of ten this is the staple :—

> Of a fair town where Dr. Rack was guide,
> His only daughter was the boast and pride.

Now that is unexceptionable verse enough, but what is the good of putting it in verse at all? Here again :—

> For he who makes me thus on business wait,
> Is not for business in a proper state.

It is obvious that you cannot trust a man who, unless he is intending a burlesque, can bring himself to write like that. Crabbe not only brings himself to it, but rejoices and luxuriates in the style. The tale from which that last luckless distich is taken, "The Elder Brother," is full of pathos and about equally full of false notes. If we turn to a far different subject, the very vigorously conceived "Natural Death of Love," we find a piece of strong and true satire, the best thing of its kind in the author, which is kept up throughout. Although, like all satire, it belongs at best but to the outer courts of poetry, it is so good that none can complain. Then the page is turned and one reads :—

CRABBE.

> "I met," said Richard, when returned to dine,
> "In my excursion with a friend of mine."

It may be childish, it may be uncritical, but I own that such verse as that excites in me an irritation which destroys all power of enjoyment, except the enjoyment of ridicule. Nor let any one say that pedestrian passages of the kind are inseparable from ordinary narrative in verse and from the adaptation of verse to miscellaneous themes. If it were so the argument would be fatal to such adaptation, but it is not. Pope seldom indulges in such passages, though he does sometimes: Dryden never does. He can praise, abuse, argue, tell stories, make questionable jests, do anything in verse that is still poetry, that has a throb and a quiver and a swell in it, and is not merely limp, rhythmed prose. In Crabbe, save in a few passages of feeling and a great many of mere description—the last an excellent setting for poetry but not necessarily poetical—this rhythmed prose is everywhere. The matter which it serves to convey is, with the limitations above given, varied, and it is excellent. No one except the greatest prose novelists has such a gallery of distinct, sharply etched characters, such another gallery of equally distinct scenes and manner-pieces, to set before the reader. Exasperating as Crabbe's style sometimes is, he seldom bores—never indeed except in his rare passages of digressive reflection. It has, I think, been observed, and if not the observation is obvious, that he has done with the pen for the neighbourhood of Aldborough and Glemham what Crome and Cotman have done for the neighbourhood of Norwich with the pencil. His observation of human nature, so far as it goes, is not less careful, true, and vivid. His pictures of manners, to those who read them at all, are perfectly fresh and in no respect grotesque or faded, dead as the manners themselves are. His pictures of motives and of facts, of vice and virtue, never can fade, because the subjects are perennial and are truly caught. Even his plays on words, which horrified Jeffrey—

CRABBE.

> Alas! your reverence, wanton thoughts I grant
> Were once my motive, now the thoughts of want,

and the like—are not worse than Milton's jokes on the guns. He has immense talent, and he has the originality which sets talent to work in a way not tried by others, and may thus be very fairly said to turn it into genius. He is all this and more. But despite the warnings of a certain precedent, I cannot help stating the case which we have discussed in the old form, and asking, was Crabbe a poet?

CRABBE.

And thus putting the question, we may try to sum up. It is the gracious habit of a summing-up to introduce, if possible, a dictum of the famous men our fathers that were before us. I have already referred to Hazlitt's criticism on Crabbe in *The Spirit of the Age*, and I need not here urge at very great length the cautions which are always necessary in considering any judgment of Hazlitt's.[1] Much that he says even in the brief space of six or eight pages which he allots to Crabbe is unjust; much is explicably, and not too creditably, unjust. Crabbe was a successful man, and Hazlitt did not like successful men: he was a clergyman of the Church of England, and Hazlitt did not love clergymen of the Church of England: he had been a duke's chaplain, and Hazlitt loathed dukes: he had been a Radical, and was still (though Hazlitt does not seem to have thought him so) a Liberal, but his Liberalism had been Torified into a tame variety. Again, Crabbe, though by no means squeamish, is the most unvoluptuous and dispassionate of all describers of inconvenient things; and Hazlitt was the author of *Liber Amoris*. Accordingly there is much that is untrue in the tissue of denunciation which the critic devotes to the poet. But there are two passages in this tirade which alone might show how great a critic Hazlitt himself was. Here in a couple of

[1] See below, Essay on Hazlitt.

lines ("they turn, one and all, on the same sort of teasing, helpless, unimaginative distress") is the germ of one of the most famous and certainly of the best passages of the late Mr. Arnold; and here again is one of those critical taps of the finger which shivers by a touch of the weakest part a whole Rupert's drop of misapprehension. Crabbe justified himself by Pope's example. "Nothing," says Hazlitt, "can be more dissimilar. Pope describes what is striking: Crabbe would have described merely what was there. . . . In Pope there was an appeal to the imagination, you see what was passing *in a poetical point of view*."

CRABBE.

Even here (and I have not been able to quote the whole passage) there is one of the flaws, which Hazlitt rarely avoided, in the use of the word "striking"; for, Heaven knows, Crabbe is often striking enough. But the description of Pope as showing things "in a poetical point of view" hits the white at once, wounds Crabbe mortally, and demolishes realism, as we have been pleased to understand it for the last generation or two. Hazlitt, it is true, has not followed up the attack, as I shall hope to show in an instant; but he has indicated the right line of it. As far as mere treatment goes, the fault of Crabbe is that he is pictorial rather than poetic, and photographic rather than pictorial. He sees his subject steadily, and even in a way he sees it whole; but he does not see it in the poetical way. You are bound in the shallows and the miseries of the individual; never do you reach the large freedom of the poet who looks at the universal. The absence of selection, of the discarding of details that are not wanted, has no doubt a great deal to do with this—Hazlitt seems to have thought that it had everything to do. I do not quite agree with him there. Dante, I think, was sometimes quite as minute as Crabbe; and I do not know that any one less hardy than Hazlitt himself would single out, as Hazlitt expressly does, the death-bed scene of Buckingham as a conquering instance in Pope to compare with Crabbe. We know that the bard of Twickenham grossly exaggerated this. But suppose he had not? Would it have been worse verse? I think not. Although the faculty of selecting instead of giving all, as Hazlitt himself justly contends, is one of the things which make *poesis non ut pictura*, it is not all, and I think myself that a poet, if he is a poet, could be almost absolutely literal. Shakespeare is so in the picture of Gloucester's corpse. Is that not poetry?

CRABBE.

The defect of Crabbe, as it seems to me, is best indicated by reference to one of the truest of all dicta on poetry, the famous maxim of Joubert—that the lyre is a winged instrument and must transport. There is no wing in Crabbe, there is no transport, because, as I hold (and this is where I go beyond Hazlitt), there is no music. In all poetry, the very highest as well as the very lowest that is still poetry, there is something which transports, and that something in my view is always the music of the verse, of the words, of the cadence, of the rhythm, of the sounds superadded to the meaning. When you get the best music married to the best meaning, then you get, say, Shakespeare: when you get some music married to even moderate meaning, you get, say, Moore. Wordsworth can, as everybody but Wordsworthians holds, and as some even of Wordsworthians admit, write the most detestable doggerel and platitude. But when any one who knows what poetry is reads—

CRABBE.

> Our noisy years seem moments in the being
> Of the eternal silence,

he sees that, quite independently of the meaning, which disturbs the soul of no less a person than Mr. John Morley, there is one note added to the articulate music of the world—a note that never will leave off resounding till the eternal silence itself gulfs it. He leaves Wordsworth, he goes straight into the middle of the eighteenth century, and he sees Thomson with his hands in his dressing-gown pockets biting at the peaches, and hears him between the mouthfuls murmuring—

> So when the shepherd of the Hebrid Isles,
> Placed far amid the melancholy main,

and there is another note, as different as possible in kind yet still alike, struck for ever. Yet again, to take example still from the less romantic poets, and in this case from a poet, whom Mr. Kebbel specially and disadvantageously contrasts with Crabbe, when we read the old schoolboy's favourite—

> When the British warrior queen,
> Bleeding from the Roman rods,

we hear the same quality of music informing words, though again in a kind somewhat lower, commoner, and less. In this matter, as in all matters that are worth handling at all, we come of course *ad mysterium*. Why certain combinations of letters, sounds, cadences, should almost without the aid of meaning, though no doubt immensely assisted by meaning, produce this effect of poetry on men no man can say. But they do; and the chief merit of criticism is that it enables us by much study of different times and different languages to recognise some part of the laws, though not the ultimate and complete causes, of the production.

Now I can only say that Crabbe does not produce, or only in the rarest instances produces, this effect on me, and what is more, that on ceasing to be a patient in search of poetical stimulant and becoming merely a gelid critic, I do not discover even in Crabbe's warmest admirers any evidence that he produced this effect on them. Both in the eulogies which Mr. Kebbel quotes, and in those that he does not quote, I observe that the eulogists either discreetly avoid saying what they mean by poetry, or specify for praise something in Crabbe that is not distinctly poetical. Cardinal Newman said that Crabbe "pleased and touched him at thirty years' interval," and pleaded that this answers to the "accidental definition of a classic." Most certainly; but not necessarily to that of a poetical classic. Jeffrey thought him "original and powerful." Granted; but there are plenty of original and powerful writers who are not poets. Wilson gave him the superlative for "original and vivid painting." Perhaps; but is Hogarth a poet? Jane Austen "thought she could have married him." She had not read his biography; but even if she had would that prove him to be a poet? Lord Tennyson is said to single out the following passage, which is certainly one of Crabbe's best, if not his very best:—

CRABBE.

Early he rose, and looked with many a sigh
On the red light that filled the eastern sky;
Oft had he stood before, alert and gay,
To hail the glories of the new-born day;
But now dejected, languid, listless, low,
He saw the wind upon the water blow,
And the cold stream curled onward as the gale
From the pine-hill blew harshly down the vale;
On the right side the youth a wood surveyed,
With all its dark intensity of shade;
Where the rough wind alone was heard to move
In this, the pause of nature and of love
When now the young are reared, and when the old,
Lost to the tie, grow negligent and cold:
Far to the left he saw the huts of men,
Half hid in mist that hung upon the fen:
Before him swallows gathering for the sea,
Took their short flights and twittered o'er the lea;
And near the bean-sheaf stood, the harvest done,
And slowly blackened in the sickly sun;
All these were sad in nature, or they took
Sadness from him, the likeness of his look
And of his mind—he pondered for a while,
Then met his Fanny with a borrowed smile.

CRABBE.

It is good: it is extraordinarily good: it could not be better of its kind. It is as nearly poetry as anything that Crabbe ever did—but is it quite? If it is (and I am not careful to deny it) the reason, as it seems to me, is that the verbal and rhythmical music here, with its special effect of "transporting" of "making the common as if it were uncommon," is infinitely better than is usual with Crabbe, that in fact there is music as well as meaning. Hardly anywhere else, not even in the best passages of the story of Peter Grimes, shall we find such music; and in its absence it may be said of Crabbe much more truly than of Dryden (who carries the true if not the finest poetical undertone with him even into the rant of Almanzor and Maximin, into the interminable arguments of "Religio Laici" and "The Hind and the Panther") that he is a classic of our prose.

Yet the qualities which are so noteworthy in him are all qualities which are valuable to the poet, and which for the most part are present in good poets. And I cannot help thinking that this was what actually deceived some of his contemporaries and made others content for the most part to acquiesce in an exaggerated estimate of his poetical merits. It must be remembered that even the latest generation which, as a whole and unhesitatingly, admired Crabbe, had been brought up on the poets of the eighteenth century, in the very best of whom the qualities which Crabbe lacks had been but sparingly and not eminently present. It must be remembered too, that from the great vice of the poetry of the eighteenth century, its artificiality and convention, Crabbe is conspicuously free. The return to nature was not the only secret of the return to poetry; but it was part of it, and that Crabbe returned to nature no one could doubt. Moreover he came just between the school of prose fiction which practically ended with *Evelina* and the school of prose fiction which opened its different branches with *Waverley* and *Sense and Sensibility*. His contemporaries found nowhere else the narrative power, the faculty of character-drawing, the genius for description of places and manners, which they found in Crabbe; and they knew that in almost all, if not in all the great poets there is narrative power, faculty of character-drawing, genius for description. Yet again, Crabbe put these gifts into verse which at its best was excellent in its own way, and at its worst was a blessed contrast to Darwin or to Hayley. Some readers may have had an uncomfortable though only half-conscious feeling that if they had not a poet in Crabbe they had not a poet at all. At all events they made up their minds that they had a poet in him.

CRABBE.

But are we bound to follow their example? I think not. You could play on Crabbe that odd trick which used, it is said, to be actually played on some mediæval verse chroniclers and unrhyme

CRABBE.

him—that is to say, put him into prose with the least possible changes—and his merits would, save in rare instances, remain very much as they are now. You could put other words in the place of his words, keeping the verse, and it would not as a rule be much the worse. You cannot do either of these things with poets who are poets. Therefore I shall conclude that save at the rarest moments, moments of some sudden gust of emotion, some happy accident, some special grace of the Muses to reward long and blameless toil in their service, Crabbe was not a poet. But I have not the least intention of denying that he was great, and all but of the greatest among English writers.

II

HOGG

HOGG.

"WHAT on earth," it was once asked "will you make of Hogg?" I think that there is something to be made of Hogg, and that it is something worth the making. In the first place, it is hardly possible, without studying "the Shepherd" pretty close, fully to appreciate three other persons, all greater, and one infinitely greater, than himself; namely, Wilson, Lockhart, and Scott. To the two first he was a client in the Roman sense, a plaything, something of a butt, and an invaluable source of inspiration or at least suggestion. Towards the last he occupied a very curious position, never I think quite paralleled elsewhere—the position of a Boswell who would fain be a Boswell and is not allowed to be, who has wild notions that he is really a greater man than Johnson and occasionally blasphemes against his idol, but who in the intervals is truly Boswellian. In the second place, he has usually hitherto been not criticised at all, but either somewhat sneered at or else absurdly over-praised. In the third place, as both Scott and Byron recognised, he is probably the most remarkable example we have of absolute self-education, or of no education: for Burns was an academically instructed student in comparison with Hogg. In the fourth, he produced, amid a mass of rubbish, some charming verse and one prose-story which, though it is almost overlooked by the general, some good judges are, I believe, agreed with me in regarding as one of the very best things of its kind, while it is also a very curious literary puzzle.

HOGG.

The anecdotic history, more or less authentic, of the Ettrick Shepherd would fill volumes, and I must try to give some of the cream of it presently. The non-anecdotic part may be despatched in a few sentences. The exact date of his birth is not known, but he was baptized on 9th December 1770. His father was a good shepherd and a bad farmer—a combination of characteristics which Hogg himself inherited unimpaired and unimproved. If he had any early education at all, he forgot it so completely that he had, as a grown-up man, to teach himself writing if not reading a second time. He pursued his proper vocation for about thirty years, during the latter part of which time he became known as a composer of very good songs, "Donald Macdonald" being ranked as the best. He printed a few as a pamphlet in the first year of the century, but met with little success. Then he fell in with Scott, to whom he had been introduced as a purveyor of ballads, not a few of which his mother, Margaret Laidlaw, knew by heart. This old lady it was who gave Scott the true enough warning that the ballads were "made for singing and no for reading." Scott in his turn set Hogg on the track of making some money by his literary work, and Constable published *The Mountain Bard* together with a treatise called *Hogg on Sheep*, which I have not read, and of which I am not sure that I should be a good critic if I had. The two books brought Hogg three hundred pounds. This sum he poured into the usual Danaids' vessel of the Scotch peasant—the taking and stocking of a farm, which he had neither judgment to select, capital to work, nor skill to manage; and he went on doing very much the same thing for the rest of his life. The exact dates of that life are very sparely given in his own *Autobiography*, in his daughter's *Memorials*, and in the other notices of him that I have seen. He would appear to have spent four or five years in the promising attempt to run, not one but two large stock-farms. Then he tried shepherding again, without much success; and finally in 1810, being forty years old and able to write, he went to Edinburgh and "commenced," as the good old academic phrase has it, literary man. He brought out a new book of songs called *The Forest Minstrel*, and then he started a periodical, *The Spy*. On this, as he tells us, Scott very wisely remonstrated with him, asking him whether he

HOGG.

HOGG.

thought he could be more elegant than Addison or Mackenzie. Hogg replied with his usual modesty that at any rate he would be "mair original." The originality appears to have consisted in personality; for Hogg acknowledges one exceedingly insolent attack on Scott himself, which Scott seems, after at first resenting it (and yet Hogg tells us elsewhere that he never resented any such thing), to have forgiven. He had also some not clearly known employments of the factorship or surveyorship kind; he was much patronised by two worthy hatters, Messrs. Grieve and Scott, and in 1813 the book which contains all his best verse, *The Queen's Wake*, was published. It was deservedly successful; but, by a species of bad luck which pursued Hogg with extraordinary assiduity, the two first editions yielded nothing, as his publisher was not solvent. The third, which Blackwood issued, brought him in good profit. Two years later he became in a way a made man. He had very diligently sought the patronage of Harriet, Duchess of Buccleuch, and, his claims being warmly supported by Scott and specially recommended by the Duchess on her deathbed to her husband, Hogg received rent free, or at a peppercorn, the farm of Mossend, Eltrive or Altrive. It is agreed even by Hogg's least judicious admirers that if he had been satisfied with this endowment and had then devoted himself, as he actually did, to writing, he might have lived and died in comfort, even though his singular luck in not being paid continued to haunt him. But he must needs repeat his old mistake and take the adjacent farm of Mount Benger, which, with a certain reckless hospitable way of living for which he is not so blamable, kept him in difficulties all the rest of his life and made him die in them. He lived twenty years longer; married a good-looking girl much his superior in rank and twenty years his junior, who seems to have made him an excellent wife; engaged in infinite magazine- and book-writing, of which more presently; became the inspirer, model and butt of *Blackwood's Magazine*; constantly threatened to quarrel with it for traducing him, and once did so; loved Edinburgh convivialities more well than wisely; had the very ill luck to survive Scott and to commit the folly of writing a pamphlet (more silly than anything else) on the "domestic manners" of that great man, which estranged Lockhart, hitherto his fast friend; paid a visit to London in 1832, whereby hang tales; and died himself on 21st November 1835.

HOGG.

Such, briefly but not I think insufficiently given, is the Hogg of history. The Hogg of anecdote is a much more considerable and difficult person. He mixes himself up with or becomes by turns (whichever phrase may be preferred) the Shepherd of the *Noctes* and the Hogg who is revealed to us, say his panegyrists, with "uncalled-for malignity" in Lockhart's *Life of Scott*. But these panegyrists seem to forget that there are two documents which happen not to be signed either "John Gibson

Lockhart" or "Christopher North," and that these documents are Hogg's *Autobiography*, published by himself, and the *Domestic Manners of Sir Walter Scott*, likewise authenticated. In these two we have the Hogg of the *ana* put forward pretty vividly. For instance, Hogg tells us how, late in Sir Walter's life, he and his wife called upon Scott. "In we went and were received with all the affection of old friends. But his whole discourse was addressed to my wife, while I was left to shift for myself. . . . In order to attract his attention from my wife to one who I thought as well deserved it, I went close up to him with a scrutinising look and said, 'Gudeness guide us, Sir Walter, but ye hae gotten a braw gown.'" The rest of the story is not bad, but less characteristic. Immediately afterwards Hogg tells his own speech about being "not sae yelegant but mair original" than Addison. Then there is the other capital legend, also self-told, how he said to Scott, "Dear Sir Walter, ye can never suppose that I belang to your school of chivalry! Ye are the king of that school, but I'm the king of the mountain and fairy school, which is a far higher ane than yours!" "This," says Professor Veitch, a philosopher, a scholar, and a man of letters, "though put with an almost sublime egotism, is in the main true." Almost equally characteristic is the fact that, after beginning his pamphlet by calling Lockhart "the only man thoroughly qualified for the task" of writing Scott's life, Hogg

HOGG.

elsewhere, in one of the extraordinary flings that distinguish him, writes: "Of Lockhart's genius and capabilities Sir Walter always spoke with the greatest enthusiasm: more than I thought he deserved. For I knew him a great deal better than Sir Walter did, and, whatever Lockhart may pretend, I knew Sir Walter a thousand times better than he did."

HOGG.

Now be it remembered that these passages are descriptive of Hogg's Hogg, to use the always useful classification of Dr. Holmes. To complete them (the actual texts are too long to give here) it is only necessary to compare the accounts of a certain dinner at Bowhill given respectively by Hogg in the *Domestic Manners* and by Lockhart in his biography, and also those given in the same places of the one-sided quarrel between Scott and Hogg, because the former, according to his almost invariable habit, refused to collaborate in Hogg's *Poetic Mirror*. In all this we have the man's own testimony about himself. It is not in the least incompatible with his having been, as his panegyrists contend, an affectionate friend, husband, and father; a very good fellow when his vanity or his whims were not touched; and inexhaustibly fertile in the kind of rough profusion of flower and weed that uncultivated soil frequently produces. But it most certainly is also not inconsistent, but on the contrary highly consistent, with the picture drawn by Lockhart in his great book; and it shows how, to say the least and mildest, the faults and foibles of the curious personage known as "the Shepherd of the *Noctes*" were not the parts of the character on which Wilson need have spent, or did spend, most of his invention. Even if the "boozing buffoon" had been a boozing buffoon and nothing more, Hogg, who confesses with a little affected remorse, but with evident pride, that he once got regularly drunk every night for some six weeks running, till "an inflammatory fever" kindly pulled him up, could not have greatly objected to this part of the matter. The wildest excesses of the *Eidolon*-Shepherd's vanity do not exceed that speech to Scott which Professor Veitch thinks so true; and the quaintest pranks played by the same shadow do not exceed in quaintness the immortal story of Hogg being introduced to Mrs. Scott for the first time, extending himself on a sofa at full length (on the excuse that he "thought he could never do wrong to copy the lady of the house," who happened at the time to be in a delicate state of health), and ending by addressing her as "Charlotte." This is the story that Mrs. Garden, Hogg's daughter, without attempting to contest its truth, describes as told by Lockhart with "uncalled-for malignity." Now when anybody who knows something of Lockhart comes across "malignant," "scorpion," or any term of the kind, he, if he is wise, merely shrugs his shoulders. All the literary copy-books have got it that Lockhart was malignant, and there is of course no more to be said.[1] But something may

HOGG.

[1] For something more, however, see the Essay on Lockhart below.

be done by a little industrious clearing away of fiction in particulars. It may be most assuredly and confidently asserted that no one reading the *Life of Scott* without knowing what Hogg's friends have said of it would dream of seeing malignity in the notices which it contains of the Shepherd. Before writing this paper I gave myself the trouble, or indulged myself in the pleasure (for perhaps that is the more appropriate phrase in reference to the most delightful of biographies, if not of books), of marking with slips of paper all the passages in Lockhart referring to Hogg, and reading them consecutively. I am quite sure that any one who does this, even knowing little or nothing of the circumstances, will wonder where on earth the "ungenerous assaults," the "virulent detraction," the "bitter words," the "false friendship," and so forth, with which Lockhart has been charged, are to be found. But any one who knows that Hogg had, just before his own death, and while the sorrow of Sir Walter's end was fresh, published the possibly not ill-intentioned but certainly ill-mannered pamphlet referred to—a pamphlet which contains among other things, besides the grossest impertinences about Lady Scott's origin, at least one insinuation that Scott wrote Lockhart's books for him—if any one further knows (I think the late Mr. Scott Douglas was the first to point out the fact) that Hogg had calmly looted Lockhart's biography of Burns, then he will think that the "scorpion," instead of using his sting, showed

HOGG.

most uncommon forbearance. This false friend, virulent detractor and ungenerous assailant describes Hogg as "a true son of nature and genius with a naturally kind and simple character." He does indeed remark that Hogg's "notions of literary honesty were exceedingly loose." But (not to mention the Burns affair, which gave me some years ago a clue to this sentence) the remark is subjoined to a letter in which Hogg placidly suggests that he shall write an autobiographic sketch, and that Scott, transcribing it and substituting the third person for the first, shall father it as his own. The other offence I suppose was the remark that "the Shepherd's nerves were not heroically strung." This perhaps might have been left out, but if it was the fact (and Hogg's defenders never seem to have traversed it) it suggested itself naturally enough in the context, which deals with Hogg's extraordinary desire, when nearly forty, to enter the militia as an ensign. Moreover the same passage contains plenty of kindly description of the Shepherd. Perhaps there is "false friendship" in quoting a letter from Scott to Byron which describes Hogg as "a wonderful creature," or in describing the Shepherd's greeting to Wilkie, "Thank God for it! I did not know you were so young a man" as "graceful," or in the citation of Jeffrey's famous blunder in selecting for special praise a fabrication of Hogg's among the "Jacobite Ballads," or in the genial description, without a touch of ridicule, of Hogg at the St. Ronan's

HOGG.

Games. The sentence on Hogg's death is indeed severe: "It had been better for his memory had his end been of earlier date; for he did not follow his benefactor until he had insulted his dust." It is even perhaps a little too severe, considering Hogg's irresponsible and childlike nature. But Lockhart might justly have retorted that men of sixty-four have no business to be irresponsible children; and it is certainly true that in this unlucky pamphlet Hogg distinctly accuses Scott of anonymously puffing himself at his, Hogg's, expense, of being over and over again jealous of him, of plagiarising his plots, of sneering at him, and, if the passage has any meaning, of joining a conspiracy of "the whole of the aristocracy and literature of the country" to keep Hogg down and "crush him to a nonentity." Neither could Lockhart have been exactly pleased at the passage where Scott is represented as afraid to clear the character of an innocent friend to the boy Duke of Buccleuch.

HOGG.

He told me that which I never knew nor suspected before; that a certain gamekeeper, on whom he bestowed his maledictions without reserve, had prejudiced my best friend, the young Duke of Buccleuch, against me by a story; and though he himself knew it to be a malicious and invidious lie, yet seeing his grace so much irritated, he durst not open his lips on the subject, further than by saying, "But, my lord duke, you must always remember that Hogg is no ordinary man, although he may have shot a stray moorcock." And then turning to me he said, "Before you had ventured to give any saucy language to a low scoundrel of an English gamekeeper, you should have thought of Fielding's tale of Black George."

"I never saw that tale," said I, "and dinna HOGG. ken ought about it. But never trouble your head about that matter, Sir Walter, for it is awthegither out o' nature for our young chief to entertain ony animosity against me. The thing will never mair be heard of, an' the chap that tauld the lees on me will gang to hell, that's aye some comfort."

Part of my reason for quoting this last passage is to recall to those who are familiar with the *Noctes Ambrosianæ* the extraordinary felicity of the imitation. This, which Hogg with his own pen represents himself as speaking with his own mouth, might be found textually in any page of the *Noctes* without seeming in the least out of keeping with the ideal Hogg.

And this brings me to the second charge of Hogg's friends, that Wilson wickedly caricatured his humble friend, if indeed he did not manufacture a Shepherd out of his own brain. This is as uncritical as the other, and even more surprising. That any one acquainted with Hogg's works, especially his autobiographic productions, should fail to recognise the resemblance is astonishing enough ; but what is more astonishing is that any one interested in Hogg's fame should not perceive that the Shepherd of the *Noctes* is Hogg magnified and embellished in every way. He is not a better poet, for the simple reason that the verses put in his mouth are usually Hogg's own and not always his best. But out of the *Confes-*

sions of a Sinner, Hogg has never signed anything half so good as the best prose passages assigned to him in the *Noctes*. They are what he might have written if he had taken pains: they are in his key and vein; but they are much above him. Again, unless any reader is so extraordinarily devoid of humour as to be shocked by the mere horse-play, it must be clear to him that the Shepherd's manners are dressed up with extraordinary skill, so as to be just what he would have liked them to be. As for the drinking and so forth, it simply comes to this—that the habits which were fashionable when the century was not yet in its teens, or just in them, were getting to be looked on askance when it was entering or had entered on its thirties. But, instead of being annoyed at this Socrates-Falstaff, as somebody has called it, one might have thought that both Hogg himself and his admirers would have taken it as an immense compliment. The only really bad turn that Wilson seems to have done his friend was posthumous and pardonable. He undertook the task of writing the Shepherd's life and editing his *Remains* for the benefit of his family, who were left very badly off; and he not only did not do it but appears to have lost the documents with which he was entrusted. It is fair to say that after the deaths, which came close together, of his wife, of Blackwood, and of Hogg himself, Wilson was never fully the same man; and that his strongly sentimental nature, joined to his now inveterate

HOGG.

habit of writing rapidly as the fancy took him, would have made the task of hammering out a biography and of selecting and editing *Remains* so distasteful from different points of view as to be practically impossible. But in that case of course he should not have undertaken it, or should have relinquished it as soon as he found out the difficulties. Allan Cunningham, it is said, would have gladly done the business; and there were few men better qualified.

HOGG.

And now, having done a by no means unnecessary task in this preliminary clearance of rubbish, let us see what sort of a person in literature and life this Ettrick Shepherd really was—the Shepherd whom Scott not only befriended with unwearied and lifelong kindness, but ranked very high as an original talent, whom Byron thought Scott's only second worth speaking of, whom Southey, a very different person from either, esteemed highly, whom Wilson selected as the mouthpiece and model for one of the most singular and (I venture to say despite a certain passing wave of unpopularity) one of the most enduring of literary character-parts, and to whom Lockhart was, as Hogg himself late in life sets down, "a warm and disinterested friend." We have seen what Professor Veitch thinks of him—that he is the king of a higher school than Scott's. On the other hand, I fear the general English impression of him is rather that given by no Englishman, but by Thomas Carlyle, at the time of Hogg's visit to

London in 1832. Carlyle describes him as talking and behaving like a "gomeril," and amusing the town by walking about in a huge gray plaid, which was supposed to be an advertisement, suggested by his publisher.

HOGG.

The king of a school higher than Scott's and the veriest gomeril — these surely, though the judges be not quite of equal competence, are judgments of a singularly contradictory kind. Let us see what middle term we can find between them.

The mighty volume (it has been Hogg's ill-fortune that the most accessible edition of his work is in two great double-columned royal octavos, heavy to the hand and not too grateful to the eye) which contains the Shepherd's collected poetical work is not for every reader. "Poets? where are they?" Wordsworth is said, on the authority of De Quincey, to have asked, with a want of graciousness of manners uncommon even in him and never forgiven by Hogg, when the latter used the plural in his presence, and in that of Wilson and Lloyd. It was unjust as well as rude, but endless allowance certainly has to be made for Hogg as a poet. I do not know to whom the epigram that "everything that is written in Scotch dialect is not necessarily poetry" is originally due, but there is certainly some justice in it. Scotch, as a language, has grand accommodations; it has richer vowels and a more varied and musical arrangement of consonants than English, while it falls not much short of English in freedom from that mere monotony which besets the richly-vowelled continental languages. It has an almost unrivalled provision of poetical *clichés* (the sternest purist may admit a French word which has no English equivalent), that is to say, the stock phrases which Heaven knows who first minted and which will pass till they are worn out of all knowledge. It has two great poets—one in the vernacular, one in the literary language—who are rich enough to keep a bank for their inferiors almost to the end of time. The depreciation of it by "glaikit Englishers" (I am a glaikit Englisher who does not depreciate), simply because it is unfamiliar and rustic-looking, is silly enough. But its best practitioners are sometimes prone to forget that nothing ready-made will do as poetry, and that you can no more take a short cut to Parnassus by spelling good "guid" and liberally using "ava," than you can execute the same journey by calling a girl a nymph and a boy a swain. The reason why Burns is a great poet, and one of the greatest, is that he seldom or never does this in Scots. When he takes to the short cut, as he does sometimes, he usually "gets to his English." Of Hogg, who wrote some charming things and many good ones, the same cannot be said. No writer known to me, not even the eminent Dr. Young, who has the root of the poetical matter in him at all, is so utterly uncritical as Hogg. He does not seem even to have known when he borrowed and when he was original. We have seen that he told Scott that he was not of

HOGG.

his school. Now a great deal that he wrote, perhaps indeed actually the major part of his verse, is simply imitation and not often very good imitation of Scott. Here is a passage :—

HOGG.

Light on her airy steed she sprung,
Around with golden tassels hung.
No chieftain there rode half so free,
Or half so light and gracefully.
How sweet to see her ringlets pale
Wide-waving in the southland gale,
Which through the broom-wood odorous flew
To fan her cheeks of rosy hue !
Whene'er it heaved her bosom's screen
What beauties in her form were seen !
And when her courser's mane it swung,
A thousand silver bells were rung.
A sight so fair, on Scottish plain,
A Scot shall never see again.

I think we know where this comes from. Indeed Hogg had a certain considerable faculty of conscious parody as well as of unconscious imitation, and his *Poetic Mirror*, which he wrote as a kind of humorous revenge on his brother bards for refusing to contribute, is a fair second to *Rejected Addresses.* The amusing thing is that he often parodied where he did not mean parody in the least, and nowadays we do not want Scott-and-water. Another vein of Hogg's, which he worked mercilessly, is a similar imitation, not of Scott, but of the weakest echoes of Percy's *Reliques* :—

O sad, sad, was young Mary's plight :
  She took the cup, no word she spake,
She had even wished that very night
  To sleep and never more to wake.

Sad, sad indeed is the plight of the poet who publishes verses like this, of which there are thousands of lines to be found in Hogg. And then one comes to "Kilmeny," and the note changes with a vengeance:—

HOGG.

Bonny Kilmeny gaed up the glen;
But it wasna to meet Duneira's men,
Nor the rosy monk of the isle to see,
For Kilmeny was pure as pure could be.
It was only to hear the yorlin sing,
And pu' the cress-flower round the spring,
The scarlet hip and the hindberry,
For Kilmeny was pure as pure could be.

. . . . .

Kilmeny looked up with a lovely grace,
But nae smile was seen on Kilmeny's face;
As still was her look and as still was her ee
As the stillness that lay on the emeraut lea,
Or the mist that sleeps on a waveless sea.
For Kilmeny had been she kent not where,
And Kilmeny had seen what she could not declare;
Kilmeny had been where the cock never crew,
Where the rain never fell and the wind never blew.

No matter that it is necessary even here to make a cento, that the untutored singer cannot keep up the song by natural force and has not skill enough to dissemble the lapses. "Kilmeny" at its best is poetry—such poetry as, to take Hogg's contemporaries only, there is none in Rogers or Crabbe, little I fear in Southey, and not very much in Moore. Then there is no doubt at all that he could write ballads. "The Witch of Fife" is long and is not improved by being written (at least in one version) in a kind of Scots that never was on land or sea, but it is quite admirable of its class. "The Good Grey Cat," his own imitation of himself in the *Poetic Mirror*, comes perhaps second to it, and "The Abbot McKinnon" (which is rather close to the imitations of Scott) third. But there are plenty of others. As for his poems of the more ambitious kind, "Mador of the Moor," "Pilgrims of the Sun," and even "Queen Hynde," let blushing glory—the glory attached to the literary department—hide the days on which he produced those. She can very well afford it, for the hiding leaves untouched the division of Hogg's poetical work which furnishes his highest claims to fame except "Kilmeny," the division of the songs. These are numerous and unequal as a matter of course. Not a few of them are merely variations on older scraps and fragments of the kind which Burns had made popular; some of them are absolute rubbish; some of them are mere imitations of Burns himself. But this leaves abundance of precious remnants, as the Shepherd's covenanting friends would have said. The before-mentioned "Donald Macdonald" is a famous song of its kind: "I'll no wake wi' Annie" comes very little short of Burns's "Green grow the rashes O!" The piece on the lifting of the banner of Buccleuch, though a curious contrast with Scott's "Up with the Banner" does not suffer too much by the comparison: "Cam' ye by Athole" and "When

HOGG.

the kye comes hame" everybody knows, and I do not know whether it is a mere delusion, but there seems to me to be a rare and agreeable humour in "The Village of Balmaquhapple."

HOGG.

D'ye ken the big village of Balmaquhapple?
The great muckle village of Balmaquhapple?
'Tis steeped in iniquity up to the thrapple,
An' what's to become o' poor Balmaquhapple?

Whereafter follows an invocation to St. Andrew, with a characteristic suggestion that he may spare himself the trouble of intervening for certain persons such as

Geordie, our deacon for want of a better,
And Bess, wha delights in the sins that beset her—

ending with the milder prayer:

But as for the rest, for the women's sake save them,
Their bodies at least, and their sauls if they have them.

. . . . .

And save, without word of confession auricular,
The clerk's bonny daughters, and Bell in particular;
For ye ken that their beauty's the pride and the stapple
Of the great wicked village of Balmaquhapple!

"Donald McGillavry," which deceived Jeffrey, is another of the half-inarticulate songs which have the gift of setting the blood coursing;

Donald's gane up the hill hard an' hungry;
Donald's come down the hill wild an' angry:
Donald will clear the gowk's nest cleverly;
Here's to the King and Donald McGillavry!

. . . . .

Donald has foughten wi' reif and roguery,
Donald has dinnered wi' banes and beggary;

Better it war for Whigs an' Whiggery
Meeting the deevil than Donald McGillavry.
Come like a tailor, Donald McGillavry,
Come like a tailor, Donald McGillavry,
Push about, in an' out, thimble them cleverly.
Here's to King James an' Donald McGillavry!

"Love is Like a Dizziness," and the "Boys' Song,"

Where the pools are bright and deep,
Where the grey trout lies asleep,
Up the river and over the lea,
That's the way for Billy and me—

and plenty more charming things will reward the explorer of the Shepherd's country. Only let that explorer be prepared for pages on pages of the most unreadable stuff, the kind of stuff which hardly any educated man, however great a "gomeril" he might be, would ever dream of putting to paper, much less of sending to press. It is fair to repeat that the educated man who thus refrained would probably be a very long time before he wrote "Kilmeny," or even "Donald McGillavry" and "The Village of Balmaquhapple."

Still (though to say it is enough to make him turn in his grave) if Hogg had been a verse-writer alone he would, except for "Kilmeny" and his songs, hardly be worth remembering, save by professed critics and literary free-selectors. A little better than Allan Cunningham, he is but for that single, sudden, and unsustained inspiration of "Kilmeny," and one or two of his songs, so far below Burns that Burns might enable us to pay no attention to him and not lose much. As for Scott, "Proud Maisie" (an unapproachable thing), the fragments that Elspeth Cheyne sings, even the single stanza in *Guy Mannering*, "Are these the Links of Forth? she said," any one of a thousand snatches that Sir Walter has scattered about his books with a godlike carelessness will "ding" Hogg and all his works on their own field. But then it is not saying anything very serious against a man to say that he is not so great as Scott. With those who know what poetry is, Hogg will keep his corner ("not a polished corner," as Sydney Smith would say) of the temple of Apollo.

HOGG.

Hogg wrote prose even more freely than he wrote verse, and after the same fashion—a fashion which he describes with equal frankness and truth by the phrases, "dashing on," "writing as if in desperation," "mingling pathos and absurdity," and so forth. Tales, novels, sketches, all were the same to him; and he had the same queer mixture of confidence in their merits and doubt about the manner in which they were written. *The Brownie of Bodsbeck*, *The Three Perils of Man* (which appears refashioned in the modern editions of his works as *The Siege of Roxburgh*), *The Three Perils of Woman*, *The Shepherd's Calendar* and numerous other uncollected tales exhibit for the most part very much the same characteristics. Hogg knew the Scottish peasantry well, he had abundant stores of unpublished folklore, he could invent more when wanted, he was not destitute of the true poetic knowledge of human nature, and at his best he could write strikingly and picturesquely. But he simply did not know what self-criticism was, he had no notion of the conduct or carpentry of a story, and though he was rather fond of choosing antique subjects, and prided himself on his knowledge of old Scots, he was quite as likely to put the baldest modern touches in the mouth of a heroine of the fourteenth or fifteenth century as not. If anybody takes pleasure in seeing how a good story can be spoilt, let him look at the sixth chapter of the *Shepherd's Calendar*, "The Souters of Selkirk;" and if any one wants to read a novel of antiquity which is not like Scott, let him read *The Bridal of Polmood.*

HOGG.

In the midst, however, of all this chaotic work, there is still to be found, though misnamed, one of the most remarkable stories of its kind ever written—a story which, as I have said before, is not only extraordinarily good of itself, but insists peremptorily that the reader shall wonder how the devil it got where it is. This is the book now called *The Private Memoirs and Confessions of a Fanatic*, but by its proper and original title, *The Confessions of a Justified Sinner*. Hogg's reference to it in his *Autobiography* is sufficiently odd. "The next year (1824)," he says, "I published *The Confessions of a Fanatic* [*Sinner*], but, it being a story replete with horrors, after I had written it

I durst not venture to put my name to it, so it was published anonymously, and of course did not sell very well—so at least I believe, for I do not remember ever receiving anything for it, and I am sure if there had been a reversion [he means return] I should have had a moiety. However I never asked anything, so on that point there was no misunderstanding." And he says nothing more about it, except to inform us that his publishers, Messrs. Longman, who had given him for his two previous books a hundred and fifty pounds each "as soon as the volumes were put to press," and who had published the *Confessions* on half profits, observed, when his next book was offered to them, that "his last publication (the *Confessions*) had been found fault with in some very material points, and they begged leave to decline the present one until they consulted some other persons." That is all. But the Reverend Thomas Thomson, Hogg's editor, an industrious and not incompetent man of letters, while admitting that it is "in excellence of plot, concentration of language and vigorous language, one of the best and most interesting [he might have said the best without a second] of Hogg's tales," observes that it "alarmed the religious portion of the community who hastily thought that the author was assailing Christianity." "Nothing could be more unfounded," says the Reverend Thomas Thomson with much justice. He might have added that it would have been much more

HOGG.

reasonable to suspect the author of practice with

HOGG.

the Evil One in order to obtain the power of writing anything so much better than his usual work.

For, in truth, *The Confessions of a Justified Sinner*, while it has all Hogg's merits and more, is quite astoundingly free from his defects. His tales are generally innocent of the most rudimentary notions of construction: this goes closely ordered, with a few pardonable enough digressions, from beginning to end. He has usually little concentrated grasp of character: the few personages of the *Confessions* are consistent throughout. His dialogue is, as a rule, extraordinarily slipshod and unequal: here there is no fault to find with it. His greatest lack, in short, is the lack of form: and here, though the story might perhaps have been curtailed, or rather "cut" in the middle, with advantage, the form is excellent. As its original edition, though an agreeable volume, is rare, and its later ones are buried amidst discordant rubbish, it may not be improper to give some account of it. The time is pitched just about the Revolution and the years following, and, according to a common if not altogether praiseworthy custom, the story consists of an editor's narrative and of the *Confessions* proper imbedded therein. The narrative tells how a drinking Royalist laird married an exceedingly precise young woman, how the dissension which was probable broke out between them, how a certain divine, the Reverend Robert

Wringhim, endeavoured to convert the sinner at the instances of the saint, and perhaps succeeded in consoling the saint at the expense of the sinner; how the laird sought more congenial society with a certain cousin of his named Arabella Logan, and how, rather out of jealousy than forgiveness, such a union or quasi-union took place between husband and wife that they had two sons, George and Robert, the elder of whom was his father's favourite and like, while the younger was pretty much left to the care of Mr. Wringhim. The tale then tells how, after hardly seeing one another in boyhood, the brothers met as young men at Edinburgh, where on extreme provocation the elder was within an ace of killing the younger. The end of it was that, after Robert had brought against George a charge of assaulting him on Arthur's Seat, George himself was found mysteriously murdered in an Edinburgh close. His mother cared naught for it; his father soon died of grief; the obnoxious Robert succeeded to the estates, and only Arabella Logan was left to do what she could to clear up the mystery, which, after certain strange passages, she did. But when warrants were made out against Robert he had disappeared, and the whole thing remained wrapped in more mystery than ever.

HOGG.

To this narrative succeed the confessions of Robert himself. He takes of course the extreme side both of his mother and of her doctrines, but for some time, though an accomplished Pharisee, he is not assured of salvation, till at last his adopted (if not real) father Wringhim announces that he has wrestled sufficiently in prayer and has received assurance.

HOGG.

Thereupon the young man sallies out in much exaltation of feeling and full of contempt for the unconverted. As he goes he meets another young man of mysterious appearance, who seems to be an exact double of himself. This wraith, however, presents himself as only a humble admirer of Robert's spiritual glory, and holds much converse with him. He meets this person repeatedly, but is never able to ascertain who he is. The stranger says that he may be called Gil Martin if Robert likes, but hints that he is some great one—perhaps the Czar Peter, who was then known to be travelling incognito about Europe. For a time Robert's Illustrious Friend (as he generally calls him) exaggerates the extremest doctrines of Calvinism, and slips easily from this into suggestions of positive crime. A minister named Blanchard, who has overheard his conversation, warns Robert against him, and Gil Martin in return points out Blanchard as an enemy to religion whom it is Robert's duty to take off. They lay wait for the minister and pistol him, the Illustrious Friend managing not only to avert all suspicion from themselves, but to throw it with capital consequences on a perfectly innocent person. After this initiation in blood Robert is fully reconciled to the "great work" and, going to Edinburgh, is led by his Illustrious Friend without difficulty into the series of plots against his brother which had to outsiders so strange an appearance, and which ended in a fresh murder. When Robert in the course of events above described becomes master of Dalchastel, the family estate, his Illustrious Friend accompanies him and the same process goes on. But now things turn less happily for Robert. He finds himself, without any consciousness of the acts charged, accused on apparently indubitable evidence, first of peccadillos, then of serious crimes. Seduction, forgery, murder, even matricide are hinted against him, and at last, under the impression that indisputable proofs of the last two crimes have been discovered, he flies from his house. After a short period of wandering, in which his Illustrious Friend alternately stirs up all men against him and tempts him to suicide, he finally in despair succumbs to the temptation and puts an end to his life. This of course ends the *Memoir*, or rather the *Memoir* ends just before the catastrophe. There is then a short postscript in which the editor tells a tale of a suicide found with some such legend attaching to him on a Border hill-side, of an account given in *Blackwood* of the searching of the grave, and of a visit to it made by himself (the editor), his friend Mr. L——t of C——d [Lockhart of Chiefswood], Mr. L——w [Scott's Laidlaw] and others. The whole thing ends with a very well written bit of rationalisation of the now familiar kind, discussing the authenticity of the *Memoirs*, and concluding that they are probably the work of some one suffering from religious mania, or perhaps a sort of parable or allegory worked out with insufficient skill.

HOGG.

Although some such account as this was necessary, no such account, unless illustrated with the most copious citation, could do justice to the book. The first part or Narrative is not of extraordinary, though it is of considerable merit, and has some of Hogg's usual faults. The *Memoirs* proper are almost wholly free from these faults. In no book known to me is the grave treatment of the topsy-turvy and improbable better managed ; although, by an old trick, it pleases the "editor" to depreciate his work in the passage just mentioned. The writer, whoever he was, was fully qualified for the task. The possibility of a young man of narrow intellect—his passion against his brother already excited, and his whole mind given to the theology of predestination—gliding into such ideas as are here described is undoubted ; and it is made thoroughly credible to the reader. The story of the pretended Gil Martin, preposterous as it is, is told by the unlucky maniac exactly in the manner in which a man deluded, but with occasional suspicions of his delusion, would tell it. The gradual change from intended and successful rascality and crime into the incurring or the supposed incurring of the most hideous guilt without any actual consciousness of guilty action may seem an almost hopeless thing to treat probably. Yet it is so treated here. And the final gathering and blackening of the clouds of despair (though here again there is a very slight touch of Hogg's undue prolongation of things) exhibits literary power of the ghastly kind infinitely different from and far above the usual raw-head-and-bloody-bones story of the supernatural.

HOGG.

Now, who wrote it?

No doubt, so far as I know, has been generally entertained of Hogg's authorship, though, since I myself entertained doubts on the subject, I have found some good judges not unwilling to agree with me. Although admitting that it appeared anonymously, Hogg claims it, as we have seen, not only without hesitation but apparently without any suspicion that it was a particularly valuable or meritorious thing to claim, and without any attempt to shift, divide, or in any way disclaim the responsibility, though the book had been a failure. His publishers do not seem to have doubted then that it was his; nor, I have been told, have their representatives any reason to doubt it now. His daughter, I think, does not so much as mention it in her *Memorials*, but his various biographers have never, so far as I know, hinted the least hesitation. At the same time I am absolutely unable to believe that it is Hogg's unadulterated and unassisted work. It is not one of those cases where a man once tries a particular style, and then from accident, disgust, or what not, relinquishes it. Hogg was always trying the supernatural, and he failed in it, HOGG. except in this instance, as often as he tried it. Why should he on this particular occasion have been saved from himself? and who saved him?—for that great part of the book at least is his there can be no doubt.

By way of answer to these questions I can at least point out certain coincidences and probabilities. It has been seen that Lockhart's name actually figures in the postscript to the book. Now at this time and for long afterwards Lockhart was one of the closest of Hogg's literary allies; and Hogg, while admitting that the author of *Peter's Letters* hoaxed him as he hoaxed everybody, is warm in his praise. He describes him in his *Autobiography* as "a warm and disinterested friend." He tells us in the book on Scott how he had a plan, even later than this, that Lockhart should edit all his (the Shepherd's) works, for discouraging which plan he was very cross with Sir Walter. Further, the vein of the *Confessions* is very closely akin to, if not wholly identical with, a vein which Lockhart not only worked on his own account but worked at this very same time. It was in these very years of his residence at Chiefswood that Lockhart produced the little masterpiece of "Adam Blair" (where the terrors and temptations of a convinced Presbyterian minister are dwelt upon), and "Matthew Wald," which is itself the history of a lunatic as full of horrors, and those of no very different kind, as the

Confessions themselves. That editing, and perhaps something more than editing, on Lockhart's part would have been exactly the thing necessary to prune and train and direct the Shepherd's disorderly luxuriance into the methodical madness of the Justified Sinner—to give Hogg's loose though by no means vulgar style the dress of his own polished manner—to weed and shape and correct and straighten the faults of the Boar of the Forest—nobody who knows the undoubted writing of the two men will deny. And Lockhart, who was so careless of his work that to this day it is difficult, if not impossible, to ascertain what he did or did not write unassisted, would certainly not have been the man to claim a share in the book, even had it made more noise ; though he may have thought of this as well as of other things when, in his wrath over the foolish blethering about Scott, he wrote that the Shepherd's views of literary morality were peculiar. As for Hogg himself, he would never have thought of acknowledging any such editing or collaboration if it did take place ; and that not nearly so much from vanity or dishonesty as from simple carelessness, dashed perhaps with something of the habit of literary *supercherie* which the society in which he lived affected, and which he carried as far at least as any one of its members.

HOGG.

It may seem rather hard after praising a man's ewe lamb so highly to question his right in her. But I do not think there is any real hardship. I should think that the actual imagination of the story is chiefly Hogg's, for Lockhart's forte was not that quality, and his own novels suffer rather for want of it. If this be the one specimen of what the Shepherd's genius could turn out when it submitted to correction and training, it gives us a useful and interesting explanation why the mass of his work, with such excellent flashes, is so flawed and formless as a whole. It explains why he wished Lockhart to edit the others. It explains at the same time why (for the Shepherd's vanity was never far off) he set apparently little store by the book. It is only a hypothesis of course, and a hypothesis which is very unlikely ever to be proved, while in the nature of things it is even less capable of disproof. But I think there is good critical reason for it.

HOGG.

At any rate, I confess for myself, that I should not take anything like the same interest in Hogg, if he were not the putative author of the *Confessions.* The book is in a style which wearies soon if it be overdone, and which is very difficult indeed to do well. But it is one of the very best things of its kind, and that is a claim which ought never to be overlooked. And if Hogg in some lucky moment did really "write it all by himself," as the children say, then we could make up for him a volume composed of it, of "Kilmeny," and of the best of the songs, which would be a very remarkable volume indeed. It would not represent a twentieth part of his collected work, and it would probably represent a still smaller fraction of what he wrote, while all the rest would be vastly inferior. But it would be a title to no inconsiderable place in literature, and we know that good judges did think Hogg, with all his personal weakness and all his literary shortcomings, entitled to such a place.

HOGG.

III

SYDNEY SMITH

SYDNEY SMITH.

THE hackneyed joke about biographers adding a new terror to death holds still as good as ever. But biography can sometimes make a good case against her persecutors; and one of the instances which she would certainly adduce would be the instance of Sydney Smith. I more than suspect that his actual works are less and less read as time goes on, and that the brilliant virulence of *Peter Plymley*, the even greater brilliance, not marred by virulence at all, of the *Letters to Archdeacon Singleton*, the inimitable quips of his articles in the *Edinburgh Review*, are familiar, if they are familiar at all, only to the professed readers of the literature of the past, and perhaps to some intelligent newspaper men who find Sydney[1] to be what Fuseli pronounced Blake,

[1] To speak of him in this way is not impertinence or familiarity. He was most generally addressed as "Mr. Sydney," and his references to his wife are nearly always to "Mrs. Sydney," seldom or never to "Mrs. Smith."

"d—d good to steal from." But the *Life* which Lady Holland, with her mother's and Mrs. Austin's aid, produced more than thirty years ago has had a different fate; and a fresh lease of popularity seems to have been secured by another *Life*, published by Mr. Stuart Reid in 1883. This was partly abridged from the first, and partly supplied with fresh matter by a new sifting of the documents which Lady Holland had used. Nor do the authors of these works, however great must be our gratitude to them, take to themselves any such share of the credit as is due to Boswell in the case of Johnson, to Lockhart in the case of Scott, to Carlyle in the case of Sterling. Neither can lay claim to the highest literary merit of writing or arrangement; and the latter of the two contains digressions, not interesting to all readers, about the nobility of Sydney's cause. It is because both books let their subject reveal himself by familiar letters, scraps of journal, or conversation, and because the revelation of self is so full and so delightful, that Sydney Smith's immortality, now that the generation which actually heard him talk has all but disappeared, is still secured without the slightest fear of disturbance or decay. With a few exceptions (the Mrs. Partington business, the apologue of the dinners at the synod of Dort, "Noodle's Oration," and one or two more), the things by which Sydney is known to the general, all come, not from his works, but from his *Life* or

Lives. No one with any sense of fun can read the

SYDNEY SMITH.

Works without being delighted ; but in the Life and the letters the same qualities of wit appear, with other qualities which in the Works hardly appear at all. A person absolutely ignorant of anything but the Works might possibly dismiss Sydney Smith as a brilliant but bitter and not too consistent partisan, who fought desperately against abuses when his party was out, and discovered that they were not abuses at all when his party was in. A reader of his Life and of his private utterances knows him better, likes him better, and certainly does not admire him less.

He was born in 1771, the son of an eccentric and apparently rather provoking person, who for no assigned reason left his wife at the church door in order to wander about the world, and who maintained his vagabond principles so well that, as his granddaughter ruefully records, he bought, spent money on, and sold at a loss, no less than nineteen different houses in England and Wales. Sydney was also the second of four clever brothers, the eldest and cleverest being the somewhat famous "Bobus," who co-operated in the *Microcosm* with Canning and Frere, survived his better known brother but a fortnight, founded a family, and has left one of those odd reputations of immense talent not justified by any producible work, to which our English life of public schools, universities, and Parliament gives peculiar facilities. Bobus and

Cecil the third brother were sent to Eton: Sydney and Courtenay, the fourth, to Winchester, after a childhood spent in precocious reading and arguing among themselves. From Winchester Sydney (of whose school-days some trifling but only trifling anecdotes are recorded,) proceeded in regular course to New College, Oxford, and being elected of right to a Fellowship, then worth about a hundred pounds a year, was left by his father to "do for himself" on that not extensive revenue. He did for himself at Oxford during the space of nine years; and it is supposed that his straitened circumstances had something to do with his dislike for universities, which however was a kind of point of conscience among his Whig friends. It is at least singular that this residence of nearly a decade has left hardly a single story or recorded incident of any kind; and that though three generations of undergraduates passed through Oxford in his time, no one of them seems in later years to have had anything to say of not the least famous and one of the most sociable of Englishmen. At that time, it is true, and for long afterwards, the men of New College kept more to themselves than the men of any other college in Oxford; but still it is odd. Another little mystery is, Why did Sydney take orders? Although there is not the slightest reason to question his being, according to his own standard, a very sincere and sufficient divine, it obviously was not quite the profession for him.

SYDNEY SMITH.

He is said to have wished for the Bar, but to have deferred to his father's wishes for the Church. That Sydney was an affectionate and dutiful son nobody need doubt: he was always affectionate, and in his own way dutiful. But he is about the last man one can think of as likely to undertake an uncongenial profession out of high-flown dutifulness to a father who had long left him to his own resources, and who had neither influence nor prospects in the Church to offer him. The Fellowship would have kept him, as it had kept him already, till briefs came. However, he did take orders; and the later *Life* gives more particulars than the first as to the incumbency which indirectly determined his career. It was the curacy of Netheravon on Salisbury Plain; and its almost complete seclusion was tempered by a kindly squire, Mr. Hicks-Beach, great-grandfather of the present Sir Michael Hicks-Beach. Mr. Hicks-Beach offered Sydney the post of tutor to his eldest son; Sydney accepted it, started for Germany with his pupil, but (as he picturesquely though rather vaguely expresses it) "put into Edinburgh under stress of war" and stayed there for five years.

SYDNEY SMITH.

The sojourn at Edinburgh began in June 1798: it ended in August 1803. It will thus be seen that Sydney was by no means a very young man even when he began reviewing, the year before leaving the Scotch capital. Indeed the aimless pro-

SYDNEY SMITH.

longation of his stay at Oxford, which brought him neither friends, money, nor professional experience of any kind, threw him considerably behindhand all his life; and this delay, much more than Tory persecution or Whig indifference, was the cause of the comparative slowness with which he made his way. His time at Edinburgh was, however, usefully spent even before that invention of the *Review*, over which there is an amicable and unimportant dispute between himself and Jeffrey. His tutorship was so successful that Mr. Hicks-Beach rewarded it with a cheque for a thousand pounds: he did duty in the Episcopal churches of Edinburgh: he made friends with all the Whigs and many of the Tories of the place: he laughed unceasingly at Scotchmen and liked them very much. Also, about the middle of his stay, he got married, but not to a Scotch girl. His wife was Miss Catherine Pybus, of Cheam, and the marriage was as harebrained a one, from the point of view of settlements, as Jeffrey's own.[1] Sydney's settlement on his wife is well known: it consisted of "six small silver teaspoons much worn," with which worldly goods he did her literally endow by throwing them into her lap. It would appear that there never was a happier marriage; but it certainly seemed for some years as if there might have been many more prosperous in point of money. When Sydney moved to

[1] See next Essay.

London he had no very definite prospect of any income whatever; and had not Mrs. Smith sold her mother's jewels (which came to her just at the time), they would apparently have had some difficulty in furnishing their house in Doughty Street. But Horner, their friend (the "parish bull" of Scott's irreverent comparison), had gone to London before them, and impressed himself, apparently by sheer gravity, on the political world as a good young man. Introduced by him, Sydney Smith soon became one of the circle at Holland House. It is indeed not easy to live on invitations and your mother-in-law's pearls; but Sydney reviewed vigorously, preached occasionally, before very long received a regular appointment at the Foundling Hospital, and made some money by lecturing very agreeably at the Royal Institution on Moral Philosophy—a subject of which he honestly admits that he knew, in the technical sense, nothing. But his hearers did not want technical ethics, and in Sydney Smith they had a moral philosopher of the practical kind who could hardly be excelled either in sense or in wit. One little incident of this time, however, throws some light on the complaints which have been made about the delay of his promotion. He applied to a London rector to license him to a vacant chapel, which had not hitherto been used for the services of the Church. The immediate answer has not been preserved; but from what followed it clearly was a civil and

SYDNEY SMITH.

rather evasive but perfectly intelligible request to be excused. The man was of course quite within his right, and a dozen good reasons can be guessed for his conduct. He may really have objected, as he seems to have said he did, to take a step which his predecessors had refused to take, and which might inconvenience his successors. But Sydney would not take the refusal, and wrote another very logical, but extremely injudicious, letter pressing his request with much elaboration, and begging the worthy Doctor of Divinity to observe that he, the Doctor, was guilty of inconsistency and other faults. Naturally this put the Doctor's back up, and he now replied with a flat and very high and mighty refusal. We know from another instance that Sydney was indisposed to take "No" for an answer. However he obtained, besides his place at the Foundling, preacherships in two proprietary chapels, and seems to have had both business and pleasure enough on his hands during his London sojourn, which was about the same length as his Edinburgh one. It was, however, much more profitable, for in three years the ministry of "All the Talents" came in, the Holland House interest was exerted, and the Chancellor's living of Foston, near York, valued at five hundred pounds a year, was given to Sydney. He paid for it, after a fashion which in a less zealous and convinced Whig might seem a little dubious, by the famous lampoons of the *Plymley Letters*, advocating the claims of Catholic emancipation, and extolling Fox and Grenville at the expense of Perceval and Canning. Very edifying is it to find Sydney Smith objecting to this latter that he is a "diner out," a "maker of jokes and parodies," a trifler on important subjects—in fact each and all of the things which the Rev. Sydney Smith himself was, in a perfection only equalled by the object of his righteous wrath. But of Peter more presently.

SYDNEY SMITH.

Even his admiring biographers have noticed, with something of a chuckle, the revenge which Perceval, who was the chief object of Plymley's sarcasm, took, without in the least knowing it, on his lampooner. Had it not been for the Clergy Residence Bill, which that very respectable, if not very brilliant, statesman passed in 1808, and which put an end to perhaps the most flagrant of all then existing abuses, Sydney, the enemy of abuses, would no doubt have continued with a perfectly clear conscience to draw the revenues of Foston, and while serving it by a curate, to preach, lecture, dine out, and rebuke Canning for making jokes, in London. As it was he had to make up his mind, though he obtained a respite from the Archbishop, to resign (which in the recurring frost of Whig hopes was not to be thought of), to exchange, which he found impossible, or to bury himself in Yorkshire. This was a real hardship upon him, because Foston, as it was, was uninhabitable, and had had no resident clergyman since the seventeenth century. But whatever bad things could be said of Sydney (and I really do not know what they are, except that the combination of a sharp wit, a ready pen, and strong political prejudices sometimes made him abuse his talents), no one could say that he ever shirked either a difficulty or a duty. When his first three years' leave expired, he went down in 1809 with his family to York, and established himself at Heslington, a village near the city and not far from his parish. And when a second term of dispensation from actual residence was over, he set to work and built the snuggest if the ugliest parsonage in England, with farm-buildings and all complete, at the cost of some four thousand pounds. Of the details of that building his own inimitable account exists, and is or ought to be well known. The brick-pit and kiln on the property, which were going to save fortunes and resulted in nothing but the production of exactly a hundred and fifty thousand unusable bricks: the four oxen, Tug, Lug, Haul and Crawl, who were to be the instruments of another economy and proved to be, at least in Sydneian language, equal to nothing but the consumption of "buckets of sal volatile:" the entry of the distracted mother of the household on her new domains with a baby clutched in her arms and one shoe left in the circumambient mud: the great folks of the neighbourhood (Lord and Lady Carlisle) coming to call graciously on the strangers,

SYDNEY SMITH.

and being whelmed, coach and four, outriders and all, in a ploughed field of despond: the "universal scratcher" in the meadows, inclined so as to let the brute creation of all heights enjoy that luxury: Bunch the butler, a female child of tender years but stout proportions: Annie Kay the factotum: the "Immortal," a chariot which was picked up at York in the last stage of decay, and carried the family for many years half over England—all these things and persons are told in divers delightful scraps of autobiography and in innumerable letters, after a fashion impossible to better and at a length too long to quote.

SYDNEY SMITH.

Sydney Smith was for more than twenty years rector of Foston, and for fully fifteen actually resided there. During this time he made the acquaintance of Lord and Lady Grey, next to Lord and Lady Holland his most constant friends, visited a little, entertained in his own unostentatious but hearty fashion a great deal, wrote many articles for the *Edinburgh Review*, found himself in a minority of one or two among the clergy of Yorkshire on the subject of Emancipation and similar matters, but was on the most friendly terms possible with his diocesan, Archbishop Vernon Harcourt. Nor was he even without further preferment, for he held for some years (on the then not discredited understanding of resignation when one of the Howards was ready for it) the neighbouring and valuable living of Londesborough. Then the death of an aunt put an end to his monetary anxieties, which for years had been considerable, by the legacy of a small but sufficient fortune. And at last, when he was approaching sixty, the good things of the Church, which he never affected to despise, came in earnest. The Tory Chancellor Lyndhurst gave him a stall at Bristol, which carried with it a small Devonshire living, and soon afterwards he was able to exchange Foston (which he had greatly improved), for Combe Florey near Taunton. When his friend Lord Grey became Prime Minister, the stall at Bristol was exchanged for a much more valuable one at St. Paul's; Halberton, the Devonshire vicarage, and Combe Florey still remaining his. These made up an ecclesiastical revenue not far short of three thousand a year, which Sydney enjoyed for the last fifteen years of his life. He never got anything more, and it is certain that for a time he was very sore at not being made a bishop, or at least offered a bishopric. Lord Holland had rather rashly explained the whole difficulty years before, by reporting a conversation of his with Lord Grenville, in which they had hoped that when the Whigs came into power they would be more grateful to Sydney than the Tories had been to Swift. Sydney's acuteness must have made him wince at the omen. For my part I do not see why either Harley or Grey should have hesitated, as far as any scruples of their own went.

SYDNEY SMITH.

SYDNEY SMITH.

But I think any fair-minded person must admit the possibility of a scruple, though he may not share it, about the effect of seeing either the *Tale of a Tub* or *Peter Plymley's Letters*, with "By the Right Rev. the Lord Bishop of——" on the title-page. The people who would have been shocked might in each case have been fools: there is nothing that I at least can see, in either book, inconsistent with sound religion and churchmanship. But they would have been honest fools, and of such a Prime Minister has to take heed. So Amen Corner (or rather, for he did not live there, certain streets near Grosvenor Square) in London, and Combe Florey in the country, were Sydney Smith's abodes till his death. In the former he gave his breakfasts and dinners in the season, being further enabled to do so by his share (some thirty thousand pounds) of his brother Courtenay's Indian fortune. The latter, after rebuilding it,—for he had either a fate or a passion for bricks and mortar,—he made on a small scale one of the most beautiful and hospitable houses in the West of England.

To Combe Florey, as to Foston, a sheaf of fantastic legends attaches itself; indeed, as Lady Holland was not very fond of dates, it is sometimes not clear to which of the two residences some of them apply. At both Sydney had a huge store-room, or rather grocer's and chemist's shop, from which he supplied the wants, not merely of his household, but of half the neighbourhood. It

SYDNEY SMITH.

appears to have been at Combe Florey (for though no longer poor he still had a frugal mind), that he hit upon the device of "putting the cheapest soaps in the dearest papers," confident of the result upon the female temper. It was certainly there that he fitted up two favourite donkeys with a kind of holiday-dress of antlers, to meet the objection of one of his lady-visitors that he had no deer; and converted certain large bay-trees in boxes into the semblance of an orangery, by fastening some dozens of fine fruit to the branches. I like to think of the mixed astonishment and disgust of a great Russian, and a not very small Frenchman, both not long deceased, M. Tourguénieff and M. Paul de Saint-Victor, if they had heard of these pleasing tomfooleries. But tomfoolery, though, when properly and not inordinately indulged, one of the best things in life, must, like the other good things of life, come to an end. After an illness of some months Sydney Smith died at his house in Green Street, of heart disease, on 22nd February 1845, in the seventy-fourth year of his age.

The memorials and evidences of his peculiar if not unique genius consist of three different kinds; reported or remembered conversations and jokes, letters, and formal literary work. He was once most famous as a talker; but conversation is necessarily the most perishable of all things, and its recorded fragments bear keeping less than any other relics. Some of the verbal jests assigned to him (notably the famous one about the tortoise, which, after being long known by the initiated not to be his, has at last been formally claimed by its rightful owner), are certainly or probably borrowed or falsely attributed, as rich conversationalists always borrow or receive. And always the things have something of the mangled air which sayings detached from their context can hardly escape. It is otherwise with the letters. The best letters are always most like the actual conversation of their writers, and probably no one ever wrote more as he talked than Sydney Smith. The specially literary qualities of his writing for print are here too in great measure; and on the whole, though of course the importance of subject is nearly always less, and the interest of sustained work is wholly absent, nowhere can the entire Sydney be better seen. Of the three satirists of modern times with whom he may not unfairly claim to rank—Pascal, Swift, and Voltaire—he is most like Voltaire in his faculty of presenting a good thing with a preface which does not in the least prepare you for it, and then leaving it without the slightest attempt to go back on it, and elaborate it, and make sure that his hearer has duly appreciated it and laughed at it. And of the two, though the palm of concentration must be given to Voltaire, the palm of absolute simplicity must be given to Sydney. Hardly any of his letters are without these unforced flashes of wit, from almost his first

SYDNEY SMITH.

SYDNEY SMITH.

epistle to Jeffrey (where, after rallying that great little man on being the "only male despondent he has met," he adds the postscript, "I beg to except the Tuxford waiter, who desponds exactly as you do") to his very last to Miss Harcourt, in which he mildly dismisses one of his brethren as "anything but a *polished* corner of the Temple." There is the "usual establishment for an eldest landed baby:" the proposition, advanced in the grave and chaste manner, that "the information of very plain women is so inconsiderable, that I agree with you in setting no store by it:" the plaintive expostulation with Lady Holland (who had asked him to dinner on the ninth of the month, after previously asking him to stay from the fifth to the twelfth), "it is like giving a gentleman an assignation for Wednesday when you are going to marry him on the previous Sunday—an attempt to combine the stimulus of gallantry with the security of connubial relations:" the simple and touching information that "Lord Tankerville has sent me a whole buck. This necessarily takes up a good deal of my time;" that "geranium-fed bacon is of a beautiful colour, but it takes so many plants to fatten one pig that such a system can never answer;" that "it is a mistake to think that Dr. Bond could be influenced by partridges. He is a man of very independent mind, with whom pheasants at least, or perhaps even turkeys, are necessary;" and scores more with references to which I find the fly-leaves of my copy of the letters covered. If any one wants to see how much solid there is with all this froth, let him turn to the passages showing the unconquerable manliness, fairness, and good sense with which Sydney treated the unhappy subject of Queen Caroline, out of which his friends were so ready to make political capital ; or to the admirable epistle in which he takes seriously, and blunts once for all, the points of certain foolish witticisms as to the readiness with which he, a man about town, had taken to catechisms and cabbages in an almost uninhabited part of the despised country. In conversation he would seem sometimes to have a little, a very little, "forced the note." The Quaker baby, and the lady "with whom you might give an assembly or populate a parish," are instances in point. But he never does this in his letters. I take particular pleasure in the following passage written to Miss Georgiana Harcourt within two years of his death : "What a charming existence ! To live in the midst of holy people ; to know that nothing profane can approach you ; to be certain that a Dissenter can no more be found in the Palace than a snake can exist in Ireland, or ripe fruit in Scotland ! To have your society strong, and undiluted by the laity ; to bid adieu to human learning ; to feast on the Canons and revel in the Thirty-Nine Articles ! Happy Georgiana ! " Now if Sydney had been what some foolish people think him, merely a scoffer, there would be no fun

SYDNEY SMITH.

in this; it would be as impertinent and in as bad taste as the stale jokes of the eighteenth century about Christianity. But he was much else.

SYDNEY SMITH.

Of course, however, no rational man will contend that in estimating Sydney Smith's place in the general memory, his deliberate literary work, or at least that portion of it which he chose to present on reflection, acknowledged and endorsed, can be overlooked. His *Life* contains (what is infinitely desirable in all such Lives and by no means always or often furnished) a complete list of his contributions to the *Edinburgh Review*, and his works contain most of them. To these have to be added the pamphlets, of which the chief and incomparably the best are, at intervals of thirty years, *Peter Plymley* and the *Letters to Archdeacon Singleton*, together with sermons, speeches, and other miscellaneous matter. The whole, except the things which he did not himself care to reprint, can be obtained now in one volume; but the print is not to be recommended to aged or weakly sight.

Sydney Smith had no false modesty, and in not a few letters to Jeffrey he speaks of his own contributions to the *Edinburgh* with the greatest freedom, combating and quite refusing to accept his editor's suggestion as to their flippancy and fantasticality, professing with much frankness that this is the way he can write and no other, and more than once telling Jeffrey that whatever they may think in solemn Scotland, his, Sydney's, articles are a great deal more read in England and elsewhere than any others. Although there are maxims to the contrary effect, the judgment of a clever man, not very young and tolerably familiar with the world, on his own work, is very seldom far wrong. I should say myself that, putting aside the historic estimate, Sydney Smith's articles are by far the most interesting nowadays of those contributed by any one before the days of Macaulay, who began just as Sydney ceased to write anonymously in 1827, on his Bristol appointment. They are also by far the most distinct and original. Jeffrey, Brougham, and the rest wrote, for the most part, very much after the fashion of the ancients: if a very few changes were made for date, passages of Jeffrey's criticism might almost be passages of Dryden, certainly passages of the better critics of the eighteenth century, as far as manner goes. There is nobody at all like Sydney Smith before him in England, for Swift's style is wholly different. To begin with, Sydney had a strong prejudice in favour of writing very short articles, and a horror of reading long ones—the latter being perhaps less peculiar to himself than the former. Then he never made the slightest pretence at systematic or dogmatic criticism of anything whatever. In literature proper he seems indeed to have had no particular principles, and I cannot say that he had very good taste. He commits the almost unpardonable sin of not merely blaspheming Madame

SYDNEY SMITH.

de Sévigné, but preferring to her that second-rate leader-writer in petticoats, Madame de Staël. On the other hand, if he had no literary principles, he had (except in rare cases where politics came in, and not often then) few literary prejudices, and his happily incorrigible good sense and good humour were proof against the frequent bias of his associates. Though he could not have been very sensible, from what he himself says, of their highest qualities, he championed Scott's novels incessantly against the Whigs and prigs of Holland House. He gives a most well-timed warning to Jeffrey that the constant running-down of Wordsworth had very much the look of persecution, though with his usual frankness he avows that he has not read the particular article in question, because the subject is "quite uninteresting to him." I think he would, if driven hard, have admitted with equal frankness that poetry, merely as poetry, was generally uninteresting. Still he had so many interests of various kinds, that few books failed to appeal to one or the other, and he, in his turn, has seldom failed to give a lively if not a very exact or critical account of his subject. But it is in his way of giving this account that the peculiarity, glanced at above as making a parallel between him and Voltaire, appears. It is, I have said, almost original, and what is more, endless as has been the periodical writing of the last eighty years, and sedulously as later writers

SYDNEY SMITH.

have imitated earlier, I do not know that it has ever been successfully copied. It consists in giving rapid and apparently business-like summaries, packed, with apparent negligence and real art, full of the flashes of wit so often noticed and to be noticed. Such are, in the article on "The Island of Ceylon," the honey-bird "into whose body the soul of a common informer seems to have migrated," and "the chaplain of the garrison, all in black, the Rev. Mr. Somebody or other whose name we have forgotten," the discovery of whose body in a serpent his ruthless clerical brother pronounces to be "the best history of the kind he remembers." Very likely there may be people who can read this, even the "all in black," without laughing, and among them I should suppose must be the somebody or other, whose name we too have forgotten, who is said to have imagined that he had more than parried Sydney's unforgiven jest about the joke and the surgical operation, by retorting, "Yes! an *English* joke." I have always wept to think that Sydney did not live to hear this retort. The classical places for this kind of summary work are the article just named on Ceylon, and that on Waterton. But the most inimitable single example, if it is not too shocking to this very proper age, is the argument of Mat Lewis's tragedy: "Ottilia becomes quite furious from the conviction that Cæsario has been sleeping with a second lady called Estella; whereas he has really been sleeping with a third lady called Amelrosa."

SYDNEY SMITH.

Among the most important of these essays are the two famous ones on Methodism and on Indian missions, which gave far more offence to the religious public of evangelical persuasion than all Sydney's jokes on bishops, or his arguments for Catholic emancipation, and which (owing to the strong influence which then, as now, Nonconformists possessed in the counsels of the Liberal party) probably had as much to do as anything else with the reluctance of the Whig leaders, when they came into power, to give their friend the highest ecclesiastical preferment. These subjects are rather difficult to treat in a general literary essay, and it may perhaps be admitted that here, as in dealing with poetry and other subjects of the more transcendental kind, Sydney showed a touch of Philistinism, and a distinct inability to comprehend exaltation of sentiment and thought. But the general sense is admirably sound and perfectly orthodox ; and the way in which so apparently light and careless a writer has laboriously supported every one of his charges, and almost every one of his flings, with chapter and verse from the writings of the incriminated societies, is very remarkable. Nor can it, I think, be doubted that the publication, in so widely read a periodical, of the nauseous follies of speech in which well-meaning persons indulged, had something to do with the gradual disuse of a style than which nothing could be more prejudicial to religion, for the simple reason that nothing else could make religion ridiculous.

The medicine did not of course operate at once, and silly people still write silly things. But I hardly think that the Wesleyan body or the Church Missionary Society would now officially publish such stuff as the passage about Brother Carey, who, while in the actual paroxysm of sea-sickness, was "wonderfully comforted by the contemplation of the goodness of God," or that about Brother Ward "in design clasping to his bosom" the magnanimous Captain Wickes, who subsequently "seemed very low," when a French privateer was in sight. Jeffrey was, it seems, a little afraid of these well-deserved exposures, which, from the necessity of abundant quotation, are an exception to the general shortness of Sydney's articles. Sydney's interest in certain subjects led him constantly to take up fresh books on them; and thus a series of series might be made out of his papers, with some advantage to the reader perhaps, if a new edition of his works were undertaken. The chief of such subjects is America, in dealing with which he pleased the Americans by descanting on their gradual emancipation from English prejudices and abuses, but infuriated them by constant denunciations of slavery, and by laughing at their lack of literature and cultivation. With India he also dealt often, his brothers' connection with it giving him an interest therein. Prisons were another favourite subject, though, in his zeal for making them uncomfortable, he committed himself to one really atrocious suggestion—

that of dark cells for long periods of time. It is odd that the same person should make such a truly diabolical proposal, and yet be in a perpetual state of humanitarian rage about man-traps and spring-guns, which were certainly milder engines of torture. It is odd, too, that Sydney, who was never tired of arguing that prisons ought to be made uncomfortable, because nobody need go there unless he chose, should have been furiously wroth with poor Mr. Justice Best for suggesting much the same thing of spring-guns. The greatest political triumph of his manner is to be found no doubt in the article "Bentham on Fallacies," in which the unreadable diatribes of the apostle of utilitarianism are somehow spirited and crisped up into a series of brilliant arguments, and the whole is crowned by the famous "Noodle's Oration," the summary and storehouse of all that ever has been or can be said on the Liberal side in the lighter manner. It has not lost its point even from the fact that Noodle has now for a long time changed his party, and has elaborated for himself, after his manner, a similar stock of platitudes and absurdities in favour of the very things for which Sydney was fighting.

SYDNEY SMITH.

The qualities of these articles appear equally in the miscellaneous essays, in the speeches, and even in the sermons, though Sydney Smith, unlike Sterne, never condescended to buffoonery or theatrical tricks in the pulpit. In *Peter Plymley's Letters* they appear concentrated and acidulated:

in the *Letters to Archdeacon Singleton*, in the *Repudiation Letters*, and the *Letters on Railways* which date from his very last days, concentrated and mellowed. More than one good judge has been of the opinion that Sydney's powers increased to the very end of his life, and it is not surprising that this should have been the case. Although he did plenty of work in his time, the literary part of it was never of an exhausting nature. Though one of the most original of commentators, he was a commentator pure and simple, and found, but did not supply, his matter. Thus there was no danger of running dry, and as his happiest style was not indignation but good-natured raillery, his increasing prosperity, not chequered, till quite the close of his life, by any serious bodily ailment, put him more and more in the right atmosphere and temper for indulging his genius. *Plymley*, though very amusing, and, except in the Canning matter above referred to, not glaringly unfair for a political lampoon, is distinctly acrimonious, and almost (as "almost" as Sydney could be) ill-tempered. It is possible to read between the lines that the writer is furious at his party being out of office, and is much more angry with Mr. Perceval for having the ear of the country than for being a respectable nonentity. The main argument, moreover, is bad in itself, and was refuted by facts. Sydney pretends to be, as his friend Jeffrey really was, in mortal terror lest the French

SYDNEY SMITH.

should invade England, and, joined by rebellious Irishmen and wrathful Catholics generally, produce an English revolution. The Tories replied, "We will take good care that the French shall *not* land, and that Irishmen shall *not* rise." And they did take the said good care, and they beat the Frenchmen thorough and thorough while Sydney and his friends were pointing their epigrams. Therefore, though much of the contention is unanswerable enough, the thing is doubtfully successful as a whole. In the *Letters to Archdeacon Singleton* the tone is almost uniformly good-humoured, and the argument, whether quite consistent or not in the particular speaker's mouth, is absolutely sound, and has been practically admitted since by almost all the best friends of the Church. Here occurs that inimitable passage before referred to.

SYDNEY SMITH.

I met the other day, in an old Dutch chronicle, with a passage so apposite to this subject, that, though it is somewhat too light for the occasion, I cannot abstain from quoting it. There was a great meeting of all the clergy at Dordrecht, and the chronicler thus describes it, which I give in the language of the translation: "And there was great store of Bishops in the town, in their robes goodly to behold, and all the great men of the State were there, and folks poured in in boats on the Meuse, the Merse, the Rhine, and the Linge, coming from the Isle of Beverlandt and Isselmond, and from all quarters in the Bailiwick of Dort; Arminians and Gomarists, with the friends of John Barneveldt and of Hugh Grote. And before my Lords the Bishops, Simon of Gloucester, who was a Bishop in those parts, disputed with Vorstius and Leoline the Monk, and many texts of Scripture were bandied to and fro; and when

SYDNEY SMITH.

this was done, and many propositions made, and it waxed towards twelve of the clock, my Lords the Bishops prepared to set them down to a fair repast, in which was great store of good things—and among the rest a roasted peacock, having in lieu of a tail the arms and banners of the Archbishop, which was a goodly sight to all who favoured the Church — and then the Archbishop would say a grace, as was seemly to do, he being a very holy man; but ere he had finished, a great mob of townspeople and folks from the country, who were gathered under the windows, cried out *Bread! bread!* for there was a great famine, and wheat had risen to three times the ordinary price of the *sleich*; and when they had done crying *Bread! bread!* they called out *No Bishops!* and began to cast up stones at the windows. Whereat my Lords the Bishops were in a great fright, and cast their dinner out of the window to appease the mob, and so the men of that town were well pleased, and did devour the meats with a great appetite; and then you might have seen my Lords standing with empty plates, and looking wistfully at each other, till Simon of Gloucester, he who disputed with Leoline the Monk, stood up among them and said, *Good my Lords, is it your pleasure to stand here fasting, and that those who count lower in the Church than you do should feast and fluster? Let us order to us the dinner of the Deans and Canons which is making ready for them in the chamber below.* And this speech of Simon of Gloucester pleased the Bishops much; and so they sent for the host, one William of Ypres, and told him it was for the public good, and he, much fearing the Bishops, brought them the dinner of the Deans and Canons; and so the Deans and Canons went away without dinner, and were pelted by the men of the town, because they had not put any meat out of the windows like the Bishops; and when the Count came to hear of it, he said it was a pleasant conceit, *and that the Bishops were right cunning men, and had ding'd the Canons well.*"

Even in the Singleton Letters, however, there

are some little lapses of the same kind (worse, indeed, because these letters were signed) as the attack on Canning in the Plymley Letters. Sydney Smith exclaiming against "derision and persiflage, the great principle by which the world is now governed," is again edifying. But in truth Sydney never had the weakness (for I have known it called a weakness) of looking too carefully to see what the enemy's advocate is going to say. Take even the famous, the immortal apologue of Mrs. Partington. It covered, we are usually told, the Upper House with ridicule, and did as much as anything else to carry the Reform Bill. And yet, though it is a watery apologue, it will not hold water for a moment. The implied conclusion is, that the Atlantic beat Mrs. Partington. Did it? It made, no doubt, a great mess in her house, it put her to flight, it put her to shame. But when I was last at Sidmouth the line of high-water mark was, I believe, much what it was before the great storm of 1824, and though the particular Mrs. Partington had no doubt been gathered to her fathers, the Mrs. Partington of the day was, equally without doubt, living very comfortably in the house which the Atlantic had threatened to swallow up.

SYDNEY SMITH.

It was, however, perhaps part of Sydney's strength that he never cared to consider too curiously, or on too many sides. Besides his inimitable felicity of expression (the Singleton Letters are simply crammed with epigram), he had the sturdiest possible common sense and the liveliest possible humour. I have known his claim to the title of "humourist" called in question by precisians: nobody could deny him the title of good-humourist. Except that the sentimental side of Toryism would never have appealed to him, it was chiefly an accident of time that he was a polemical Liberal. He would always and naturally have been on the side opposite to that on which most of the fools were. When he came into the world, as the straitest Tory will admit, there were in that world a great many abuses as they are called, that is to say, a great many things which, once useful and excellent, had either decayed into positive nuisances, or dried up into neutral and harmless but obstructive rubbish. There were also many silly and some mischievous people, as well as some wise and useful ones, who defended the abuses. Sydney Smith was an ideal soldier of reform for his time, and in his way. He was not extraordinarily long-sighted—indeed (as his famous and constantly-repeated advice to "take short views of life" shows) he had a distinct distrust of taking too anxious thought for political or any other morrows. But he had a most keen and, in many cases, a most just scent and sight for the immediate inconveniences and injustices of the day, and for the shortest and most effective ways of mending them. He was perhaps more destitute of romance and of reverence (though he had too much good taste to be positively irreverent) than

SYDNEY SMITH.

any man who ever lived. He never could have paralleled, he never could have even understood, Scott's feelings about the Regalia, or that ever-famous incident of Sir Walter's life, when returning with Jeffrey and other Whig friends from some public meeting, he protested against the innovations which, harmless or even beneficial individually and in themselves, would by degrees destroy every thing that made Scotland Scotland. I am afraid that his warmest admirers, even those of his own political complexion, must admit that he was, as has been said, more than a little of a Philistine; that he expressed, and expressed capitally in one way, that curious middle-class sentiment, or denial of sentiment, which won its first triumph in the first Reform Bill and its last in the Exhibition of twenty years later, which destroyed no doubt much that was absurd, and some things that were noxious, but which induced in England a reign of shoddy in politics, in philosophy, in art, in literature, and, when its own reign was over, left England weak and divided, instead of, as it had been under the reign of abuses, united and strong. The bombardment of Copenhagen may or may not have been a dreadful thing: it was at any rate better than the abandonment of Khartoum. Nor can Sydney any more than his friends be acquitted of having held the extraordinary notion that you can "rest and be thankful" in politics, that you can set Demos at bishops, but stave and tail him off

SYDNEY SMITH.

SYDNEY SMITH.

when he comes to canons; that you can level beautifully down to a certain point, and then stop levelling for ever afterwards; that because you can laugh Brother Ringletub out of court, laughter will be equally effective with Cardinal Newman; and that though it is the height of "anility" (a favourite word of his) to believe in a country gentleman, it is the height of rational religion to believe in a ten-pound householder.

But however open to exception his principles may be, and that not merely from the point of view of highflying Toryism, his carrying out of them in life and in literature had the two abiding justifications of being infinitely amusing, and of being amusing always in thoroughly good temper. It is, as I have said, impossible to read Sydney Smith's *Life*, and still more impossible to read his letters, without liking him warmly and personally, without seeing that he was not only a man who liked to be comfortable (that is not very rare), that he was not only one who liked others to be comfortable (that is rarer), but one who in every situation in which he was thrown, did his utmost to make others as well as himself comfortable (which is rarest of all). If the references in *Peter Plymley* to Canning were unjustifiable from him, there is little or no reason to think that they were prompted by personal jealousy; and though, as has been said, he was undoubtedly sore, and unreasonably sore, at not receiving the preferment which he thought he had deserved, he does not seem to have been personally jealous of any man who had received it. The parson of Foston and Combe Florey may not have been (his latest biographer, admiring though he be, pathetically laments that he was not) a spiritually minded man. But happy beyond almost all other parishioners of the time were the parishioners of Combe Florey and Foston, though one of them did once throw a pair of scissors at his provoking pastor. He was a fast and affectionate friend; and though he was rather given to haunting rich men, he did it not only without servility, but without that alternative of bearishness and freaks which has sometimes been adopted. As a prince of talkers he might have been a bore to a generation which (I own I think in that perhaps single point), wiser than its fathers, is not so ambitious as they were to sit as a bucket and be pumped into. But in that infinitely happier system of conversation by books, which any one can enjoy as he likes and interrupt as he likes at his own fireside, Sydney is still a prince. There may be living somewhere some one who does not think so very badly of slavery, who is most emphatically of opinion that "the fools were right," in the matters of Catholic emancipation and Reform, who thinks well of public schools and universities, who even, though he may not like spring-guns much, thinks that John Jones had only himself to blame if, after ample warning and with no business except the business of supplying

SYDNEY SMITH.

a London poulterer with his landlord's game, he trespassed and came to the worst. Yet even this monster, if he happened to be possessed of the sense of fun and literature, (which is perhaps impossible), could not read even the most acrid of Sydney's political diatribes without shrieking with laughter, if, in his ogreish way, he were given to such violent demonstrations ; could certainly not read the *Life* and the letters without admitting, in a moment of unwonted humanity, that here was a man who, for goodness as well as for cleverness, for sound practical wisdom as well as for fantastic verbal wit, has had hardly a superior and very few equals.

SYDNEY SMITH.

IV

JEFFREY

"JEFFREY and I," says Christopher North in one of his more malicious moments, "do nothing original; it's porter's work." A tolerably experienced student of human nature might almost, without knowing the facts, guess the amount of truth contained in this fling. North, as North, had done nothing that the world calls original: North, as Wilson, had done a by no means inconsiderable quantity of such work in verse and prose. But Jeffrey really did underlie the accusation contained in the words. A great name in literature, nothing stands to his credit in permanent literary record but a volume (a sufficiently big one, no doubt[1]) of criticisms on the work of other men; and though this volume is only a selection from his actual writings, no further gleaning could be made of any different material. Even his cele-

JEFFREY.

[1] To prevent mistakes it may be as well to say that Jeffrey's *Contributions to the Edinburgh Review* appeared first in four volumes, then in three, then in one.

brated, or once celebrated, "Treatise on Beauty" is but a review article, worked up into an encyclopædia article, and dealing almost wholly with pure criticism. Against him, if against any one, the famous and constantly repeated gibe about the fellows who have failed in literature and art, falls short and harmless. In another of its forms, "the corruption of a poet is the generation of a critic," it might be more appropriate. For Jeffrey, as we know from his boyish letters, once thought, like almost every boy who is not an idiot, that he might be a poet, and scribbled verses in plenty. But the distinguishing feature in this case was, that he waited for no failure, for no public ridicule or neglect, not even for any private nipping of the merciful, but so seldom effective, sort, to check those sterile growths. The critic was sufficiently early developed in him to prevent the corruption of the poet from presenting itself, in its usual disastrous fashion, to the senses of the world. Thus he lives (for his political and legal renown, though not inconsiderable, is comparatively unimportant) as a critic pure and simple.

JEFFREY.

His biographer, Lord Cockburn, tells us that "Francis Jeffrey, the greatest of British critics, was born in Edinburgh on 23d October 1773." It must be at the end, not the beginning, of this paper that we decide whether Jeffrey deserves the superlative. He seems certainly to have begun his critical practice very early. He was the son of a depute-clerk of the Court of Session, and

JEFFREY.

respectably, though not brilliantly, connected. His father was a great Tory, and, though it would be uncharitable to say that this was the reason why Jeffrey was a great Liberal, the two facts were probably not unconnected in the line of causation. Francis went to the High School when he was eight, and to the College at Glasgow when he was fourteen. He does not appear to have been a prodigy at either; but he has an almost unequalled record for early work of the self-undertaken kind. He seems from his boyhood to have been addicted to filling reams of paper, and shelves full of note-books, with extracts, abstracts, critical annotations, criticisms of these criticisms, and all manner of writing of the same kind. I believe it is the general experience that this kind of thing does harm in nineteen cases, for one in which it does good; but Jeffrey was certainly a striking exception to the rule, though perhaps he might not have been so if his producing, or at least publishing, time had not been unusually delayed. Indeed, his whole mental history appears to have been of a curiously piecemeal character; and his scrappy and self-guided education may have conduced to the priggishness which he showed early, and never entirely lost, till fame, prosperity, and the approach of old age mellowed it out of him. He was not sixteen when his sojourn at Glasgow came to an end; and, for more than two years, he seems to have been left to a kind of studious independence, attending only a couple of law classes at Edinburgh University. Then his father insisted on his going to Oxford: a curious step, the reasons for which are anything but clear. For the paternal idea seems to have been that Jeffrey was to study not arts, but law; a study for which Oxford may present facilities now, but which most certainly was quite out of its way in Jeffrey's time, and especially in the case of a Scotch boy of ordinary freshman's age.

JEFFREY.

It is painful to have to say that Jeffrey hated Oxford, because there are few instances on record in which such hatred does not show the hater to have been a very bad man indeed. There are, however, some special excuses for the little Scotchman. His college (Queen's) was not perhaps very happily selected; he had been sent there in the teeth of his own will, which was a pretty strong will; he was horrified, after the free selection of Scotch classes, to find a regular curriculum which he had to take or leave as a whole; the priggishness of Oxford was not his priggishness, its amusements (for he hated sport of every kind) were not his amusements; and, in short, there was a general incompatibility. He came up in September and went down in July, having done nothing except having, according to a not ill-natured jest, "lost the broad Scotch, but gained only the narrow English,"—a peculiarity which sometimes brought a little mild ridicule on him both from Scotchmen and Englishmen.

Very soon after his return to Edinburgh, he

seems to have settled down steadily to study for the Scotch bar, and during his studies distinguished himself as a member of the famous Speculative Society, both in essay-writing and in the debates. He was called on 16th December 1794.

JEFFREY.

Although there have never been very quick returns at the bar, either of England or Scotland, the smaller numbers of the latter might be thought likely to bring young men of talent earlier to the front. This advantage, however, appears to have been counterbalanced partly by the strong family interests which made a kind of aristocracy among Scotch lawyers, and partly by the influence of politics and of Government patronage. Jeffrey was, comparatively speaking, a "kinless loon"; and, while he was steadily resolved not to put himself forward as a candidate for the Tory manna of which Dundas was the Moses, his filial reverence long prevented him from declaring himself a very violent Whig. Indeed, he gave an instance of this reverence which might serve as a pretty text for a casuistical discussion. Henry Erskine, Dean of the Faculty of Advocates, was in 1796 deprived by vote of that, the most honourable position of the Scotch bar, for having presided at a Whig meeting. Jeffrey, like Gibbon, sighed as a Whig, but obeyed as a son, and stayed away from the poll. His days were certainly long in the land; but I am inclined to think that, in a parallel case, some Tories at least would have taken the chance of shorter life with less speckled honour. However, it is hard to quarrel with a man for obeying his parents; and perhaps, after all, the Whigs did not think the matter of so much importance as they affected to do. It is certain that Jeffrey was a little dashed by the slowness of his success at the bar. Towards the end of 1798, he set out for London with a budget of letters of introduction, and thoughts of settling down to literature. But the editors and publishers to whom he was introduced did not know what a treasure lay underneath the scanty surface of this Scotch advocate, and they were either inaccessible or repulsive. He returned to Edinburgh, and, for another two years, waited for fortune philosophically enough, though with lingering thoughts of England, and growing ones of India. It was just at the turn of the century, that his fortunes began, in various ways, also to take a turn. For some years, though a person by no means given to miscellaneous acquaintances, he had been slowly forming the remarkable circle of friends from whose combined brains was soon to start the *Edinburgh Review*. He fell in love, and married his second cousin, Catherine Wilson, on 1st November 1801—a bold and by no means canny step, for his father was ill-off, the bride was tocherless, and he says that he had never earned a hundred pounds a year in fees. They did not, however, launch out greatly, and their house in Buccleuch Place (not the least famous locality in literature) was fur-

JEFFREY.

nished on a scale which some modern colleges, conducted on the principles of enforced economy, would think Spartan for an undergraduate. Shortly afterwards, and very little before the appearance of the Blue and Yellow, Jeffrey made another innovation, which was perhaps not less profitable to him, by establishing a practice in ecclesiastical causes; though he met with a professional check in his rejection, on party principles, for the so-called collectorship, a kind of reporter's post of some emolument and not inconsiderable distinction.

The story of the *Edinburgh Review* and its foundation has been very often told on the humorous, if not exactly historical, authority of Sydney Smith. It is unnecessary to repeat it. It is undoubted that the idea was Sydney's. It is equally undoubted that, but for Jeffrey, the said idea might never have taken form at all, and would never have retained any form for more than a few months. It was only Jeffrey's long-established habit of critical writing, the untiring energy into which he whipped up his no doubt gifted but quite untrained contributors, and the skill which he almost at once developed in editing proper,—that is to say in selecting, arranging, adapting, and, even to some extent, re-writing contributions—which secured success. Very different opinions have been expressed at different times on the intrinsic merits of this celebrated production; and perhaps, on the whole, the principal feeling of explorers into the long and dusty ranges of its early volumes, has been one of disappointment. I believe myself that, in similar cases, a similar result is very common indeed, and that it is due to the operation of two familiar fallacies. The one is the delusion as to the products of former times being necessarily better than those of the present; a delusion which is not the less deluding because of its counterpart, the delusion about progress. The other is a more peculiar and subtle one. I shall not go so far as a very experienced journalist who once said to me commiseratingly, "My good sir, I won't exactly say that literary merit hurts a newspaper." But there is no doubt that all the great successes of journalism, for the last hundred years, have been much more due to the fact of the new venture being new, of its supplying something that the public wanted and had not got, than to the fact of the supply being extraordinarily good in kind. In nearly every case, the intrinsic merit has improved as the thing went on, but it has ceased to be a novel merit. Nothing would be easier than to show that the early *Edinburgh* articles were very far from perfect. Of Jeffrey we shall speak presently, and there is no doubt that Sydney at his best was, and is always, delightful. But the blundering bluster of Brougham, the solemn ineffectiveness of Horner (of whom I can never think without also thinking of Scott's delightful Shandean jest on him), the respectable erudition of the Scotch

JEFFREY.

professors, cannot for one single moment be compared with the work which, in Jeffrey's own later days, in those of Macvey Napier, and in the earlier ones of Empson, was contributed by Hazlitt, by Carlyle, by Stephen, and, above all, by Macaulay. The *Review* never had any one who could emulate the ornateness of De Quincey or Wilson, the pure and perfect English of Southey, or the inimitable insolence, so polished and so intangible, of Lockhart. But it may at least claim that it led the way, and that the very men who attacked its principles and surpassed its practice had, in some cases, been actually trained in its school, and were in all, imitating and following its model. To analyse, with chemical exactness, the constituents of a literary novelty is never easy, if it is ever possible. But some of the contrasts between the style of criticism most prevalent at the time, and the style of the new venture are obvious and important. The older rivals of the *Edinburgh* maintained for the most part a decent and amiable impartiality; the *Edinburgh*, whatever it pretended to be, was violently partisan, unhesitatingly personal, and more inclined to find fault, the more distinguished the subject was. The reviews of the time had got into the hands either of gentlemen and ladies who were happy to be thought literary, and only too glad to write for nothing, or else into those of the lowest booksellers' hacks, who praised or blamed according to orders, wrote without interest and

JEFFREY.

without vigour, and were quite content to earn the smallest pittance. The *Edinburgh* started from the first on the principle that its contributors should be paid, and paid well, whether they liked it or not, thus establishing at once an inducement to do well and a check on personal eccentricity and irresponsibility; while whatever partisanship there might be in its pages, there was at any rate no mere literary puffery.

JEFFREY.

From being, but for his private studies, rather an idle person, Jeffrey became an extremely busy one. The *Review* gave him not a little occupation, and his practice increased rapidly. In 1803 the institution, at Scott's suggestion, of the famous Friday Club, in which, for the greater part of the first half of this century, the best men in Edinburgh, Johnstone and Maxwell, Whig and Tory alike, met in peaceable conviviality, did a good deal to console Jeffrey, who was now as much given to company as he had been in his early youth to solitude, for the partial breaking up of the circle of friends—Allen, Horner, Smith, Brougham, Lord Webb Seymour—in which he had previously mixed. In the same year he became a volunteer, an act of patriotism the more creditable, that he seems to have been sincerely convinced of the probability of an invasion, and of the certainty of its success if it occurred. But I have no room here for anything but a rapid review of the not very numerous or striking events of his life. Soon, however, after the date last mentioned, he met with two afflictions peculiarly trying to a man whose domestic affections were unusually strong. These were the deaths of his favourite sister in May 1804, and of his wife in October 1805. The last blow drove him nearly to despair; and the extreme and open-mouthed "sensibility" of his private letters, on this and similar occasions, is very valuable as an index of character, oddly as it contrasts, in the vulgar estimate, with the supposed cynicism and savagery of the critic. In yet another year occurred the somewhat ludicrous duel, or beginning of a duel, with Moore, in which several police constables did perform the friendly office which Mr. Winkle vainly deprecated, and in which Jeffrey's, not Moore's, pistol was discovered to be leadless. There is a sentence in a letter of Jeffrey's concerning the thing which is characteristic and amusing: "I am glad to have gone through this scene, both because it satisfies me that my nerves are good enough to enable me to act in conformity to my notions of propriety without any suffering, and because it also assures me that I am really as little in love with life as I have been for some time in the habit of professing." It is needless to say that this was an example of the excellence of beginning with a little aversion, for Jeffrey and Moore fraternised immediately afterwards and remained friends for life. The quarrel, or half quarrel, with Scott as to the review of "Marmion," the planning and producing of the *Quarterly Review*, *English Bards and Scotch Reviewers*, not a few other events of the same kind, must be passed over rapidly. About six years after the death of his first wife, Jeffrey met, and fell in love with, a certain Miss Charlotte Wilkes, great-niece of the patriot, and niece of a New York banker, and of a Monsieur and Madame Simond, who were travelling in Europe. He married her two years later, having gone through the very respectable probation of crossing and re-crossing the Atlantic (he was a very bad sailor) in a sailing ship, in winter, and in time of war, to fetch his bride. Nor had he long been married before he took the celebrated country house of Craigcrook, where, for more than thirty years, he spent all the spare time of an exceedingly happy life. Then we may jump some fifteen years to the great Reform contest which gave Jeffrey the reward, such as it was, of his long constancy in opposition, in the shape of the Lord Advocateship. He was not always successful as a debater; but he had the opportunity of adding a third reputation to those which he had already gained in literature and in law. He had the historical duty of piloting the Scotch Reform Bill through Parliament, and he had the, in his case, pleasurable and honourable pain of taking the official steps in Parliament necessitated by the mental incapacity of Sir Walter Scott. Early in 1834 he was provided for by promotion to the Scotch Bench. He had five years before, on being appointed Dean of

JEFFREY.

Faculty, given up the editorship of the *Review*, which he had held for seven-and-twenty years. For some time previous to his resignation, his own contributions, which in early days had run up to half a dozen in a single number, and had averaged two or three for more than twenty years, had become more and more intermittent. After that resignation he contributed two or three articles at very long intervals. He was perhaps more lavish of advice than he need have been to Macvey Napier, and after Napier's death it passed into the control of his own son-in-law, Empson. Long, however, before the reins passed from his own hands, a rival more galling if less formidable than the *Quarterly* had arisen in the shape of *Blackwood's Magazine*. The more ponderous and stately publication always affected, to some extent, to ignore its audacious junior; and Lord Cockburn (perhaps instigated not more by prudence than by regard for Lockhart and Wilson, both of whom were living) passes over in complete silence the establishment of the magazine, the publication of the Chaldee manuscript, and the still greater hubbub which arose around the supposed attacks of Lockhart on Playfair, and the *Edinburgh* reviewers generally, with regard to their religious opinions. How deep the feelings really excited were, may be seen from a letter of Jeffrey's, published, not by Cockburn, but by Wilson's daughter in the life of her father. In this Jeffrey practically

JEFFREY.

drums out a new and certainly most promising recruit for his supposed share in the business, and inveighs in the most passionate terms against the imputation. It is undesirable to enter at length into any such matters here. It need only be said that Allen, one of the founders of the *Edinburgh*, and always a kind of standing counsel to it, is now acknowledged to have been something uncommonly like an atheist, that Sydney Smith (as I believe most unjustly) was often, and is sometimes still, regarded as standing towards his profession very much in the attitude of a French *abbé* of the eighteenth century, that almost the whole staff of the *Review*, including Jeffrey, had, as every Edinburgh man of position knew, belonged to the so-called Academy of Physics, the first principle of which was that only three facts (the words are Lord Cockburn's) were to be admitted without proof: (1) Mind exists; (2) matter exists; (3) every change indicates a cause. Nowadays the most orthodox of metaphysicians would admit that this limitation of position by no means implied atheism. But seventy years ago it would have been the exception to find an orthodox metaphysician who did admit it; and Lockhart, or rather Baron von Lauerwinkel, was perfectly justified in taking the view which ordinary opinion took.

JEFFREY.

These jars, however, were long over when Jeffrey became Lord Jeffrey, and subsided upon the placid bench. He lived sixteen years longer, alternating between Edinburgh, Craigcrook, and divers houses which he hired from time to time, on Loch Lomond, on the Clyde, and latterly at some English watering-places in the west. His health was not particularly good, though hardly worse than any man who lives to nearly eighty, with constant sedentary and few out-of-door occupations, and with a cheerful devotion to the good things of this life, must expect. And he was on the whole singularly happy, being passionately devoted to his wife, his daughter, and his grandchildren ; possessing ample means, and making a cheerful and sensible use of them ; seeing the increasing triumph of the political principles to which he had attached himself ; knowing that he was regarded by friends and foes alike, as the chief living English representative of an important branch of literature ; and retaining to the last an almost unparalleled juvenility of tastes and interests. His letters to Dickens are well known, and, though I should be very sorry to stake his critical reputation upon them, there could not be better documents for his vivid enjoyment of life. He died on 26th January 1850, in his seventy-seventh year, having been in harness almost to the very last. He had written a letter the day before to Empson, describing one of those curious waking visions known to all sick folk, in which there had appeared part of a proof-sheet of a new edition of the Apocrypha, and a new political paper filled with discussions on Free Trade.

JEFFREY.

In reading Jeffrey's work[1] nowadays, the critical reader finds it considerably more difficult to gain and keep the author's own point of view than in the case of any other great English critic. With Hazlitt, with Coleridge, with Wilson, with Carlyle, with Macaulay, we very soon fall into step, so to speak, with our author. If we cannot exactly prophesy what he will say on any given subject, we can make a pretty shrewd guess at it; and when, as it seems to us, he stumbles and shies, we have a sort of feeling beforehand that he is going to do it, and a decided inkling of the reason. But my own experience is, that a modern reader of Jeffrey, who takes him systematically, and endeavours to trace cause and effect in him, is liable to be constantly thrown out before he finds the secret. For Jeffrey, in the most puzzling way, lies between the ancients and the moderns in matter of criticism, and we never quite know where to have him. It is ten to one, for instance, that the novice approaches him with the idea that he is a "classic" of the old rock. Imagine the said novice's confusion, when he finds Jeffrey not merely exalting Shakespeare to the skies, but warmly praising Elizabethan poetry in general, anticipating

[1] In the following remarks, reference is confined to the *Contributions to the Edinburgh Review*, 1 vol. London, 1853. This is not merely a matter of convenience; the selection having been made with very great care by Jeffrey himself at a time when his faculties were in perfect order, and including full specimens of every kind of his work.

Mr. Matthew Arnold almost literally, in the estimate of Dryden and Pope as classics of our prose, and hailing with tears of joy the herald of the emancipation in Cowper. Surely our novice may be excused if, despite certain misgiving memories of such reviews as that of "The Lay of the Last Minstrel," he concludes that Jeffrey has been maligned, and that he was really a Romantic before Romanticism. Unhappy novice! he will find his new conclusion not less rapidly and more completely staggered than his old. Indeed, until the clue is once gained, Jeffrey must appear to be one of the most incomprehensibly inconsistent of writers and of critics. On one page he declares that Campbell's extracts from Chamberlayne's "Pharonnida" have made him "quite impatient for an opportunity of perusing the whole poem,"—Romantic surely, quite Romantic. "The tameness and poorness of the serious style of Addison and Swift,"—Romantic again, quite Romantic. Yet when we come to Jeffrey's own contemporaries, he constantly appears as much bewigged and befogged with pseudo-classicism as M. de Jouy himself. He commits himself, in the year of grace 1829, to the statement that "the rich melodies of Keats and Shelley, and the fantastical emphasis of Wordsworth are melting fast from the field of our vision," while he contrasts with this "rapid withering of the laurel" the "comparative absence of marks of decay" on Rogers and Campbell. The poets of his own time whom he praises most heartily, and with least reserve, are Campbell and Crabbe; and he is quite as enthusiastic over "Theodric" and "Gertrude" as over the two great war-pieces of the same author, which are worth a hundred "Gertrudes" and about ten thousand "Theodrics." Reviewing Scott, not merely when they were personal friends (they were always that), but when Scott was a contributor to the *Edinburgh*, and giving general praise to "The Lay," he glances with an unmistakable meaning at the "dignity of the subject," regrets the "imitation and antiquarian researches," and criticises the versification in a way which shows that he had not in the least grasped its scheme. It is hardly necessary to quote his well-known attacks on Wordsworth; but, though I am myself anything but a Wordsworthian, and would willingly give up to chaos and old night nineteen-twentieths of the "extremely valooable chains of thought" which the good man used to forge, it is in the first place quite clear that the twentieth ought to have saved him from Jeffrey's claws; in the second, that the critic constantly selects the wrong things as well as the right for condemnation and ridicule; and in the third, that he would have praised, or at any rate not blamed, in another, the very things which he blames in Wordsworth. Even his praise of Crabbe, excessive as it may now appear, is diversified by curious patches of blame which seem to me at any rate,

JEFFREY.

singularly uncritical. There are, for instance, a very great many worse jests in poetry than,

JEFFREY.

> Oh, had he learnt to make the wig he wears!

—which Jeffrey pronounces a misplaced piece of buffoonery. I cannot help thinking that if Campbell instead of Southey had written the lines,

> To see brute nature scorn him and renounce
> Its homage to the human form divine,

Jeffrey would, to say the least, not have hinted that they were "little better than drivelling." But I do not think that when Jeffrey wrote these things, or when he actually perpetrated such almost unforgivable phrases as "stuff about dancing daffodils," he was speaking away from his sincere conviction. On the contrary, though partisanship may frequently have determined the suppression or the utterance, the emphasising or the softening, of his opinions, I do not think that he ever said anything but what he sincerely thought. The problem, therefore, is to discover and define, if possible, the critical standpoint of a man whose judgment was at once so acute and so purblind; who could write the admirable surveys of English poetry contained in the essays on Mme. de Staël and Campbell, and yet be guilty of the stuff (we thank him for the word) about the dancing daffodils; who could talk of "the splendid strains of Moore" (though I have myself a relatively high opinion of Moore) and pronounce "The White Doe of

Rylstone" (though I am not very fond of that animal as a whole) "the very worst poem he ever saw printed in a quarto volume"; who could really appreciate parts even of Wordsworth himself, and yet sneer at the very finest passages of the poems he partly admired. It is unnecessary to multiply inconsistencies, because the reader who does not want the trouble of reading Jeffrey must be content to take them for granted, and the reader who does read Jeffrey will discover them in plenty for himself. But they are not limited, it should be said, to purely literary criticism; and they appear, if not quite so strongly, in his estimates of personal character, and even in his purely political arguments.

JEFFREY.

The explanation, as far as there is any, (and perhaps such explanations, as Hume says of another matter, only push ignorance a stage farther back), seems to me to lie in what I can only call the Gallicanism of Jeffrey's mind and character. As Horace Walpole has been pronounced the most French of Englishmen, so may Francis Jeffrey be pronounced the most French of Scotchmen. The reader of his letters, no less than the reader of his essays, constantly comes across the most curious and multiform instances of this Frenchness. The early priggishness is French; the effusive domestic affection is French; the antipathy to dogmatic theology, combined with general recognition of the Supreme Being, is French; the talk (I had almost said the chatter) about virtue and sympathy, and so forth, is French ; the Whig recognition of the rights of man, joined to a kind of bureaucratical distrust and terror of the common people (a combination almost unknown in England), is French. Everybody remembers the ingenious argument in *Peter Simple* that the French were quite as brave as the English, indeed more so, but that they were extraordinarily ticklish. Jeffrey, we have seen, was very far from being a coward, but he was very ticklish indeed. His private letters throw the most curious light possible on the secret, as far as he was concerned, of the earlier Whig opposition to the war, and of the later Whig advocacy of reform. Jeffrey by no means thought the cause of the Revolution divine, like the Friends of Liberty, or admired Napoleon like Hazlitt, or believed in the inherent right of Manchester and Birmingham to representation like the zealots of 1830. But he was always dreadfully afraid of invasion in the first place, and of popular insurrection in the second ; and he wanted peace and reform to calm his fears. As a young man he was, with a lack of confidence in his countrymen probably unparalleled in a Scotchman, sure that a French corporal's guard might march from end to end of Scotland, and a French privateer's boat's crew carry off "the fattest cattle and the fairest women" (these are his very words) "of any Scotch seaboard county." The famous, or infamous, Cevallos article—an ungenerous and pusillanimous attack on the Spanish patriots, JEFFREY. which practically founded the *Quarterly Review*, by finally disgusting all Tories and many Whigs with the *Edinburgh*—was, it seems, prompted merely by the conviction that the Spanish cause was hopeless, and that maintaining it, or assisting it, must lead to mere useless bloodshed. He felt profoundly the crime of Napoleon's rule; but he thought Napoleon unconquerable, and so did his best to prevent him being conquered. He was sure that the multitude would revolt if reform was not granted; and he was, therefore, eager for reform. Later, he got into his head the oddest crotchet of all his life, which was that a Conservative government, with a sort of approval from the people generally, and especially from the English peasantry, would scheme for a *coup d'état*, and (his own words again) "make mincemeat of their opponents in a single year." He may be said almost to have left the world in a state of despair over the probable results of the Revolutions of 1848-49; and it is impossible to guess what would have happened to him if he had survived to witness the Second of December. Never was there such a case, at least among Englishmen, of timorous pugnacity and plucky pessimism. But it would be by no means difficult to parallel the temperament in France; and, indeed, the comparative frequency of it there, may be thought to be no small cause of the political and military disasters of the country.

In literature, and especially in criticism, Jeffrey's characteristics were still more decidedly and unquestionably French. He came into the world almost too soon to feel the German impulse, even if he had been disposed to feel it. But, as a matter of fact, he was not at all disposed. The faults of taste of the German Romantic School, its alternate homeliness and extravagance, its abuse of the supernatural, its undoubted offences against order and proportion, scandalised him only a little less than they would have scandalised Voltaire and did scandalise the later Voltairians. Jeffrey was perfectly prepared to be Romantic up to a certain point,—the point which he had himself reached in his early course of independent reading and criticism. He was even a little inclined to sympathise with the reverend Mr. Bowles on the great question whether Pope was a poet; and, as I have said, he uses, about the older English literature, phrases which might almost satisfy a fanatic of the school of Hazlitt or of Lamb. He is, if anything, rather too severe on French as compared with English drama. Yet, when he comes to his own contemporaries, and sometimes even in reference to earlier writers, we find him slipping into those purely arbitrary severities of condemnation, those capricious stigmatisings of this as improper, and that as vulgar, and the other as unbecoming, which are the characteristics of the pseudo-correct and pseudo-classical school of

JEFFREY.

criticism. He was a great admirer of Cowper, and yet he is shocked by Cowper's use, in his translation of Homer, of the phrases, "to entreat Achilles to a calm" (evidently he had forgotten Shakespeare's "pursue him and entreat him to a peace"), "this wrangler here," "like a fellow of no worth." He was certainly not likely to be unjust to Charles James Fox. So he is unhappy, rather than contemptuous, over such excellent phrases as "swearing away the lives," "crying injustice," "fond of ill-treating." These appear to Mr. Aristarchus Jeffrey too "homely and familiar," too "low and vapid"; while a harmless and rather agreeable Shakespearian parallel of Fox's seems to him downright impropriety. The fun of the thing is that the passage turns on the well-known misuse of "flat burglary"; and if Jeffrey had had a little more sense of humour (his deficiency in which, for all his keen wit, is another Gallic note in him), he must have seen that the words were ludicrously applicable to his own condemnation and his own frame of mind. These settings-up of a wholly arbitrary canon of mere taste, these excommunicatings of such and such a thing as "low" and "improper," without assigned or assignable reason, are eminently Gallic. They may be found not merely in the older school before 1830, but in almost all French critics up to the present day: there is perhaps not one, with the single exception of Sainte-Beuve, who is habitually free from them. The critic may be

JEFFREY.

quite unable to say why *tarte à la crême* is such a shocking expression, or even to produce any important authority for the shockingness of it. But he is quite certain that it is shocking. Jeffrey is but too much given to protesting against *tarte à la crême*; and the reasons for his error are almost exactly the same as in the case of the usual Frenchman; that is to say, a very just and wholesome preference for order, proportion, literary orthodoxy, freedom from will-worship and eccentric divagations, unfortunately distorted by a certain absence of catholicity, by a tendency to regard novelty as bad, merely because it is novelty, and by a curious reluctance, as Lamb has it of another great man of the same generation, to go shares with any newcomer in literary commerce.

JEFFREY.

But when these reservations have been made, when his standpoint has been clearly discovered and marked out, and when some little tricks, such as the affectation of delivering judgments without appeal, which is still kept up by a few, though very few, reviewers, have been further allowed for, Jeffrey is a most admirable essayist and critic. As an essayist, a writer of *causeries*, I do not think he has been surpassed among Englishmen in the art of interweaving quotation, abstract, and comment. The best proof of his felicity in this respect is that in almost all the books which he has reviewed, (and he has reviewed many of the most interesting books in literature) the passages and traits, the anecdotes and phrases, which have made most mark in the general memory, and which are often remembered with very indistinct consciousness of their origin, are to be found in his reviews. Sometimes the very perfection of his skill in this respect makes it rather difficult to know where he is abstracting or paraphrasing, and where he is speaking outright and for himself; but that is a very small fault. Yet his merits as an essayist, though considerable, are not to be compared, even to the extent to which Hazlitt's are to be compared, with his merits as a critic, and especially as a literary critic. It would be interesting to criticise his political criticism; but it is always best to keep politics out where it can be managed. Besides, Jeffrey as a political critic is a subject of almost exclusively historical interest, while as a literary critic he is important at this very day, and perhaps more important than he was in his own. For the spirit of merely æsthetic criticism, which was in his day only in its infancy, has long been full grown and rampant; so that, good work as it has done in its time, it decidedly needs chastening by an admixture of the dogmatic criticism, which at least tries to keep its impressions together and in order, and to connect them into some coherent doctrine and creed.

JEFFREY.

Of this dogmatic criticism Jeffrey, with all his shortcomings, is perhaps the very best example that we have in English. He had addressed himself more directly and theoretically to literary criticism than Lockhart. Prejudiced as he often was, he was not affected by the wild gusts of personal and political passion which frequently blew Hazlitt a thousand miles off the course of true criticism. He keeps his eye on the object, which De Quincey seldom does. He is not affected by that desire to preach on certain pet subjects which affects the admirable critical faculty of Carlyle. He never blusters and splashes at random like Wilson. And he never indulges in the mannered and rather superfluous graces which marred, to some tastes, the work of his successor in critical authority, if there has been any such, the author of *Essays in Criticism*.

JEFFREY.

Let us, as we just now looked through Jeffrey's work to pick out the less favourable characteristics which distinguish his position, look through it again to see those qualities which he shares, but in greater measure than most, with all good critics. The literary essay which stands first in his collected works is on Madame de Staël. Now that good lady, of whom some judges in these days do not think very much, was a kind of goddess on earth in literature, however much she might bore them in life, to the English Whig party in general; while Jeffrey's French tastes must have made her, or at least her books, specially attractive to him. Accordingly he has written a great deal about her, no less than three essays appearing in the collected works. Writing at least partly in her lifetime and under the influences just glanced at, he is of course profuse in compliments. But it is very amusing and highly instructive to observe how, in the intervals of these compliments, he contrives to take the good Corinne to pieces, to smash up her ingenious Perfectibilism, and to put in order her rather rash literary judgments. It is in connection also with her, that he gives one of the best of not a few general sketches of the history of literature which his work contains. Of course there are here, as always, isolated expressions as to which, however much we admit that Jeffrey was a clever man, we cannot agree with Jeffrey. He thinks Aristophanes "coarse" and "vulgar" just as a living pundit thinks him "base," while (though nobody of course can deny the coarseness) Aristophanes and vulgarity are certainly many miles asunder. We may protest against the chronological, even more than against the critical, blunder which couples Cowley and Donne, putting Donne, moreover, who wrote long before Cowley was born, and differs from him in genius almost as the author of the *Iliad* does from the author of the *Henriade*, second. But hardly anything in English criticism is better than Jeffrey's discussion of the general French imputation of "want of taste and politeness" to English and German writers, especially English. It is a very general, and a very mistaken notion that the Romantic movement in France has done away with this imputation to a great extent. On the contrary,

JEFFREY.

JEFFREY.

though it has long been a kind of fashion in France to admire Shakespeare, and though since the labours of MM. Taine and Montégut, the study of English literature generally has grown and flourished, it is, I believe, the very rarest thing to find a Frenchman who, in his heart of hearts, does not cling to the old "pearls in the dung-heap" idea, not merely in reference to Shakespeare, but to English writers, and especially English humorists, generally. Nothing can be more admirable than Jeffrey's comments on this matter. They are especially admirable because they are not made from the point of view of a *Romantique à tous crins*; because, as has been already pointed out, he himself is largely penetrated by the very preference for order and proportion which is at the bottom of the French mistake; and because he is, therefore, arguing in a tongue understanded of those whom he censures. Another essay which may be read with especial advantage is that on Scott's edition of Swift. Here, again, there was a kind of test subject, and perhaps Jeffrey does not come quite scatheless out of the trial: to me, at any rate, his account of Swift's political and moral conduct and character seems both uncritical and unfair. But here, too, the value of his literary criticism shows itself. He might very easily have been tempted to extend his injustice from the writer to the writings, especially since, as has been elsewhere shown, he was by no means a fanatical admirer of the Augustan age, and thought the serious style of Addison and Swift tame and poor. It is possible of course, here also, to find things that seem to be errors, both in the general sketch which Jeffrey, according to his custom, prefixes, and in the particular remarks on Swift himself. For instance, to deny fancy to the author of the *Tale of a Tub*, of *Gulliver*, and of the *Polite Conversation*, is very odd indeed. But there are few instances of a greater triumph of sound literary judgment over political and personal prejudice than Jeffrey's description, not merely of the great works just mentioned (it is curious, and illustrates his defective appreciation of humour, that he likes the greatest least, and is positively unjust to the *Tale of a Tub*), but also of those wonderful pamphlets, articles, lampoons, skits (libels if any one likes), which proved too strong for the generalship of Marlborough and the administrative talents of Godolphin ; and which are perhaps the only literary works that ever really changed, for a not inconsiderable period, the government of England. "Considered," he says, "with a view to the purposes for which they were intended, they have probably never been equalled in any period of the world." They certainly have not ; but to find a Whig, and a Whig writing in the very moment of Tory triumph after Waterloo, ready to admit the fact, is not a trivial thing. Another excellent example of Jeffrey's strength, by no means

JEFFREY.

unmixed with examples of his weakness, is to be found in his essays on Cowper. I have already given some of the weakness: the strength is to be found in his general description of Cowper's revolt, thought so daring at the time, now so apparently moderate, against poetic diction. These instances are to be found under miscellaneous sections, biographical, historical, and so forth; but the reader will naturally turn to the considerable divisions headed Poetry and Fiction. Here are the chief rocks of offence already indicated, and here also are many excellent things which deserve reading. Here is the remarkable essay, quoted above, on Campbell's *Specimens*. Here is the criticism of Weber's edition of Ford, and another of those critical surveys of the course of English literature which Jeffrey was so fond of doing, and which he did so well, together with some remarks on the magnificently spendthrift style of our Elizabethan dramatists which would deserve almost the first place in an anthology of his critical beauties. The paper on Hazlitt's *Characters of Shakespeare* (Hazlitt was an *Edinburgh* reviewer, and his biographer, not Jeffrey's, has chronicled a remarkable piece of generosity on Jeffrey's part towards his wayward contributor) is a little defaced by a patronising spirit, not, indeed, of that memorably mistaken kind which induced the famous and unlucky sentence to Macvey Napier about Carlyle, but something in the spirit of the

JEFFREY.

schoolmaster who observes, "See this clever boy of mine, and only think how much better I could do it myself." Yet it contains some admirable passages on Shakespeare, if not on Hazlitt; and it would be impossible to deny that its hinted condemnation of Hazlitt's "desultory and capricious acuteness" is just enough. On the other hand, how significant is it of Jeffrey's own limitations that he should protest against Hazlitt's sympathy with such "conceits and puerilities" as the immortal and unmatchable

JEFFREY.

> Take him and cut him out in little stars,

with the rest of the passage. But there you have the French spirit. I do not believe that there ever was a Frenchman since the seventeenth century (unless perchance it was Gérard de Nerval, and he was not quite sane), who could put his hand on his heart and deny that the little stars seemed to him puerile and conceited.

Jeffrey's dealings with Byron (I do not now speak of the article on *Hours of Idleness*, which was simply a just rebuke of really puerile and conceited rubbish) are not, to me, very satisfactory. The critic seems, in the rather numerous articles which he has devoted to the "noble Poet," as they used to call him, to have felt his genius unduly rebuked by that of his subject. He spends a great deal, and surely an unnecessarily great deal, of time in solemnly, and no doubt quite sincerely, rebuking Byron's morality; and in doing so he is sometimes almost absurd. He calls him "not more obscene perhaps than Dryden or Prior," which is simply ludicrous, because it is very rare that this particular word can be applied to Byron at all, while even his staunchest champion must admit that it applies to glorious John and to dear Mat Prior. He helps, unconsciously no doubt, to spread the very contagion which he denounces, by talking about Byron's demoniacal power, going so far as actually to contrast *Manfred* with Marlowe to the advantage of the former. And he is so completely overcome by what he calls the "dreadful tone of sincerity" of this "puissant spirit," that he never seems to have had leisure or courage to apply the critical tests and solvents of which few men have had a greater command. Had he done so, it is impossible not to believe that, whether he did or did not pronounce Byron's sentiment to be as theatrical, as vulgar, and as false as it seems to some later critics, he would at any rate have substituted for his edifying but rather irrelevant moral denunciations some exposure of those gross faults in style and metre, in phrase and form, which now disgust us.

JEFFREY.

There are many essays remaining on which I should like to comment if there were room enough. But I have only space for a few more general remarks on his general characteristics, and especially those which, as Sainte-Beuve said to the altered Jeffrey of our altered days, are "important to us." Let me repeat then that the peculiar value of Jeffrey is not, as is that of Coleridge, of Hazlitt, or of Lamb, in very subtle, very profound, or very original views of his subjects. He is neither a critical Columbus nor a critical Socrates; he neither opens up undiscovered countries, nor provokes and stimulates to the discovery of them. His strength lies in the combination of a fairly wide range of sympathy with an extraordinary shrewdness and good sense in applying that sympathy. Tested for range alone, or for subtlety alone, he will frequently be found wanting; but he almost invariably catches up those who have thus outstripped him, when the subject of the trial is shifted to soundness of estimate, intelligent connection of view, and absence of eccentricity. And it must be again and again repeated that Jeffrey is by no means justly chargeable with the Dryasdust failings so often attributed to academic criticism. They said that on the actual Bench he worried counsel a little too much, but that his decisions were almost invariably sound. Not quite so much perhaps can be said for his other exercise of the judicial function. But however much he may sometimes seem to carp and complain, however much we may sometimes wish for a little more equity and a little less law, it is astonishing how weighty Jeffrey's critical judgments are after three quarters of a century which has seen so many

JEFFREY.

seeming heavy things grow light. There may be much that he does not see; there may be some things which he is physically unable to see; but what he does see, he sees with a clearness, and co-ordinates in its bearings on other things seen with a precision, which are hardly to be matched among the fluctuating and diverse race of critics.

JEFFREY.

V

HAZLITT

THE following paper was in great part composed, when I came across some sentences on Hazlitt, written indeed before I was born, but practically unpublished until the other day. In a review of the late Mr. Horne's *New Spirit of the Age*, contributed to the *Morning Chronicle* in 1845 and but recently included in his collected works, Thackeray writes thus of the author of the book whose title Horne had rather rashly borrowed :

HAZLITT.

The author of the *Spirit of the Age* was one of the keenest and brightest critics that ever lived. With partialities and prejudices innumerable, he had a wit so keen, a sensibility so exquisite, an appreciation of humour, or pathos, or even of the greatest art, so lively, quick, and cultivated, that it was always good to know what were the impressions made by books or men or pictures on such a mind ; and that, as there were not probably a dozen men in England with powers so varied, all the rest of the world might be rejoiced to listen to the opinions of this accomplished critic. He was of so different a caste to the people who gave authority in his day—the pompous big-wigs and

> schoolmen, who never could pardon him his familiarity of manner so unlike their own—his popular—too popular habits—and sympathies so much beneath their dignity; his loose, disorderly education gathered round those bookstalls or picture galleries where he laboured a penniless student, in lonely journeys over Europe tramped on foot (and not made, after the fashion of the regular critics of the day, by the side of a young nobleman in a postchaise), in every school of knowledge from St. Peter's at Rome to St. Giles's in London. In all his modes of life and thought, he was so different from the established authorities, with their degrees and white neckcloths, that they hooted the man down with all the power of their lungs, and disdained to hear truth that came from such a ragged philosopher.
>
> HAZLITT.

Some exceptions, no doubt, must be taken to this enthusiastic, and in the main just, verdict. Hazlitt himself denied himself wit, yet if this was mock humility, I am inclined to think that he spoke truth unwittingly. His appreciation of humour was fitful and anything but impartial, while, biographically speaking, the hardships of his apprenticeship are very considerably exaggerated. It was not, for instance, in a penniless or pedestrian manner that he visited St. Peter's at Rome; but journeying with comforts of wine, *vetturini*, and partridges, which his second wife's income paid for. But this does not matter much, and, on the whole, the estimate is as just as it is generous. Perhaps something of its inspiration may be set down to fellow-feeling, both in politics and in the unsuccessful cultivation of the arts of design. But as high an estimate of Hazlitt is quite compatible with the strongest political dissent from his opinions, and with a total freedom from the charge of wearing the willow for painting.

HAZLITT.

There is indeed no doubt that Hazlitt is one of the most absolutely unequal writers in English, if not in any, literature, Wilson being perhaps his only compeer. The term absolute is used with intention and precision. There may be others who, in different parts of their work, are more unequal than he is; but with him the inequality is pervading, and shows itself in his finest passages, in those where he is most at home, as much as in his hastiest and most uncongenial taskwork. It could not, indeed, be otherwise, because the inequality itself is due less to an intellectual than to a moral defect. The clear sunshine of Hazlitt's admirably acute intellect is always there; but it is constantly obscured by driving clouds of furious prejudice. Even as the clouds pass, the light may still be seen on distant and scattered parts of the landscape; but wherever their influence extends, there is nothing but thick darkness, gusty wind and drenching rain. And the two phenomena, the abiding intellectual light, and the fits and squalls of moral darkness, appear to be totally independent of each other, or of any single will or cause of any kind. It would be perfectly easy, and may perhaps be in place later, to give a brief collection of some of the most absurd and outrageous sayings that any writer, not a mere fool, can be charged with: of sentences not representing quips and cranks of humour, or judgments temporary and one-sided, though having a certain relative validity, but containing blunders and calumnies so gross and palpable, that the man who set them down might seem to have forfeited all claim to the reputation either of an intelligent or a responsible being. And yet, side by side with these, are other passages (and fortunately a much greater number) which justify, and more than justify, Hazlitt's claims to be as Thackeray says, "one of the keenest and brightest critics that ever lived"; as Lamb had said earlier, "one of the wisest and finest spirits breathing."

HAZLITT.

The only exception to be taken to the well-known panegyric of Elia is, that it bestows this eulogy on Hazlitt "in his natural and healthy state." Unluckily, it would seem, by a concurrence of all testimony, even the most partial, that the unhealthy state was quite as natural as the healthy one. Lamb himself plaintively wishes that "he would not quarrel with the world at the rate he does"; and De Quincey, in his short, but very interesting, biographical notice of Hazlitt (a notice entirely free from the malignity with which De Quincey has been sometimes charged), declares with quite as much truth as point, that Hazlitt's guiding principle was, "Whatever is, is wrong." He was the very ideal of a literary Ishmael; and after the fullest admission of the almost incredible virulence and unfairness of his foes, it has to be admitted, likewise, that he was quite as ready to quarrel with his friends. He succeeded, at least once, in forcing a quarrel even upon Lamb. His relations with Leigh Hunt (who, whatever his faults were, was not unamiable) were constantly strained, and at least once actually broken by his infernal temper. Nor were his relations with women more fortunate or more creditable than those with men. That the fault was entirely on his side in the rupture with his first wife is, no doubt, not the case; for Mrs. Hazlitt's, or Miss Stoddart's, own friends admit that she was of a peculiar and rather trying disposition. It is indeed evident that she was the sort of person (most teasing of all others to a man of Hazlitt's temperament) who would put her head back as he was kissing her, to ask if he would like another cup of tea, or interrupt a declaration to suggest shutting the window. As for the famous and almost legendary episode of Sarah Walker, the lodging-house keeper's daughter, and the *Liber Amoris*, the obvious and irresistible attack of something like erotic madness which it implies absolves Hazlitt partly—but only partly, for there is a kind of shabbiness about the affair which shuts it out from all reasonable claim to be regarded as a new act of the endless drama of *All for Love, or The World Well Lost!* Of his second marriage, the only persons who might be expected to give us some information either can or will say next to nothing. But when a man with such antecedents marries a

HAZLITT.

woman of whom no one has anything bad to say, lives with her for a year, chiefly on her money, and is then quitted by her with the information that she will have nothing more to do with him, it is not, I think, uncharitable to conjecture that most of the fault is his.

HAZLITT.

It is not, however, only of Hazlitt's rather imperfectly known life, or of his pretty generally acknowledged character, that I wish to speak here. His strange mixture of manly common-sense and childish prejudice, the dislike of foreigners which accompanied his Liberalism and his Bonapartism, and other traits, are very much more English than Irish. But Irish, at least on the father's side, his family was, and had been for generations. He was himself the son of a Unitarian minister, was born at Maidstone in 1778, accompanied his parents as a very little boy to America, but passed the greater part of his youth at Wem in Shropshire, where the interview with Coleridge, which decided his fate, took place. Yet for some time after that, he was mainly occupied with studies, not of literature, but of art. He had been intended for his father's profession, but had early taken a disgust to it. At such schools as he had been able to frequent, he had gained the character of a boy rather insusceptible of ordinary teaching; and his letters (they are rare throughout his life) show him to us as something very like a juvenile prig. According to his own account, he "thought for at least eight years" without being able to pen a line, or at least a page; and the worst accusation that

HAZLITT.

can truly be brought against him is that, by his own confession, he left off reading when he began to write. Those who (for their sins or for their good) are condemned to a life of writing for the press know that such an abstinence as this is almost fatal. Perhaps no man ever did good work in periodical writing, unless he had previously had a more or less prolonged period of reading, with no view to writing. Certainly no one ever did other than very faulty work if, not having such a store to draw on, when he began writing he left off reading.

The first really important event in Hazlitt's life, except the visit from Coleridge in 1798, was his own visit to Paris after the Peace of Amiens in 1802—a visit authorised and defrayed by certain commissions to copy pictures at the Louvre, which was then, in consequence of French conquests, the picture-gallery of Europe. The chief of these commissioners was a Mr. Railton, a person of some fortune at Liverpool, and the father of a daughter who, if she was anything like her portrait, had one of the most beautiful faces of modern times. Miss Railton was one of Hazlitt's many loves: it was, perhaps, fortunate for her that the course of the love did not run smooth. Almost immediately on his return, he made acquaintance with the Lambs, and, as Mr. W. C. Hazlitt, his grandson and biographer, thinks, with Miss Stoddart, his future wife. Miss Stoddart, there is no doubt, was an elderly coquette, though perfectly "proper." Besides the "William" of her early correspondence with Mary Lamb, we hear of three or four other lovers of hers between 1803 and 1808, when she married Hazlitt. It so happens that one, and only one, letter of his to her has been preserved. His biographer seems to think it in another sense unique; but it is, in effect, a very typical letter from a literary lover of a rather passionate temperament. The two were married, in defiance of superstition, on Sunday, the first of May; and certainly the superstition had not the worst of it.

HAZLITT.

At first, however, no evil results seemed likely. Miss Stoddart had a certain property settled on her at Winterslow, on the south-eastern border of Salisbury Plain, and for nearly four years the couple seem to have dwelt there (once, at least, entertaining the Lambs), and producing children, of whom only one lived. It was not till 1812 that they removed to London, and that Hazlitt engaged in writing for the newspapers. From this time till the end of his life, some eighteen years, he was never at a loss for employment—a succession of daily and weekly papers, with occasional employment on the *Edinburgh Review*, providing him, it would seem, with sufficiently abundant opportunities for copy. The *London*, the *New Monthly* (where Campbell's dislike did him no harm), and other magazines also employed him. For a time, he seems to have joined "the gallery," and written ordinary press-work. During this time, which was very short, and this time only, his friends admit a certain indulgence in drinking, which he gave up completely, but which was used against him with as much pitilessness as indecency in *Blackwood*; though heaven only knows how the most Tory soul alive could see fitness of things in the accusation of gin-drinking brought against Hazlitt by the whiskey-drinkers of the *Noctes*. For the greater part of his literary life he seems to have been almost a total abstainer, indulging only in the very strongest of tea. He soon gave up miscellaneous press-work, as far as politics went; but his passion for the theatre retained him as a theatrical critic almost to the end of his life. He gradually drifted into the business really best suited to him, that of essay-writing, and occasionally lecturing on literary and miscellaneous subjects. During the greatest part of his early London life, he was resident in a famous house, now destroyed, in York Street, Westminster, next door to Bentham and reputed to have once been tenanted by Milton; and he was a constant attendant on Lamb's Wednesday evenings. The details of his life, it has been said, are not much known. The chief of them, besides the breaking out of his lifelong war with *Blackwood* and the *Quarterly*, was, perhaps, his unlucky participation in the duel which proved fatal to Scott, the editor of the *London*. It is impossible to imagine a

HAZLITT.

more deplorable muddle than this affair. Scott, after refusing the challenge of Lockhart,[1] with whom he had, according to the customs of those days, a sufficient ground of quarrel, accepted that of Christie, Lockhart's second, with whom he had no quarrel at all. Moreover, when his adversary had deliberately spared him in the first fire, he insisted (it is said owing to the stupid conduct of his own second) on another, and was mortally wounded. Hazlitt, who was more than indirectly concerned in the affair, had a professed objection to duelling, which would have been more creditable to him if he had not been avowedly of a timid temper. But, most unfortunately, he was said, and believed, to have spurred Scott on to the acceptance of the challenge, nor do his own champions deny it. The scandal is long bygone, but is, unluckily, a fair sample of the ugly stories which cluster round Hazlitt's name, and which have hitherto prevented that justice being done to him which his abilities deserve and demand.

HAZLITT.

This wretched affair occurred in February 1821, and, shortly afterwards, the crowning complications of Hazlitt's own life, the business of the *Liber Amoris* and the divorce with his first wife, took place. The first could only be properly described by an abundance of extracts, for which there is here no room. Of the second, which, it must be

[1] For some further remarks on this duel as it concerns Lockhart see Appendix.

remembered, went on simultaneously with the first, HAZLITT. it is sufficient to say that the circumstances are nearly incredible. It was conducted under the Scotch law with a blessed indifference to collusion: the direct means taken to effect it were, if report may be trusted, scandalous; and the parties met during the whole time, and placidly wrangled over money matters, with a callousness which is ineffably disgusting. I have hinted, in reference to Sarah Walker, that the tyranny of "Love unconquered in battle" may be taken by a very charitable person to be a sufficient excuse. In this other affair there is no such palliation; unless the very charitable person should hold that a wife, who could so forget her own dignity, justified any forgetfulness on the part of her husband; and that a husband, who could haggle and chaffer about the terms on which he should be disgracefully separated from his wife, justified any forgetfulness of dignity on the wife's part.

Little has to be said about the rest of Hazlitt's life. Miss Sarah Walker would have nothing to say to him; and it has been already mentioned that the lady whom he afterwards married, a Mrs. Bridgewater, had enough of him after a year's experience. He did not outlive this last shock more than five years; and unfortunately his death was preceded by a complete financial break-down, though he was more industrious during these later years than at any other time, and though he had abundance of well-paid work. The failure of the publishers, who were to have paid him five hundred pounds for his *magnum opus*, the partisan and almost valueless *Life of Napoleon*, had something to do with this, and the dishonesty of an agent is said to have had more, but details are not forthcoming. He died on the eighteenth of September 1830, saying, "Well, I have had a happy life"; and despite his son's assertion that, like Goldsmith, he had something on his mind, I believe this to have been not ironical but quite sincere. He was only fifty-two, so that the infirmities of age had not begun to press on him. Although, except during the brief duration of his second marriage, he had always lived by his wits, it does not appear that he was ever in any want, or that he had at any time to deny himself his favourite pleasures of wandering about and being idle when he chose. If he had not been completely happy in his life, he had lived it; if he had not seen the triumph of his opinions, he had been able always to hold to them. He was one of those men, such as an extreme devotion to literature now and then breeds, who, by the intensity of their enjoyment of quite commonplace delights—a face passed in the street, a sunset, a quiet hour of reflection, even a well-cooked meal—make up for the suffering of not wholly commonplace woes. I do not know whether even the joy of literary battle did not overweigh the pain of the dishonest wounds which he received

HAZLITT.

from illiberal adversaries. I think that he had a happy life, and I am glad that he had. For he was in literature a great man. I am myself disposed to hold that, for all his accesses of hopelessly uncritical prejudice, he was the greatest critic that England has yet produced; and there are some who hold (though I do not agree with them) that he was even greater as a miscellaneous essayist than as a critic. It is certainly upon his essays, critical and other, that his fame must rest; not on the frenzied outpourings of the *Liber Amoris* (full as these are of flashes of genius), or upon the one-sided and ill-planned *Life of Napoleon*; still less on his clever-boy essay on the *Principles of Human Action*, or on his attempts in grammar, in literary compilation and abridgment, and the like. Seven volumes of Bohn's Standard Library, with another published elsewhere containing his writings on Art, contain nearly all the documents of Hazlitt's fame: a few do not seem to have been yet collected from his *Remains* and from the publications in which they originally appeared.

HAZLITT.

These books—the *Spirit of the Age*, *Table Talk*, *The Plain Speaker*, *The Round Table* (including the *Conversations with Northcote* and *Characteristics*), *Lectures on the English Poets and Comic Writers*, *Elizabethan Literature* and *Characters of Shakespeare*, *Sketches and Essays* (including *Winterslow*)—represent the work, roughly speaking, of the last twenty years of Hazlitt's life; for in the earlier and longer period he wrote very little, and, indeed, declares that for a long time he had a difficulty in writing at all. They are all singularly homogeneous in general character, the lectures written as lectures differing very little from the essays written as essays, and even the frantic diatribes of the "Letter to Gifford" bearing a strong family likeness to the good-humoured *reportage* of "On going to a Fight," or the singularly picturesque and pathetic egotism of the "Farewell to Essay-writing." This family resemblance is the more curious because, independently of the diversity of subject, Hazlitt can hardly be said to possess a style or, at least, a manner — indeed, he somewhere or other distinctly disclaims the possession. Yet, irregular as he is in his fashion of writing, no less than in the merit of it, the germs of some of the most famous styles of this century may be discovered in his casual and haphazard work. Everybody knows Jeffrey's question to Macaulay, "Where the devil did you get that style?" If any one will read Hazlitt (who, be it remembered, was a contributor to the *Edinburgh*) carefully, he will see where Macaulay got that style, or at least the beginning of it, much as he improved on it afterwards. Nor is there any doubt that, in a very different way, Hazlitt served as a model to Thackeray, to Dickens, and to many not merely of the most popular, but of the greatest, writers of the middle of the century. Indeed, in the *Spirit*

HAZLITT.

of the Age there are distinct anticipations of Carlyle.

HAZLITT.

He had the not uncommon fate of producing work which, little noted by the public, struck very strongly those of his juniors who had any literary faculty. If he had been, just by a little, a greater man than he was, he would, no doubt, have elaborated an individual manner, and not have contented himself with the hints and germs of manners. As it was, he had more of seed than of fruit. And the secret of this is, undoubtedly, to be found in the obstinate individuality of thought which characterised him all through. Hazlitt may sometimes have adopted an opinion partly because other people did not hold it, but he never adopted an opinion because other people did hold it. And all his opinions, even those which seem to have been adopted simply to quarrel with the world, were genuine opinions. He has himself drawn a striking contrast in this point, between himself and Lamb, in one of the very best of all his essays, the beautiful "Farewell to Essay-writing" reprinted in *Winterslow.* The contrast is a remarkable one, and most men, probably, who take great interest in literature or politics, or indeed in any subject admitting of principles, will be able to furnish similar contrasts from their own experience.

In matters of taste and feeling, one proof that my conclusions have not been quite shallow and hasty, is the circumstance of their having been lasting. I have the same favourite books, pictures, passages that I ever had; I may therefore presume that they will last me my life—nay, I may indulge a hope that my thoughts will survive me. This continuity of impression is the only thing on which I pride myself. Even Lamb, whose relish of certain things is as keen and earnest as possible, takes a surfeit of admiration, and I should be afraid to ask about his select authors or particular friends after a lapse of ten years. As for myself, any one knows where to have me. What I have once made up my mind to, I abide by to the end of the chapter.

HAZLITT.

This is quite true if we add a proviso to it—a proviso, to be sure, of no small importance. Hazlitt is always the same when he is not different, when his political or personal ails and angers do not obscure his critical judgment. His uniformity of principle extends only to the two subjects of literature and of art; unless a third may be added, to wit, the various good things of this life, as they are commonly called. He was not so great a metaphysician as he thought himself. He "shows to the utmost of his knowledge, and that not deep"; a want of depth not surprising when we find him confessing that he had to go to Taylor, the Platonist, to tell him something of Platonic ideas. It may be more than suspected that he had read little but the French and English philosophers of the eighteenth century; a very interesting class of persons, but, except Condillac, Hume, and Berkeley, scarcely metaphysicians. As for his politics, Hazlitt seems to me to have had no clear political creed at all. He hated something called "the hag legitimacy," but for the hag despotism, in the person of Bonaparte, he had nothing but love. How any one possessed of brains could combine Liberty and the first Napoleon in one common worship is, I confess, a mystery too great for me; and I fear that any one who could call "Jupiter Scapin" "the greatest man who ever lived," must be entirely blind to such constituents of greatness as justice, mercy, chivalry, and all that makes a gentleman. Indeed, I am afraid that "gentleman" is exactly what cannot be predicated of Hazlitt. No gentleman could have published the *Liber Amoris*, not at all because of its so-called voluptuousness, but because of its shameless kissing and telling. But the most curious example of Hazlitt's weaknesses is the language he uses in regard to those men with whom he had both political and literary differences. That he had provocation in some cases (he had absolutely none from Sir Walter Scott) is perfectly true. But what provocation will excuse such things as the following, all taken from one book, the *Spirit of the Age*? He speaks of Scott's "zeal to restore the spirit of loyalty, of passive obedience, and of non-resistance," as an acknowledgment for his having been "created a baronet by a prince of the House of Brunswick." Alas for dates and circumstances, for times and seasons, when they stand in the way of a fling of Hazlitt's! In the character of Scott himself an entire page and a half is devoted to an elaborate peroration in one huge sentence, denouncing him in such terms as "pettifogging," "littleness," "pique," "secret and envenomed blows," "slime of rankling malice and mercenary scorn," "trammels of servility," "lies," "garbage," etc. etc. The Duke of Wellington he always speaks of as a brainless noodle, forgetting apparently that the description does not make his idol's defeat more creditable to the vanquished. As for the character of Gifford, and the earlier "Letter to Gifford," I should have to print them entire to show the state of Hazlitt's mind in regard to this notorious, and certainly not very amiable person. His own words, "the dotage of age and the fury of a woman," form the best short description of both. He screams, he foams at the mouth, he gnashes and tears and kicks, rather than fights. Nor is it only on living authors and living persons (as some of his unfavourable critics have said) that he exercises his spleen. His remarks on Burke (*Round Table*, p. 150) suggest temporary insanity. Sir Philip Sidney (as Lamb, a perfectly impartial person who had no politics at all, pointed out) was a kind of representative of the courtly monarchist school in literature. So down must Sir Philip go; and not only the *Arcadia*, that "vain and amatorious poem" which Milton condemned, but the sonnets which one would have thought such a lover of poetry as Hazlitt must have spared, go down also before his remorseless bludgeon.

But there is no need to say any more of these faults of his, and there is no need to say much of another and more purely literary fault with which he has been charged—the fault of excessive quotation. In him the error lies rather in the constant repetition of the same, than in a too great multitude of different borrowings. Almost priding himself on limited study, and (as he tells us) very rarely reading his own work after it was printed, he has certainly abused his right of press most damnably in some cases. "Dry as a remainder biscuit," and "of no mark or likelihood," occur to me as the most constantly recurrent tags; but there are many others.

HAZLITT.

These various drawbacks, however, only set off the merits which almost every lover of literature must perceive in him. In most writers, in all save the very greatest, we look for one or two, or for a few special faculties and capacities, and we know perfectly well that other (generally many other) capacities and faculties will not be found in them at all. We do not dream of finding rollicking mirth in Milton, or gorgeous embroidery of style in Swift, or unadorned simplicity in Browne. But in Hazlitt you may find something of almost everything, except the finer kinds of wit and humour; to which last, however, he makes a certain side-approach by dint of his appreciation of the irony of Nature and Fate. Almost every other grace of matter and form that can be found in prose may be found at times in his. He is generally thought of as, and for the most part is, a rather plain and straightforward writer, with few tricks and frounces of phrase and style. Yet most of the fine writing of these latter days is but as crumpled tarlatan to brocaded satin beside the passage on Coleridge in the *English Poets*, or the description of Winterslow and its neighbourhood in the "Farewell to Essay-writing," or "On a Landscape of Nicolas Poussin" in the *Table-Talk*. Read these pieces and nothing else, and an excusable impression might be given that the writer was nothing if not florid. But turn over a dozen pages, and the most admirable examples of the grave and simple manner occur. He is an inveterate quoter, yet few men are more original. No man is his superior in lively, gossiping description, yet he could, within his limits, reason closely and expound admirably. It is, indeed, almost always necessary, when he condemns anything, to inquire very carefully as to the reasons of the condemnation. But nothing that he likes (except Napoleon) is ever bad: everything that he praises will repay the right man who, at the right time, examines it to see for what Hazlitt likes it. I have, for my part, no doubt that Miss Sarah Walker was a very engaging young woman; but (though the witness is the same) I have the gravest doubts as to Hazlitt's charges against her.

HAZLITT.

We shall find this same curious difference everywhere in Hazlitt. He has been talking, for instance, with keen relish of the "Conversation of Authors" (it is he, be it remembered, who has handed down to us the immortal debate at one of

Lamb's Wednesdays on "People one would Like to have Seen"), and saying excellent things about it. Then he changes the key, and tells us that the conversation of "Gentlemen and Men of Fashion" will not do. Perhaps not; but the wicked critic stops and asks himself whether Hazlitt had known much of the conversation of "Gentlemen and Men of Fashion"? We can find no record of any such experiences of his. In his youth he had no opportunity: in his middle age he was notoriously recalcitrant to all the usages of society, would not dress, and scarcely ever dined out except with a few cronies. This does not seem to be the best qualification for a pronouncement on the question. Yet this same essay is full of admirable things, the most admirable being, perhaps, the description of the man who "had you at an advantage by never understanding you." I find, indeed, in looking through my copies of his books, re-read for the purpose of this paper, an innumerable and bewildering multitude of essays, of passages, and of short phrases, marked for reference. In the seven volumes above referred to (to which, as has been said, not a little has to be added) there must be hundreds of separate articles and conversations; not counting as separate the short maxims and thoughts of the *Characteristics*, and one or two other similar collections, in which, indeed, several passages are duplicated from the Essays. At least two out of every three are characteristic of Hazlitt:

HAZLITT.

not one in any twenty is not well worth reading and, if occasion served, commenting on. They are, indeed, as far from being consecutive as (according to the Yankee) was the conversation of Edgar Poe; and the multitude and diversity of their subjects fit them better for occasional than for continuous reading.[1] Perhaps, if any single volume deserves to be recommended to a beginner in Hazlitt it had better be *The Plain Speaker*, where there is the greatest range of subject, and where the author is seen in an almost complete repertory of his numerous parts. But there is not much to choose between it and *The Round Table* (where, however, the papers are shorter as a rule), *Table-Talk*, and the volume called, though not by the author, *Sketches and Essays*. I myself care considerably less for the *Conversations with Northcote*, the personal element in which has often attracted readers; and the attempts referred to above as *Characteristics*, avowedly in the manner of La Rochefoucauld, are sometimes merely extracts from the essays, and rarely have the self-containedness, the exact and chiselled proportion, which distinguishes the true *pensée* as La Rochefoucauld and some other Frenchmen, and as Hobbes perhaps alone of Englishmen, wrote it. But to criticise these numerous papers is like sifting a cluster of motes, and the mere enumeration of their titles

[1] Since this paper was first published Mr. Alexander Ireland has edited a most excellent selection from Hazlitt.

would fill up more than half the room which I have to spare. They must be criticised or characterised in two groups only, the strictly critical and the miscellaneous, the latter excluding politics. As for art, I do not pretend to be more than a connoisseur according to Blake's definition, that is to say, one who refuses to let himself be connoisseured out of his senses. I shall only, in reference to this last subject, observe that the singularly germinal character of Hazlitt's work is noticeable here also; for no one who reads the essay on Nicolas Poussin will fail to add Mr. Ruskin to Hazlitt's fair herd of literary children.

HAZLITT.

His criticism is scattered through all the volumes of general essays; but is found by itself in the series of lectures, or essays (they are rather the latter than the former), on the characters of Shakespeare, on Elizabethan Literature, on the English Poets, and on the English Comic Writers. I cannot myself help thinking that in these four Hazlitt is at his best; though there may be nothing so attractive to the general, and few such brilliant passages as may be found in the "Farewell to Essay-writing," in the paper on Poussin, in "Going to a Fight," in "Going a Journey," and others of the same class. The reason of the preference is by no means a greater interest in the subject of one class, than in the subject of another. It is that, from the very nature of the case, Hazlitt's unlucky prejudices

HAZLITT.

interfere much more seldom with his literary work. They interfere sometimes, as in the case of Sidney, as in some remarks about Coleridge and Wordsworth, and elsewhere; but these instances are rare indeed compared with those that occur in the other division. On the other hand, there are always present Hazlitt's enthusiastic appreciation of what is good in letters, his combination of gusto with sound theory as to what is excellent in prose and verse, his felicitous method of expression, and the acuteness that kept him from that excessive and paradoxical admiration which both Lamb and Coleridge affected, and which has gained many more pupils than his own moderation. Nothing better has ever been written as a general view of the subject than his introduction to his Lectures on Elizabethan Literature; and almost all the faults to be found in it are due merely to occasional deficiency of information, not to error of judgment. He is a little paradoxical on Jonson; but not many critics could furnish a happier contrast than his enthusiastic praise of certain passages of Beaumont and Fletcher, and his cool toning down of Lamb's extravagant eulogy on Ford. He is a little unfair to the Caroline poets; but here the great disturbing influence comes in. If his comparison of ancient and modern literature is rather weak, that is because Hazlitt was anything but widely acquainted with either; and, indeed, it may be said in general that wherever he goes wrong, it is not because he judges wrongly on known facts, but because he either does not know the facts, or is prevented from seeing them by distractions of prejudice. To go through his Characters of Shakespeare would be impossible, and besides, it is a point of honour for one student of Shakespeare to differ with all others. I can only say that I know no critic with whom on this point I differ so seldom as with Hazlitt. Even better, perhaps, are the two sets of lectures on the Poets and Comic Writers. The generalisations are not always sound, for, as must be constantly repeated, Hazlitt was not widely read in literatures other than his own, and his standpoint for comparison is therefore rather insufficient. But take him where his information is sufficient, and how good he is! Of the famous four treatments of the dramatists of the Restoration—Lamb's, Hazlitt's, Leigh Hunt's, and Macaulay's—his seems to me by far the best. In regard to Butler, his critical sense has for once triumphed over his political prejudice; unless some very unkind devil's advocate should suggest that the supposed ingratitude of the King to Butler reconciled Hazlitt to him. He is admirable on Burns; and nothing can be more unjust or sillier than to pretend, as has been pretended, that Burns's loose morality engaged Hazlitt on his side. De Quincey was often a very acute critic, but anything more uncritical than his attack on Hazlitt's comparison of Burns and

HAZLITT.

Wordsworth in relation to passion, it would be difficult to find. Hazlitt "could forgive Swift for being a Tory," he tells us—which is at any rate more than some other people, who have a better reputation for impartiality than his, seem to have been able to do. No one has written better than he on Pope, who still seems to have the faculty of distorting some critical judgments. His chapter on the English novelists (that is to say, those of the last century) is perhaps the best thing ever written on the subject; and is particularly valuable nowadays when there is a certain tendency to undervalue Smollett in order to exalt Fielding, who certainly needs no such illegitimate and uncritical leverage. I do not think that he is, on the whole, unjust to Campbell; though his Gallican, or rather Napoleonic mania made him commit the literary crime of slighting "The Battle of the Baltic." But in all his criticism of English literature (and he has attempted little else, except by way of digression) he is, for the critic, a study never to be wearied of, always to be profited by. His very aberrations are often more instructive than other men's right-goings; and if he sometimes fails to detect or acknowledge a beauty, he never praises a defect.

HAZLITT.

It is less easy to sum up the merits of the miscellaneous pieces, for the very obvious reason that they can hardly be brought under any general form or illustrated by any small number of typical instances. Perhaps the best way of "sampling" this undisciplined multitude is to select a few papers by name, so as to show the variety of Hazlitt's interests. The one already mentioned, "On Going to a Fight," which shocked some proprieties even in its own day, ranks almost first; but the reader should take care to accompany it with the official record of that celebrated contest between Neate and the Gasman. All fights are good reading; but this particular effort of Hazlitt's makes one sigh for a *Boxiana* or *Pugilistica* edited by him. Next, I think, must be ranked "On Going a Journey," with its fine appreciation of solitary travelling which does not exclude reminiscences of pleasant journeys in company. But these two, with the article on Poussin and the "Farewell to Essay-writing," have been so often mentioned that it may seem as if Hazlitt's store were otherwise poor. Nothing could be farther from the truth. The "Character of Cobbett" is the best thing the writer ever did of the kind, and the best thing known to me on Cobbett. "Of the Past and the Future" is perhaps the height of the popular metaphysical style—the style from which, as was noted, Hazlitt may never have got free as far as philosophising is concerned, but of which he is a master. "On the Indian Jugglers" is a capital example of what may be called improving a text; and it contains some of the most interesting and genial examples of Hazlitt's honest delight in games such as rackets and fives, a

HAZLITT.

delight which (heaven help his critics) was frequently regarded at the time as "low." "On Paradox and Commonplace" is less remarkable for its contribution to the discussion of the subject, than as exhibiting one of Hazlitt's most curious critical megrims—his dislike of Shelley. I wish I could think that he had any better reason for this than the fact that Shelley was a gentleman by birth and his own contemporary. Most disappointing of all, perhaps, is "On Criticism," which the reader (as his prophetic soul, if he is a sensible reader, has probably warned him beforehand) soon finds to be little but an open or covert diatribe against the contemporary critics whom Hazlitt did not like, or who did not like Hazlitt. The apparently promising "On the Knowledge of Character" chiefly yields the remark that Hazlitt could not have admired Cæsar if he had resembled (in face) the Duke of Wellington. But "My first Acquaintance with Poets" is again a masterpiece; and to me, at least, "Merry England" is perfect. Hazlitt is almost the only person up to his own day who dared to vindicate the claims of nonsense, though he seems to have talked and written as little of it as most men. The chapter "On Editors" is very amusing, though perhaps not entirely in the way in which Hazlitt meant it; but I cannot think him happy "On Footmen," or on "The Conversation of Lords," for reasons already sufficiently stated. A sun-dial is a much more promising subject than a broomstick, yet many essays might be written on sun-dials without there being any fear of Hazlitt's being surpassed. Better still is "On Taste," which, if the twenty or thirty best papers in Hazlitt were collected (and a most charming volume they would make), would rank among the very best. "On Reading New Books" contains excellent sense, but perhaps is, as Hazlitt not seldom is, a little deficient in humour; while the absence of any necessity for humour makes the discussion "Whether Belief is Voluntary" a capital one. Hazlitt is not wholly of the opinion of that Ebrew Jew who said to M. Renan, "*On fait ce qu'on veut mais on croit ce qu'on peut.*"

HAZLITT.

The shorter papers of the *Round Table* yield perhaps a little less freely in the way of specially notable examples. They come closer to a certain kind of Addisonian essay, a short lay-sermon, without the charming divagation of the longer articles. To see how nearly Hazlitt can reach the level of a rather older and cleverer George Osborne, turn to the paper here on Classical Education. He is quite orthodox for a wonder: perhaps because opinion was beginning to veer a little to the side of Useful Knowledge; but he is as dry as his own favourite biscuit, and as guiltless of freshness. He is best in this volume where he notes particular points such as Kean's Iago, Milton's versification (here, however, he does not get quite to the heart of the matter), "John

Buncle," and "The Excursion." In this last he far outsteps the scanty confines of the earlier papers of the *Round Table*, and allows himself that score of pages which seems to be with so many men the normal limit of a good essay. Of his shortest style one sample from "Trifles light as Air" is so characteristic, in more ways than one, that it must be quoted whole.

HAZLITT.

> I am by education and conviction inclined to Republicanism and Puritanism. In America they have both. But I confess I feel a little staggered as to the practical efficacy and saving grace of first principles, when I ask myself, Can they throughout the United States from Boston to Baltimore, produce a single head like one of Titian's Venetian Nobles, nurtured in all the pride of aristocracy and all the blindness of popery? Of all the branches of political economy the human face is perhaps the best criterion of value.

If I were editing Hazlitt's works I should put these sentences on the title-page of every volume; for, dogmatist as he thought himself, it is certain that he was in reality purely æsthetic, though, I need hardly say, not in the absurd sense, or nosense, which modern misuse of language has chosen to fix on the word. Therefore he is very good (where few are good at all) on Dreams; and, being a great observer of himself, singularly instructive on Application to Study. "On Londoners and Country People" is one of his liveliest efforts; and the pique at his own inclusion in the Cockney School fortunately evaporates in some delightful reminiscences, including one of the few classic passages on the great game of marbles. His remarks on the company at the Southampton coffee-house, which have been often and much praised, please me less: they are too much like attempts in the manner of the Queen Anne men, and Hazlitt is always best when he imitates nobody. "Hot and Cold" (which might have been more intelligibly called "North and South") is distinctly curious, bringing out again what may be called Hazlitt's fanciful observation; and it may generally be said that, however alarming and however suggestive of commonplace the titles "On Respectable People," "On People of Sense," "On Novelty and Familiarity," may be, Hazlitt may almost invariably be trusted to produce something that is not commonplace, that is not laboured paradox, that is eminently literature.

HAZLITT.

I know that a haphazard catalogue of the titles of essays (for it is little more) such as fills the last paragraph or two may not seem very succulent. But within moderate space there is really no other means of indicating the author's extraordinary range of subject, and at the same time the pervading excellence of his treatment. To exemplify a difference which has sometimes been thought to require explanation, his work as regards system, connection with anything else, immediate occasion (which with him was generally what his friend, Mr. Skimpole, would have called "pounds") is always Journalism: in result, it is almost always Literature. Its staple subjects, as far as there can be said to be any staple where the thread is so various, are very much those which the average newspaper-writer since his time has had to deal with—politics, book-reviewing, criticism on plays and pictures, social etceteras, the minor morals, the miscellaneous incidents of daily life. It is true that Hazlitt was only for a short time in the straitest shafts, the most galling traces, of periodical hack-work. His practice was rather that of George Warrington, who worked till he had filled his purse, and then lay idle till he had emptied it. He used (an indulgence agreeable in the mouth, but bitter in the belly) very frequently to receive money beforehand for work which was not yet done. Although anything but careful, he was never an extravagant man, his tastes being for the most part simple; and he never, even during his first married life, seems to have been burdened by an expensive household. Moreover, he got rid of Mrs. Hazlitt on very easy terms. Still he must constantly have had on him the sensation that he lived by his work, and by that only. It seems to be (as far as one can make it out) this sensation which more than anything else jades and tires what some very metaphorical men of letters are pleased to call their Pegasus. But Hazlitt, though he served in the shafts, shows little trace of the harness. He has frequent small carelessnesses of style, but he would probably have had as many or more if he had been the easiest and gentlest of easy-writing gentlemen. He never seems to have allowed himself to be cramped in his choice of his subjects, and wrote for the editors, of whom he speaks so amusingly, with almost as much freedom of speech as if he had had a private press of his own, and had issued dainty little tractates on Dutch paper to be fought for by bibliophiles. His prejudices, his desultoriness, his occasional lack of correctness of fact (he speaks of "Fontaine's Translation" of Æsop, and makes use of the extraordinary phrase, "The whole Council of Trent with Father Paul at their head," than which a more curious blunder is hardly conceivable), his wayward inconsistencies, his freaks of bad taste, would in all probability have been aggravated rather than alleviated by the greater freedom and less responsibility of an independent or an endowed student. The fact is that he was a born man of letters, and that he could not help turning whatsoever he touched into literature, whether it was criticism on books or on pictures, a fight or a supper, a game at marbles, a political diatribe, or the report of a literary conversation. He doubtless had favourite subjects; but I do not know that it can be said that he treated one class of subjects better than another, with the exception that I must hold him to have been first of all a literary critic. He certainly could not write a work of great length; for the faults of his *Life of Napoleon* are grave even when its view of the subject is taken as undisputed, and it holds among his productions about the same place (that of longest and worst)

HAZLITT.

which the book it was designed to counterwork holds among Scott's. Nor was he, as it seems to me, quite at home in very short papers—in papers of the length of the average newspaper article. What he could do, as hardly any other man has ever done it in England, was a *causerie* of about the same length as Sainte-Beuve's or a little shorter, less limited in range, but also less artfully proportioned than the great Frenchman's literary and historical studies, giving scope for considerable digression, but coming to an end before the author was wearied of his subject, or had exhausted the fresh thoughts and the happy borrowings and analogies which he had ready for it. Of what is rather affectedly called "architectonic," Hazlitt has nothing. No essay of his is ever an exhaustive or even a symmetrical treatment of its nominal, or of any, theme. He somewhere speaks of himself as finding it easy to go on stringing pearls when he has once got the string; but, for my part, I should say that the string was much more doubtful than the pearls. Except in a very few set pieces, his whole charm consists in the succession of irregular, half-connected, but unending and infinitely variegated thoughts, fancies, phrases, quotations, which he pours forth not merely at a particular "Open Sesame," but at "Open barley," "Open rye," or any other grain in the cornchandler's list. No doubt the charm of these is increased by the fact that they are never quite

HAZLITT.

haphazard, never absolutely promiscuous, despite their desultory arrangement; no doubt also a certain additional interest arises from the constant revelation which they make of Hazlitt's curious personality, his enthusiastic appreciation flecked with spots of grudging spite, his clear intellect clouded with prejudice, his admiration of greatness and nobility of character co-existing with the faculty of doing very mean and even disgraceful things, his abundant relish of life contrasted with almost constant repining. He must have been one of the most uncomfortable of all English men of letters, who can be called great, to know as a friend. He is certainly, to those who know him only as readers, one of the most fruitful both in instruction and in delight.

HAZLITT.

VI

MOORE

IT would be interesting, though perhaps a little impertinent, to put to any given number of well-informed persons under the age of forty or fifty the sudden query, who was Thomas Brown the Younger? And it is very possible that a majority of them would answer that he had something to do with Rugby. It is certain that with respect to that part of his work in which he was pleased so to call himself, Moore is but little known. The considerable mass of his hack-work has gone whither all hack-work goes, fortunately enough for those of us who have to do it. The vast monument erected to him by his pupil, friend, and literary executor, Lord Russell, or rather Lord John Russell, is a monument of such a Cyclopean order of architecture, both in respect of bulk and in respect of style, that most honest biographers and critics acknowledge themselves to have explored its recesses but cursorily. Less of him, even as a poet proper, is now read than of any of the

MOORE.

brilliant group of poets of which he was one, with the possible exceptions of Crabbe and Rogers; while, more unfortunate than Crabbe, he has had no Mr. Courthope to come to his rescue. But he has recently had what is an unusual thing for an English poet, a French biographer.[1] I shall not have very much to say of the details of M. Vallat's very creditable and useful monograph. It would be possible, if I were merely reviewing it, to pick out some of the curious errors of hasty deduction which are rarely wanting in a book of its nationality. If (and no shame to him) Moore's father sold cheese and whisky, *le whisky d'Irlande* was no doubt his staple commodity in the one branch, but scarcely *le fromage de Stilton* in the other. An English lawyer's studies are not even now, except at the universities and for purposes of perfunctory examination, very much in "Justinian," and in Moore's time they were still less so. And if Bromham Church is near Sloperton, then it will follow as the night the day that it is not *dans le Bedfordshire.* But these things matter very little. They are found, in their different kinds, in all books; and if we English bookmakers (at least some of us) are not likely to make a Bordeaux wine merchant sell Burgundy as his chief commodity, or say that a village near Amiens is *dans*

MOORE.

[1] *Etude sur la Vie et les Œuvres de Thomas Moore;* by Gustave Vallat. Paris: Rousseau. London: Asher and Co. Dublin: Hodges, Figgis, and Co. 1887.

le Béarn, we no doubt do other things quite as bad. On the whole, M. Vallat's sketch, though of moderate length, is quite the soberest and most trustworthy sketch of Moore's life and of his books, as books merely, that I know. In matters of pure criticism M. Vallat is less blameless. He quotes authorities with that apparent indifference to, or even ignorance of, their relative value which is so yawning a pit for the feet of the foreigner in all cases; and perhaps a wider knowledge of English poetry in general would have been a better preparation for the study of Moore's in particular. "Never," says M. Renan very wisely, "never does a foreigner satisfy the nation whose history he writes"; and this is as true of literary history as of history proper. But M. Vallat satisfies us in a very considerable degree; and even putting aside the question whether he is satisfactory altogether, he has given us quite sufficient text in the mere fact that he has bestowed upon Moore an amount of attention and competence which no compatriot of the author of "Lalla Rookh" has cared to bestow for many years.

MOORE.

I shall also here take the liberty of neglecting a very great—as far as bulk goes, by far the greatest—part of Moore's own performance. He has inserted so many interesting autobiographical particulars in the prefaces to his complete works, that visits to the great mausoleum of the Russell memoirs are rarely necessary, and still more rarely profitable. His work for the booksellers was done

MOORE.

at a time when the best class of such work was much better done than the best class of it is now; but it was after all work for the booksellers. His *History of Ireland*, his *Life of Lord Edward Fitzgerald*, etc., may be pretty exactly gauged by saying that they are a good deal better than Scott's work of a merely similar kind (in which it is hardly necessary to say that I do not include the *Tales of a Grandfather* or the introductions to the Dryden, the Swift, and the Ballantyne novels), not nearly so good as Southey's, and not quite so good as Campbell's. The Life of Byron holds a different place. With the poems, or some of them, it forms the only part of Moore's literary work which is still read; and though it is read much more for its substance than for its execution, it is still a masterly performance of a very difficult task. The circumstances which brought it about are well known, and no discussion of them would be possible without plunging into the Byron controversy generally, which the present writer most distinctly declines to do. But these circumstances, with other things among which Moore's own comparative faculty for the business may be not unjustly mentioned, prevent it from taking rank at all approaching that of Boswell's or Lockhart's inimitable biographies. The chief thing to note in it as regards Moore himself, is the help it gives in a matter to which we shall have to refer again, his attitude towards those whom his time still called "the great."

MOORE.

And so we are left with the poems—not an inconsiderable companion seeing that its stature is some seven hundred small quarto pages closely packed with verses in double columns. Part of this volume is, however, devoted to the "Epicurean," a not unremarkable example of ornate prose in many respects resembling the author's verse. Indeed, as close readers of Moore know, there exists an unfinished verse form of it which, in style and general character, is not unlike a more serious "Lalla Rookh." As far as poetry goes, almost everything that will be said of "Lalla Rookh" might be said of "Alciphron": this latter, however, is a little more Byronic than its more famous sister, and in that respect not quite so successful.

Moore's life, which is not uninteresting as a key to his personal character, is very fairly treated by M. Vallat, chiefly from the poet's own authority; but it need not detain us very long. He was born at Dublin on 28th May 1779. There is no mystery about his origin. His father, John Moore, was a small grocer and liquor-shop keeper who received later the place of barrack-master from a patron of his son. The mother, Anastasia Codd, was a Wexford girl, and seems to have been well educated and somewhat above her husband in station. Thomas was sent to several private schools, where he appears to have attained to some scholarship and to have early practised composition in the tongue of the hated Saxon. When he was fourteen, the first measure of Catholic Emancipation opened Trinity College to him, and that establishment, "the intellectual eye of Ireland" as Sir William Harcourt has justly called it, received him a year later. The "silent sister" has fostered an always genial, if sometimes inexact, fashion of scholarship, in which Moore's talents were well suited to shine, and a pleasant social atmosphere wherein he was also not misplaced. But the time drew near to '98, and Moore, although he had always too much good sense to dip deeply into sedition, was, from his sentimental habits, likely to run some risk of being thought to have dipped in it. Although it is certain that he would have regarded what is called Nationalism in our days with disgust and horror, he cannot be acquitted of using, to the end of his life, the loosest of language on subjects where precision is particularly to be desired. Robert Emmet was his contemporary, and the action which the authorities took was but too well justified by the outbreak of the insurrection later. A Commission was named for purifying the college. Its head was Lord Clare, one of the greatest of Irishmen, the base or ignorant vilifying of whom by some persons in these days has been one of the worst results of the Home Rule movement. It had a rather comic assessor in Dr. Duigenan, the same, I believe, of whom it has been recorded that, at an earlier stage of his academic career and when a

MOORE.

junior Fellow, he threatened to "bulge the Provost's eye." The oath was tendered to each examinate, and on the day before Moore's appearance Emmet and others had gone by default, while it was at least whispered that there had been treachery in the camp. Moore's own performance was, by his own account, heroic and successful: by another, which he very fairly gives, a little less heroic but still successful. Both show clearly that Clare was nothing like the stage-tyrant which the imagination of the seditious has chosen to represent him as being. That M. Vallat should talk rather foolishly about Emmet was to be expected; for Emmet's rhetorical rubbish was sure to impose, and has always imposed, on Frenchmen. The truth of course is that this young person—though one of those whom every humane man would like to keep mewed up till they arrived, if they ever did arrive, which is improbable, at years of discretion—was one of the most mischievous of agitators. He was one of those who light a bonfire and then are shocked at its burning, who throw a kingdom into anarchy and misery and think that they are cleared by a reference to Harmodius and Aristogeiton. It is one of the most fearful delights of the educated Tory to remember what the grievance of Harmodius and Aristogeiton really was. Moore (who had something of the folly of Emmet, but none of his reckless conceit) escaped, and his family must

MOORE.

have been exceedingly glad to send him over to the Isle of Britain. He entered at the Middle Temple in 1799, but hardly made even a pretence of reading law. His actual experience is one of those puzzles which continually meet the student of literary history in the days when society was much smaller, the makers of literature fewer, and the resources of patronage greater. Moore toiled not, neither did he spin. He slipped, apparently on the mere strength of an ordinary introduction, into the good graces of Lord Moira, who introduced him to the exiled Royal Family of France, and to the richest members of the Whig aristocracy—the Duke of Bedford, the Marquis of Lansdowne and others, not to mention the Prince of Wales himself. The young Irishman had indeed, as usual, his "proposals" in his pocket —proposals for a translation of Anacreon which appeared in May 1800. The thing which thus founded one of the easiest, if not the most wholly triumphant, of literary careers is not a bad thing. The original, now abandoned as a clever though late imitation, was known even in Moore's time to be in parts of very doubtful authenticity, but it still remains, as an original, a very pretty thing. Moore's version is not quite so pretty, and is bolstered out with paraphrase and amplification to a rather intolerable extent. But there was considerable fellow-feeling between the author, whoever he was, and the translator, and the result is not

MOORE.

MOORE.

despicable. Still there is no doubt that work as good or better might appear now, and the author would be lucky if he cleared a hundred pounds and a favourable review or two by the transaction. Moore was made for life. These things happen at one time and do not happen at another. We are inclined to accept them as ultimate facts into which it is useless to inquire. There does not appear to be among the numerous fixed laws of the universe any one which regulates the proportion of literary desert to immediate reward, and it is on the whole well that it should be so. At any rate the publication increased Moore's claims as a "lion," and encouraged him to publish next year the *Poems of the late Thomas Little* (he always stuck to the Christian name), which put up his fame and rather put down his character.

In later editions Thomas Little has been so much subjected to the fig-leaf and knife that we have known readers who wondered why on earth any one should ever have objected to him. He was a good deal more uncastrated originally, but there never was much harm in him. It is true that the excuse made by Sterne for Tristram Shandy, and often repeated for Moore, does not quite apply. There is not much guilt in Little, but there is certainly very little innocence. He knows that a certain amount of not too gross indecency will raise a snigger, and, like Voltaire and Sterne himself, he sets himself to raise it. But he does not do it very wickedly. The propriety of the nineteenth century, moreover, had not then made the surprisingly rapid strides of a few years later, and some time had to pass before Moore was to go out with Jeffrey, and nearly challenge Byron, for questioning his morality. The rewards of his harmless iniquity were at hand; and in the autumn of 1803 he was made Secretary of the Admiralty in Bermuda. Bermuda, it is said, is an exceedingly pleasant place; but either there is no Secretary of the Admiralty there now, or they do not give the post to young men four-and-twenty years old who have written two very thin volumes of light verses. The Bermoothes are not still vexed with that kind of Civil Servant. The appointment was not altogether fortunate for Moore, inasmuch as his deputy (for they not only gave nice berths to men of letters then, but let them have deputies) embezzled public and private moneys, with disastrous results to his easy-going principal. But for the time it was all, as most things were with Moore, plain sailing. He went out in a frigate, and was the delight of the gun-room. As soon as he got tired of the Bermudas, he appointed his deputy and went to travel in America, composing large numbers of easy poems. In October 1804 he was back in England, still voyaging at His Majesty's expense, and having achieved his fifteen months' trip wholly on those terms. Little is heard of him for the next two

MOORE.

years, and then the publication of his American and other poems, with some free reflections on the American character, brought down on him the wrath of *The Edinburgh*, and provoked the famous leadless or half-leadless duel at Chalk Farm. It was rather hard on Moore, if the real cause of his castigation was that he had offended democratic principles, while the ostensible cause was that, as Thomas Little, he had five years before written loose and humorous verses. So thinks M. Vallat, with whom we are not wholly disposed to agree, for Jeffrey, though a Whig, was no Democrat, and he was a rather strict moralist. However, no harm came of the meeting in any sense, though its somewhat burlesque termination made the irreverent laugh. It was indeed not fated that Moore should smell serious powder, though his courage seems to have been fully equal to any such occasion. The same year brought him two unquestioned and unalloyed advantages, the friendship of Rogers and the beginning of the Irish Melodies, from which he reaped not a little solid benefit, and which contain by far his highest and most lasting poetry. It is curious, but by no means unexampled, that, at the very time at which he was thus showing that he had found his right way, he also diverged into one wholly wrong—that of the serious and very ineffective Satires, "Corruption," "Intolerance," and others. The year 1809 brought "English Bards and Scotch Reviewers" with a gibe from Byron and a challenge from Moore. But Moore's challenges were fated to have no other result than making the challenged his friends for life. All this time he had been more or less "about town." In 1811 he married Elizabeth Dyke ("Bessy"), an actress of virtue and beauty, and wrote the very inferior comic opera of "The Blue Stocking." Lord Moira gave the pair a home first in his own house, then at Kegworth near Donington, whence they moved to Ashbourne. Moore was busy now. The politics of "The Two-penny Postbag" are of course sometimes dead enough to us; but sometimes also they are not, and then the easy grace of the satire, which is always pungent and never venomed, is not much below Canning. Its author also did a good deal of other work of the same kind, besides beginning to review for *The Edinburgh.* Considering that he was in a way making his bread and butter by lampooning, however good-humouredly, the ruler of his country, he seems to have been a little unreasonable in feeling shocked that Lord Moira, on going as viceroy to India, did not provide for him. In the first place he was provided for already; and in the second place you cannot reasonably expect to enjoy the pleasures of independence and those of dependence at the same time. At the end of 1817 he left Mayfield (his cottage near Ashbourne) and Lord Moira, for Lord Lansdowne and Sloperton, a cottage near Bowood, the end of the one sojourn

MOORE.

and the beginning of the other being distinguished by the appearance of his two best works, next to the Irish Melodies—"Lalla Rookh" and "The Fudge Family at Paris." His first and almost his only heavy stroke of ill-luck now came on him: his deputy at Bermuda levanted with some six thousand pounds, for which Moore was liable. Many friends came to his aid, and after some delay and negotiations, during which he had to go abroad, Lord Lansdowne paid what was necessary. But Moore afterwards paid Lord Lansdowne, which makes a decided distinction between his conduct and that of Theodore Hook in a similar case.

MOORE.

Although the days of Moore lasted for half an ordinary lifetime after this, they saw few important events save the imbroglio over the Byron memoirs. They saw also the composition of a great deal of literature and journalism, all very well paid, notwithstanding which, Moore seems to have been always in a rather unintelligible state of pecuniary distress. That he made his parents an allowance, as some allege in explanation, will not in the least account for this; for, creditable as it was in him to make it, this allowance did not exceed one hundred pounds a year. He must have spent little in an ordinary way, for his Sloperton establishment was of the most modest character, while his wife was an excellent manager, and never went into society. Probably he might have endorsed, if he had been asked, the great principle which somebody or other has formulated, that the most expensive way of living is staying in other people's houses. At any rate his condition was rather precarious till 1835, when Lord John Russell and Lord Lansdowne obtained for him a Civil List pension of three hundred pounds a year. In his very last days this was further increased by an additional hundred a year to his wife. His end was not happy. The softening of the brain, which set in about 1848, and which had been preceded for some time by premonitory symptoms, can hardly, as in the cases of Scott and Southey, be set down to overwork, for though Moore had not been idle, his literary life had been mere child's play to theirs. He died on 26th February 1852.

MOORE.

Of Moore's character not much need be said, nor need what is said be otherwise than favourable. Not only to modern tastes, but to the sturdier tastes of his own day, and even of the days immediately before his, there was a little too much of the parasite and the hanger-on about him. It is easy to say that a man of his talents, when he had once obtained a start, might surely have gone his own way and lived his own life, without taking up the position of a kind of superior gamekeeper or steward at rich men's gates. But race, fashion, and a good many other things have to be taken into account; and it is fair to Moore to remember that he was, as it were from the first, bound to the

MOORE.

chariot-wheels of "the great," and could hardly liberate himself from them without churlishness and violence. Moreover, it cannot possibly be denied by any fair critic that if he accepted to some extent the awkward position of led-poet, he showed in it as much independence as was compatible with the function. Both in money matters, in his language to his patrons, and in a certain general but indefinable tone of behaviour, he contrasts not less favourably than remarkably, both with the ultra-Tory Hook, to whom we have already compared him, and with the ultra-Radical Leigh Hunt. Moore had as little of Wagg as he had of Skimpole about him; though he allowed his way of life to compare in some respects perilously with theirs. It is only necessary to look at his letters to Byron—always ready enough to treat as spaniels those of his inferiors in station who appeared to be of the spaniel kind—to appreciate his general attitude, and his behaviour in this instance is by no means different from his behaviour in others. As a politician there is no doubt that he at least thought himself to be quite sincere. It may be that, if he had been, his political satires would have galled Tories more than they did then, and could hardly be read by persons of that persuasion with such complete enjoyment as they can now. But the insincerity was quite unconscious, and indeed can hardly be said to have been insincerity at all. Moore had not a political head, and in English as in Irish politics his beliefs were probably not founded on any clearly comprehended principles. But such as they were he held to them firmly. Against his domestic character nobody has ever said anything; and it is sufficient to observe that not a few of the best as well as of the greatest men of his time, Scott as well as Byron, Lord John Russell as well as Lord Moira, appear not only to have admired his abilities and liked his social qualities, but to have sincerely respected his character. And so we may at last find ourselves alone with the plump volume of poems in which we shall hardly discover with the amiable M. Vallat "the greatest lyric poet of England," but in which we shall find a poet certainly, and if not a very great poet, at any rate a poet who has done many things well, and one particular thing better than anybody else.

MOORE.

The volume opens with "Lalla Rookh," a proceeding which, if not justified by chronology, is completely justified by the facts that Moore was to his contemporaries the author of that poem chiefly, and that it is by far the most considerable thing not only in mere bulk, but in arrangement, plan, and style, that he ever did. Perhaps I am not quite a fair judge of "Lalla Rookh." I was brought up in what is called a strict household where, though the rule was not, as far as I can remember, enforced by any penalties, it was a point of honour that in the nursery and school-room none but "Sunday books" should be read on Sunday. But this severity was tempered by one of the easements often occurring in a world which, if not the best, is certainly not the worst of all possible worlds. For the convenience of servants, or for some other reason, the children were much more in the drawing-room on Sundays than on any other day, and it was an unwritten rule that any book that lived in the drawing-room was fit Sunday-reading. The consequence was that from the time I could read, till childish things were put away, I used to spend a considerable part of the first day of the week in reading and re-reading a collection of books, four of which were Scott's poems, "Lalla Rookh," *The Essays of Elia* (First Edition,—I have got it now), and Southey's *Doctor*. Therefore it may be that I rank "Lalla Rookh" rather too high. At the same time, I confess that it still seems to me a very respectable poem indeed of the second rank. Of course it is artificial. The parade of second, or third, or twentieth-hand learning in the notes makes one smile, and the whole reminds one (as I daresay it has reminded many others before) of a harp of the period with the gilt a little tarnished, the ribbons more than a little faded, and the silk stool on which the young woman in ringlets used to sit much worn. All this is easy metaphorical criticism, if it is criticism at all. For I am not sure that,

MOORE.

MOORE.

when the last age has got a little farther off from our descendants, they will see anything more ludicrous in such a harp than we see in the faded spinets of a generation earlier still. But much remains to Lalla if not to Feramorz. The prose interludes have lost none of their airy grace. Even Mr. Burnand has not been able to make Mokanna ridiculous, nor have the recent accounts of the actual waste of desert and felt huts banished at least the poetical beauty of "Merou's bright palaces and groves." There are those who laugh at the bower of roses by Bendemeer's stream: I do not. "Paradise and the Peri" is perhaps the prettiest purely sentimental poem that English or any other language can show. "The Fire Worshippers" are rather long, but there is a famous fight—more than one indeed—in them to relieve the monotony. For "The Light of the Harem" alone I have never been able to get up much enthusiasm; but even "The Light of the Harem" is a great deal better than Moore's subsequent attempt in the style of "Lalla Rookh," or something like it, "The Loves of the Angels." There is only one good thing that I can find to say of that: it is not so bad as the poem which similarity of title makes one think of in connection with it—Lamartine's disastrous "Chute d'un Ange."

As "Lalla Rookh" is far the most important of Moore's serious poems, so "The Fudge Family in Paris" is far the best of his humorous poems. I

MOORE.

do not forget "The Two-penny Postbag," nor many capital later verses of the same kind, the best of which perhaps is the Epistle from Henry of Exeter to John of Tchume. But "The Fudge Family" has all the merits of these, with a scheme and framework of dramatic character which they lack. Miss Biddy and her vanities, Master Bob and his guttling, the eminent turncoat Phil Fudge, Esq. himself and his politics, are all excellent. But I avow that Phelim Connor is to me the most delightful, though he has always been rather a puzzle. If he is intended to be a satire on the class now represented by the O'Briens and the McCarthys he is exquisite, and it is small wonder that Young Ireland has never loved Moore much. But I do not think that Thomas Brown the Younger meant it, or at least wholly meant it, as satire, and this is perhaps the best proof of his unpractical way of looking at politics. For Phelim Connor is a much more damning sketch than any of the Fudges. Vanity, gluttony, the scheming intrigues of eld, may not be nice things, but they are common to the whole human race. The hollow rant which enjoys the advantages of liberty and declaims against the excesses of tyranny is in its perfection Irish alone. However this may be, these lighter poems of Moore are great fun, and it is no small misfortune that the younger generation of readers pays so little attention to them. For they are full of acute observation of manners, politics, and society by an accomplished man of the world, put into pointed and notable form by an accomplished man of letters. Our fathers knew them well, and many a quotation familiar enough at second hand is due originally to the Fudge Family in their second appearance (not so good, but still good) many years later, to "The Two-penny Postbag" and to the long list of miscellaneous satires and skits. The last sentence is however to be taken as most strictly excluding "Corruption," "Intolerance," and "The Sceptic." "Rhymes on the Road," travel-pieces out of Moore's line, may also be mercifully left aside: and "Evenings in Greece;" and "The Summer Fête" (any universal provider would have supplied as good a poem with the supper and the rout-seats) need not delay the critic and will not extraordinarily delight the reader. Not here is Moore's spur of Parnassus to be found.

MOORE.

For that domain of his we must go to the songs which, in extraordinary numbers, make up the whole of the divisions headed Irish Melodies, National Airs, Sacred Songs, Ballads and Songs, and some of the finest of which are found outside these divisions in the longer poems from "Lalla Rookh" downwards. The singular musical melody of these pieces has never been seriously denied by any one, but it seems to be thought, especially nowadays, that because they are musically melodious they are not poetical. It is probably useless to protest against a prejudice which, where it is not due to simple thoughtlessness or to blind following of fashion, argues a certain constitutional defect of the understanding powers. But it may be just necessary to repeat pretty firmly that any one who regards, even with a tincture of contempt, such work (to take various characteristic examples) as Dryden's lyrics, as Shenstone's, as Moore's, as Macaulay's Lays, because he thinks that, if he did not contemn them, his worship of Shakespeare, of Shelley, of Wordsworth would be suspect, is most emphatically not a critic of poetry and not even a catholic lover of it. Which said, let us betake ourselves to seeing what Moore's special virtue is. It is acknowledged that it consists partly in marrying music most happily to verse; but what is not so fully acknowledged as it ought to be is, that it also consists in marrying music not merely to verse, but to poetry. Among the more abstract questions of poetical criticism few are more interesting than this, the connection of what may be called musical music with poetical music; and it is one which has not been much discussed. Let us take the two greatest of Moore's own contemporaries in lyric, the two greatest lyrists as some think (I give no opinion on this) in English, and compare their work with his. Shelley has the poetical music in an unsurpassable and sometimes in an almost unapproached degree, but his verse is admittedly very difficult to set to music. I should myself go farther

MOORE.

and say that it has in it some indefinable quality antagonistic to such setting. Except the famous Indian Serenade, I do not know any poem of Shelley's that has been set with anything approaching to success, and in the best setting that I know of this the honeymoon of the marriage turns into a "red moon" before long. That this is not merely due to the fact that Shelley likes intricate metres any one who examines Moore can see. That it is due merely to the fact that Shelley, as we know from Peacock, was almost destitute of any ear for music is the obvious and common explanation. But neither will this serve, for we happen also to know that Burns, whose lyric, of a higher quality than Moore's, assorts with music as naturally as Moore's own, was quite as deficient as Shelley in this respect. So was Scott, who could yet write admirable songs to be sung. It seems therefore almost impossible, on the comparison of these three instances, to deny the existence of some peculiar musical music in poetry, which is distinct from poetical music, though it may coexist with it or may be separated from it, and which is independent both of technical musical training and even of what is commonly called "ear" in the poet. That Moore possessed it in probably the highest degree, will I think, hardly be denied. It never seems to have mattered to him whether he wrote the words for the air or altered the air to suit the words. The two fit like

MOORE.

MOORE.

a glove, and if, as is sometimes the case, the same or a similar poetical measure is heard set to another air than Moore's, this other always seems intrusive and wrong. He draws attention in one case to the extraordinary irregularity of his own metre (an irregularity to which the average pindaric is a mere jog-trot), yet the air fits it exactly. Of course the two feet which most naturally go to music, the anapæst and the trochee, are commonest with him ; but the point is that he seems to find no more difficulty, if he does not take so much pleasure, in setting combinations of a very different kind. Nor is this peculiar gift by any means unimportant from the purely poetical side, the side on which the verse is looked at without any regard to air or accompaniment. For the great drawback to "songs to be sung" in general since Elizabethan days (when, as Mr. Arber and Mr. Bullen have shown, it was very different) has been the constant tendency of the verse-writer to sacrifice to his musical necessities either meaning or poetic sound or both. The climax of this is of course reached in the ineffable balderdash which usually does duty for the libretto of an opera, but it is quite as noticeable in the ordinary songs of the drawing-room. Now Moore is quite free from this blame. He may not have the highest and rarest strokes of poetic expression ; but at any rate he seldom or never sins against either reason or poetry for the sake of rhythm and rhyme. He is always the master not the servant, the artist not the clumsy craftsman. And this I say not by any means as one likely to pardon poetical shortcomings in consideration of musical merit, for, shameful as the confession may be, a little music goes a long way with me; and what music I do like, is rather of the kind opposite to Moore's facile styles. Yet it is easy, even from the musical view, to exaggerate his facility. Berlioz is not generally thought a barrel-organ composer, and he bestowed early and particular pains on Moore.

MOORE.

To many persons, however, the results are more interesting than the analysis of their qualities and principles; so let us go to the songs themselves. To my fancy the three best of Moore's songs, and three of the finest songs in any language, are "Oft in the stilly Night," "When in Death I shall calm recline," and "I saw from the Beach." They all exemplify what has been pointed out above, the complete adaptation of words to music and music to words, coupled with a decidedly high quality of poetical merit in the verse, quite apart from the mere music. It can hardly be necessary to quote them, for they are or ought to be familiar to everybody; but in selecting these three I have no intention of distinguishing them in point of general excellence from scores, nay hundreds of others. "Go where Glory waits thee" is the first of the Irish melodies, and one of those most hackneyed by the enthusiasm of bygone Pogsons.

But its merit ought in no way to suffer on that account with persons who are not Pogsons. It ought to be possible for the reader, it is certainly possible for the critic, to dismiss Pogson altogether, to wave Pogson off, and to read anything as if it had never been read before. If this be done we shall hardly wonder at the delight which our fathers, who will not compare altogether badly with ourselves, took in Thomas Moore. "When he who adores thee" is supposed on pretty good evidence to have been inspired by the most hollow and senseless of all pseudo-patriotic delusions, a delusion of which the best thing that can be said is that "the pride of thus dying for" it has been about the last thing that it ever did inspire, and that most persons who have suffered from it have usually had the good sense to take lucrative places from the tyrant as soon as they could get them, and to live happily ever after. But the basest, the most brutal, and the bloodiest of Saxons may recognise in Moore's poem the expression of a possible, if not a real, feeling given with infinite grace and pathos. The same string reverberates even in the thrice and thousand times hackneyed Harp of Tara. "Rich and rare were the Gems she wore" is chiefly comic opera, but it is very pretty comic opera; and the two pieces "There is not in the wide world" and "How dear to me" exemplify, for the first but by no means for the last time, Moore's extraordinary command of the

MOORE.

last phase of that curious thing called by the century that gave him birth Sensibility. We have turned Sensibility out of doors; but he would be a rash man who should say that we have not let in seven worse devils of the gushing kind in her comparatively innocent room.

MOORE.

Then we may skip not a few pieces, only referring once more to "The Legacy" ("When in Death I shall calm recline"), an anacreontic quite unsurpassable in its own kind. We need dwell but briefly on such pieces as "Believe me if all those endearing young Charms," which is typical of much that Moore wrote, but does not reach the true devil-may-care note of Suckling, or as "By the Hope within us springing," for Moore's war-like pieces are seldom or never good. But with "Love's Young Dream" we come back to the style of which it is impossible to say less than that it is quite admirable in its kind. Then after a page or two we come to the chief *cruces* of Moore's pathetic and of his comic manner, "The Last Rose of Summer," "The Young May Moon," and "The Minstrel Boy." I cannot say very much for the last, which is tainted with the unreality of all Moore's Tyrtean efforts; but "The Young May Moon" could not be better, and I am not going to abandon the Rose, for all her perfume be some-thing musty—a *pot-pourri* rose rather than a fresh one. The song of O'Ruark with its altogether fatal climax—

On our side is virtue and Erin,
On theirs is the Saxon and guilt—

(which carries with it the delightful reflection that it was an Irishman running away with an Irishwoman that occasioned this sweeping moral contrast) must be given up; but surely not so "Oh had we some bright little Isle of our own." For indeed if one only had some bright little isle of that kind, some *rive fidèle où l'on aime toujours*, and where things in general are adjusted to such a state, then would Thomas Moore be the Laureate of that bright and tight little island.

But it is alarming to find that we have not yet got through twenty-five pages out of some hundred or two, and that the Irish Melodies are not yet nearly exhausted. Not a few of the best known of Moore's songs, including "Oft in the stilly Night," are to be found in the division of National Airs, which is as a whole a triumph of that extraordinary genius for setting which has been already noticed. Here is "Flow on thou shining River," here the capital "When I touch the String," on which Thackeray loved to make variations. But "Oft in the stilly Night" itself is far above the others. We do not say "stilly" now: we have been taught by Coleridge (who used to use it freely himself before he laughed at it) to laugh at "stilly" and "paly" and so forth. But the most acrimonious critic may be challenged to point out another weakness of the same kind, and on the whole the straightforward simplicity of the phrase equals the melody of the rhythm.

MOORE.

The Sacred Songs need not delay us long; for they are not better than sacred songs in general, which is saying remarkably little. Perhaps the most interesting thing in them is the well-known couplet,

> This world is but a fleeting show
> For man's illusion given—

which, as has justly been observed, contains one of the most singular estimates of the divine purpose anywhere to be found. But Moore might, like Mr. Midshipman Easy, have excused himself by remarking, "Ah! well, I don't understand these things." The miscellaneous division of Ballads, Songs, etc., is much more fruitful. "The Leaf and the Fountain," beginning "Tell me, kind seer, I pray thee," though rather long, is singularly good of its kind—the kind of half-narrative ballad. So in a lighter strain is "The Indian Bark." Nor is Moore less at home after his own fashion in the songs from the Anthology. It is true that the same fault which has been found with his Anacreon may be found here, and that it is all the more sensible because at least in some cases the originals are much higher poetry than the pseudo-Teian. To the form and style of Meleager Moore could not pretend; but as these are rather songs on Greek motives than translations from the Greek, the slackness and dilution matter less. But the strictly miscellaneous division holds some of the best work. We could no doubt dispense with the well-known ditty (for once very nearly the "rubbish" with which Moore is so often and so unjustly charged) where Posada rhymes of necessity to Granada, and where, quite against the author's habit, the ridiculous term "Sultana" is fished out to do similar duty in reference to the Dulcinea, or rather to the Maritornes, of a muleteer. But this is quite an exception, and as a rule the facile verse is as felicitous as it is facile. Perhaps no one stands out very far above the rest; perhaps all have more or less the mark of easy variations on a few well-known themes. The old comparison that they are as numerous as motes, as bright, as fleeting, and as individually insignificant, comes naturally enough to the mind. But then they are very numerous, they are very bright, and if they are fleeting, their number provides plenty more to take the place of that which passes away. Nor is it by any means true that they lack individual significance.

MOORE.

This enumeration of a few out of many ornaments of Moore's muse will of course irritate those who object to the "brick-of-the-house" mode of criticising; while it may not be minute enough, or sufficiently bolstered by actual quotation, to please those who hold that simple extract is the best, if not the only tolerable form of criticism. But the critic is not alone in finding that, whether he carry his ass or ride upon it, he cannot please all his public. What has been said is probably enough, in the case of a writer whose work, though as a whole rather unjustly forgotten, survives in parts more securely even than the work of greater men, to remind readers of at least the outlines and bases of his claim to esteem. And the more those outlines are followed up, and the structure founded on those bases is examined, the more certain, I think, is Moore of recovering, not the position which M. Vallat would assign to him of the greatest lyrist of England (a position which he never held and never could hold except with very prejudiced or very incompetent judges), not that of the equal of Scott or Byron or Shelley or Wordsworth, but still a position high enough and singularly isolated at its height. Viewed from the point of strictly poetical criticism, he no doubt ranks only with those poets who have expressed easily and acceptably the likings and passions and thoughts and fancies of the average man, and who have expressed these with no extraordinary cunning or witchery. To go further in limitation, the average man, of whom he is thus the bard, is a rather sophisticated average man, without very deep thoughts or feelings, without a very fertile or fresh imagination or fancy, with even a touch—a little touch—of cant and "gush" and other defects incident to average and sophisticated humanity. But this humanity is at any time and every time no small portion of humanity at large, and it is to Moore's credit that he sings its feelings and its thoughts so as always to

MOORE.

MOORE.

get the human and durable element in them visible and audible through the "trappings of convention." Again, he has that all-saving touch of humour which enables him, sentimentalist as he is, to be an admirable comedian as well. Yet again, he has at least something of the two qualities which one must demand of a poet who is a poet, and not a mere maker of rhymes. His note of feeling, if not full or deep, is true and real. His faculty of expression is not only considerable, but it is also distinguished ; it is a faculty which in the same measure and degree nobody else has possessed. On one side he had the gift of singing those admirable songs of which we have been talking. On the other, he had the gift of right satiric verse to a degree which only three others of the great dead men of this century in England—Canning, Praed, and Thackeray—have reached. Besides all this, he was a "considerable man of letters." But your considerable men of letters, after flourishing, turn to dust in their season, and other considerable or inconsiderable men of letters spring out of it. The true poets and even the true satirists abide, and both as a poet and a satirist Thomas Moore abides and will abide with them.

VII

LEIGH HUNT

LEIGH HUNT.

To compare the peaceful and home-keeping art of criticism to the adventurous one of lighthouse-building may seem an excursion into the heroi-comic, if not into the tragic-burlesque. Neither is it in the least my intention to dwell on a tolerably obvious metaphorical resemblance between the two. It is certainly the business of the critic to warn others off from the mistakes which have been committed by his forerunners, and perhaps (for let us anticipate the crushing wit) from his own. But that is not my reason for the suggestion. There is a story of I forget what lighthouse which Smeaton, or Stevenson, or somebody else, had unusual difficulty in establishing. The rock was too near the surface for it to be safe or practicable to moor barges over it ; and it was uncovered for too short a time to enable any solid foundations to be laid or even begun during one tide. So the engineer, with other adventurous persons, got himself landed on it, succeeded after a vain attempt or two in working an iron rod into the middle, and then hung on bodily while the tide was up, that he and his men might begin again as soon as it receded. In a mild and unexciting fashion, that is what the critic has to do—to dig about till he makes a lodgment in his author, hang on to it, and then begin to build. It is not always very easy work, and it is never less easy than in the case of the author whom somebody has kindly called "the Ariel of criticism." Leigh Hunt is an extremely difficult person upon whom to make any critical lodgment, for the reason that (I do not intend any disrespect by the comparison) he has much less of the rock about him than of the shifting sand. I do not now speak of the great Skimpole problem—we shall come to that presently—but merely of the writer as shown in his works.

The works themselves are not particularly easy to get together in any complete form, some of them being almost inextricably entangled in defunct periodicals, and others reappearing in different guises in the author's many published volumes. Mr. Kent's bibliography gives forty-six different entries; Mr. Alexander Ireland's (to which he refers) gives, I think, over eighty. Some years ago I remember receiving the catalogue of a second-hand bookseller who offered what he very frankly confessed to be far from a complete collection of the first editions, at the price of a score or two of pounds; and here at least the first are in some cases the only issues. Probably this is one reason why selections from Leigh Hunt, of which Mr. Kent's is the latest and best, have been frequent. I have seen two certainly, and I think three, within as many years. Luckily, however, quite enough for the reader's if not for the critic's purpose is easily obtainable. The poems can be bought in more forms than one; Messrs. Smith and Elder have reprinted cheaply the "Autobiography," "Men, Women, and Books," "Imagination and Fancy," "The Town," "Wit and Humour," "Table Talk," and "A Jar of Honey." Other reprints of "One Hundred Romances of Real Life" (one of his merest pieces of book-making) and of his "Stories from the Italian Poets," one of his worst pieces of criticism, but agreeably reproduced in every respect save the hideous American spelling, have recently appeared. The complete and uniform issue, the want of which to some lovers of books (I own myself among them) is never quite made up by a scratch company of volumes of all dates, sizes, and prints, is indeed wanting. But still you can get a working Leigh Hunt together.

LEIGH HUNT.

It is when you have got him that your trouble begins; and before it is done the critic, if he be one of those who are not satisfied with a mere *compte rendu*, is likely to acknowledge that Leigh Hunt, if "Ariel" be in some respects too complimentary a name for him, is at any rate a most tricksy spirit. The finest taste in some ways, contrasting with what can only be called the most horrible vulgarity in others; a light hand tediously boring again and again at obviously miscomprehended questions of religion, philosophy, and politics; a keen appetite for humour condescending to thin and repeated jests; a reviler of kings going out of his way laboriously to beslaver royalty; a man of letters, of talent almost touching genius, who seldom writes a dozen consecutive good pages:—these are only some of the inconsistencies that meet us in Leigh Hunt.

LEIGH HUNT.

He has related the history of his immediate and remoter forbears with considerable minuteness—with more minuteness indeed by far than he has bestowed upon all but a few passages of his own life. For the general reader, however, it is quite sufficient to know that his father, the Reverend Isaac Hunt, who belonged to a clerical family in Barbados, went for his education to the still British Provinces of North America, married a Philadelphia girl, Mary Shewell, practised as a lawyer till the Revolution broke out, and then being driven from his adopted country as a loyalist, settled in England, took orders, drifted into Unitarianism or anythingarianism, and ended his days, after not infrequent visits to the King's Bench, comfortably enough, but hanging rather loose on society, his friends, and a pension. Leigh Hunt (his godfathers and godmothers gave him also the names of James Henry, which he dropped) was the youngest son, and was born on 19th October 1784. His best youthful remembrance, and one of the most really humorous things he ever said, was that he used, after a childish indulgence in bad language, to think to himself with a shudder when he received any mark of favour, "Ah! they little suspect I'm the boy who said 'd——n.'" But at seven years old he went to Christ's Hospital, and continued there for another seven. His reminiscences of that seminary, put down pretty early, and afterwards embodied in the "Autobiography," are even better known from the fact that they served as a text, and as the occasion of a little gentle raillery, to Elia's famous essay than in themselves. For some years after leaving school he did nothing definite but write verses, which his father (who seems to have been gifted with a plentiful lack of judgment in most incidents and relations of life) published when the boy was but sixteen. They are as nearly as possible valueless, but they went through three editions in a very short time. It ought to be remembered that except Cowper, who was just dead, and Crabbe, who had for years intermitted writing, the public had only Rogers and Southey for poets, for it would none of the "Lyrical Ballads," and the "Lay of the Last Minstrel" had not yet been published. So that it did not make one of its worst mistakes in taking up Leigh Hunt, who

LEIGH HUNT.

certainly had poetry in him, if he did not put it forth quite so early as this. He was made a kind of lion, but, fortunately or unfortunately for him, only in middle-class circles where there were no patrons. He was quite an old man—nearly twenty—when he made regular entry into the periodical writing which kept him (with the aid of his friends) for nearly sixty years. "Mr. Town, Junior" (altered from an old signature of Colman's) contributed theatrical criticisms, which do not seem to have been paid for, to an evening paper, the *Traveller*, now surviving as a second title to the *Globe*. His bent in this direction was assisted by the fact that his elder brother John had been apprenticed to a printer, and had desires to be a publisher. In January 1808 the two brothers started the *Examiner*, and Leigh Hunt edited it with a great deal of courage for fourteen years. He threw away for this the only piece of solid preferment that he ever had, a clerkship in the War Office which Addington gave him. The references to this act of recklessness or self-sacrifice in the Autobiography are rather enigmatical. His two functions were no doubt incompatible at best, especially considering the violent Opposition tone which the *Examiner* took. But Leigh Hunt, whatever faults he had, was not quite a hypocrite; and he hints pretty broadly that if he had not resigned he might have been asked to do so, not from any political reasons, but simply because he

LEIGH HUNT.

did his work very badly. He was much more at home in the *Examiner* (with which for a short time was joined the quarterly *Reflector*), though his warmest admirers candidly admit that he knew nothing about politics. In 1809 he married a Miss Marianne Kent, whose station was not very exalted, and whose son admits with unusual frankness that she was "the reverse of handsome, and without accomplishments," adding rather whimsically that this person, "the reverse of handsome," had "a pretty figure, beautiful black hair and magnificent eyes," and though "without accomplishments" had "a very strong natural turn for plastic art." At any rate she seems to have suited Leigh Hunt admirably. The *Examiner* soon became ill-noted with Government, but it was not till the end of 1812 that a grip could be got of it. Leigh Hunt's offence is in the ordinary books rather undervalued. That he (or his contributor) called the Prince Regent, as is commonly said, "a fat Adonis of fifty" (the exact words are, "this Adonis in loveliness is a corpulent man of fifty") may have been the chief sting, but was certainly not the chief legal offence. Leigh Hunt called the ruler of his country "a violator of his word, a libertine over head and ears in disgrace, a despiser of domestic ties, the companion of demireps, a man who had just closed half a century without one single claim on the gratitude of his country or the respect of posterity." It might be

LEIGH HUNT.

true or it might be false; but certainly there was then not a country in Europe where it would have been allowed to be said of the chief of the state. And I am not sure that it could be said now anywhere but in Ireland, where considerably worse things were said with impunity of Lord Spencer and Sir George Trevelyan. At any rate the brothers were prosecuted and fined five hundred pounds each, with two years' imprisonment. The sentence was carried out; but Leigh Hunt's imprisonment in Horsemonger Lane Gaol was the merest farce of incarceration. He could not indeed go beyond the prison walls. But he had a comfortable suite of rooms which he was permitted to furnish and decorate just as he liked; he was allowed to have his wife and family with him; he had a tiny garden of his own, and free access to that of the prison; there was no restriction on visitors, who brought him presents just as they chose; and he became a kind of fashion with the Opposition. Jeremy Bentham came and played at battledore and shuttlecock with him—an almost appalling idea, for it will not do to trust too implicitly to Leigh Hunt's declaration that Jeremy's object was to suggest "an improvement in the constitution of shuttlecocks." The *Examiner* itself continued undisturbed, and except for the "I can't get out" feeling, which even of itself cannot be compared for one moment to that of a modern prisoner condemned to his cell and

LEIGH HUNT.

the exercising-ground, it is rather difficult to see much reason for Leigh Hunt's complaints. The imprisonment may have affected his health, but it certainly brought him troops of friends, and gave him leisure to do not only his journalist's work, but things much more serious. Here he wrote and published his first poem since the Juvenilia, "A Feast of the Poets" (not much of a thing), and here he wrote, though he did not publish it till his liberation, the "Story of Rimini," by far his most important poem, both for intrinsic character and for influence on others. He had known Lamb from boyhood, and Shelley some years; he now made the acquaintance of Keats, Hazlitt, and Byron.

In the next five years after his liberation he did a great deal of work, the best by far being the periodical called the *Indicator*, a weekly paper which ran for sixty-six numbers. The *Indicator* was the first thing that I ever read of Hunt's, and, by no means for that reason only, I think it the best. Its buttonholing papers, of a kind since widely imitated, were the most popular; but there are romantic things in it, such as "The Daughter of Hippocrates" (paraphrased and expanded from Sir John Mandeville with Hunt's peculiar skill), which seem to me better. It was at the end of these five years that Leigh Hunt resolved upon the second adventure (his imprisonment being the first and involuntary) of his otherwise easy-going life—an adventure the immediate consequences of which were unfortunate in many ways, LEIGH HUNT. but which supplied him with a good deal of literary material. This was his visit to Italy as a kind of literary *attaché* to Lord Byron, and editor of a quarterly magazine, the *Liberal.* The idea was Shelley's, and if Shelley had lived, it might not have resulted quite so disastrously, for Shelley was absolutely untiring as a helper of lame dogs over stiles. As it was, the excursion distinctly contradicted the saying (condemned by some as immoral) that a bad beginning makes a good ending. The Hunt family, which now included several children, embarked, in November of all months in the year, on a small ship bound for Italy. They were something like a month getting down the Channel in tremendous weather, and at last when their ship had to turn tail from near Scilly and run into Dartmouth, Hunt, whose wife was extremely ill of lung-disease, made up his mind to stay for the winter in Devonshire. He passed the time pleasantly enough at Plymouth, which they left once more in May 1822, reaching Leghorn at the end of June. Shelley's death happened within ten days of their arrival, and Byron and Leigh Hunt were left to get on together. How badly they got on is pretty generally known, might have been foreseen from the beginning, and is not very profitable to dwell on. Leigh Hunt's mixture of familiarity and "airs" could not have been worse mixed to suit the taste of Byron. The "noble poet" too was not a person who liked to be spunged upon; and his coolest admirers may sympathise with his disgust when he found that he had upon his hands a man of letters with a large family whom he was literally expected to keep, whose society was disagreeable to him, who lampooned his friends, who differed with him on every point of taste, and who did not think it necessary to be grateful. For Leigh Hunt, somewhat on Lamb's system of compensation for coming late by going away early, combined his readiness to receive favours with a practice of not acknowledging the slightest obligation for them. Byron's departure for Greece was in its way lucky, but it left Hunt stranded. He remained in Italy for rather more than three years and then returned home across the Continent. The *Liberal*, which contains work of his, of Byron's, of Shelley's, and of Hazlitt's, is interesting enough and worth buying in its original form, but it did not pay. Of the unlucky book on his relations with Byron which followed—the worst act by far of his life—I shall not say much. No one has attempted to defend it, and he himself apologises for it frankly and fully in his Autobiography. It is impossible, however, not to remark that the offence was much aggravated by its deliberate character. For the book was not published in the heat of the moment, but three years after Hunt's return to England and four after Byron's death.

LEIGH HUNT.

LEIGH HUNT.

The remaining thirty years of Hunt's life were wholly literary. As for residences, he hovered about London, living successively at Highgate, Epsom, Brompton, Chelsea, Kensington, and divers other places. At Chelsea he was very intimate with the Carlyles, and, while he was perhaps of all living men of letters most leniently judged by those not particularly lenient judges, we have nowhere such vivid glimpses of Hunt's peculiar weaknesses as in the memoirs of Carlyle and his wife. Why Leigh Hunt was always in such difficulties is not at first obvious, for he was the reverse of an idle man; he seems, though thriftless, to have been by no means very sumptuous in his way of living; everybody helped him, and his writing was always popular. He appears to have felt not a little sore that nothing was done for him when his political friends came into power after the Reform Bill—and remained there for almost the whole of the rest of his life. He had certainly in some senses borne the burden and heat of the day for Liberalism. But he was one of those reckless people who, without meaning to offend anybody in particular, offend friends as well as foes; the days of sinecures were even then passing or passed; and it is very difficult to conceive any office, even with the lightest duties, in which Leigh Hunt would not have come to grief. As for his writing, his son's earnest plea as to his not being an idle man is no doubt true enough, but he never seems to have reconciled himself to the regular drudgery of miscellaneous article writing for newspapers which is almost the only kind of journalism that really pays, and his books did not sell very largely. In his latter days, however, things became easier for him. The unfailing kindness of the Shelley family gave him (in 1844 when Sir Percy Shelley came into his property) a regular annuity of £120; two royal gifts of £200 each and in 1847 a pension of the same amount were added; and two benefit nights of Dickens's famous amateur company brought him in something like a cool thousand, as Dickens himself would have said. Of his last years Mr. Kent, who was intimate with him, gives much the pleasantest account known to me. He died on 28th August 1859, surviving his wife only two years.

LEIGH HUNT.

I can imagine some one, at the name of Dickens in the preceding paragraph, thinking or saying, that if the author of *Bleak House* raised a thousand pounds for his old friend, he took the value of it and infinitely more out of him. It is impossible to shirk the Skimpole affair in any really critical notice of Leigh Hunt. To put unpleasant things briefly, that famous character was at once recognised by every one as a caricature, perhaps ill-natured but certainly brilliant, of what an enemy might have said of the author of "Rimini." Thornton Hunt, the eldest of Leigh Hunt's children, and a writer of no small power, took the matter up and forced from Dickens a contradiction, or disavowal, with which I am afraid the recording angel must have had some little difficulty. Strangely enough the last words of Macaulay's that we have concern this affair; and they may be quoted as Sir George Trevelyan gives them, written by his uncle in those days at Holly Lodge when the shadow of death was heavy on him.

LEIGH HUNT.

December 23, 1859. An odd declaration by Dickens that he did not mean Leigh Hunt by Harold Skimpole. Yet he owns that he took the light externals of the character from Leigh Hunt, and surely it is by those light externals that the bulk of mankind will always recognise character. Besides, it is to be observed that the vices of H. S. are vices to which L. H. had, to say the least, some little leaning, and which the world generally attributed to him most unsparingly. That he had loose notions of *meum* and *tuum;* that he had no high feeling of independence; that he had no sense of obligation; that he took money wherever he could get it; that he felt no gratitude for it; that he was just as ready to defame a person who had relieved his distress as a person who had refused him relief—these were things which, as Dickens must have known, were said, truly or falsely, about L. H., and had made a deep impression on the public mind.

Now Macaulay has not always been leniently judged; but I do not think that, with the single exception of Croker's case, he can be accused of having borne hardly on the moral character of any one of his contemporaries. He had befriended Leigh Hunt in every way; he had got him into the *Edinburgh;* he had lent (that is to say given) him money freely, and I do not think that his fiercest enemy can seriously think that he bore Hunt a grudge for having told him, as he himself records, that the "Lays" were not so good as Spenser, whom Macaulay in one of the rare lapses of his memory had unjustly blasphemed, and whom Leigh Hunt adored. To my mind, if there were any doubt about Dickens's intention, or about the fitting in a certain sense of the cap, this testimony of Macaulay's would settle it. But I cannot conceive any doubt remaining in the mind of any person who has read Leigh Hunt's works, who has even read the Autobiography. Of the grossest faults in Skimpole's character, such as the selling of Jo's secret, Leigh Hunt was indeed incapable, and the insertion of these is at once a blot on Dickens's memory and a kind of excuse for his disclaimer; but as regards the lighter touches the likeness is unmistakable. Skimpole's most elaborate jests about "pounds" are hardly an exaggeration of the man who gravely and more than once tells us that his difficulties and irregularities with money came from a congenital incapacity to appreciate arithmetic, and who admits that Shelley (whose affairs he knew very well) once gave him no less than fourteen hundred pounds (that is to say some sixteen months of Shelley's income at his wealthiest) to clear him, and that he was not cleared, though apparently he gave Shelley to understand that he was.

LEIGH HUNT.

There are many excuses for him which Skimpole had not. His own pleas of tropical blood and so forth will not greatly avail. But the old patron-

theory and its more subtle transformation (the influence of which is sometimes shown even by Thackeray in the act of denouncing it), to the effect that the State or the public, or somebody, is bound to look after your man of genius, had bitten deep into the being of the literary man of our grandfathers' time. Anybody who has read *Thomas Poole and his Friends* must have seen how not merely Coleridge, of whose known liability to the weakness the book furnished new proofs, but even, to some extent and vicariously, the austere Wordsworth, cherished the idea. But for the most part, men kept it to themselves. Leigh Hunt never could keep anything to himself, and he has left record on record of the easy manner in which he acted on his beliefs.

LEIGH HUNT.

For this I own that I care little, especially since he never borrowed money of me. There is a Statute of Limitations for all such things in letters as well as in law. What is much harder to forgive is the ill-bred pertness, often if not always innocent enough in intention, but rather the worse than the better for that, which mars so much of his actual literary work. When almost an old man he wrote —when a very old man he quotes, with childlike surprise that any one should see anything objectionable in them—the following lines :

> Perhaps you have known what it is to feel longings,
> To pat buxom shoulders at routs and mad throngings—
> Well—think what it was at a vision like that !
> A grace after dinner ! a Venus grown fat !

LEIGH HUNT.

It would be almost unbelievable of any man but Leigh Hunt that he placidly remarks in reference to this impertinence that "he had not the pleasure of Lady Blessington's acquaintance," as if that did not make things ten times worse. He had laid the foundation of not a few of the literary enmities he suffered from, by writing, thirty years earlier, a "Feast of the Poets," on the pattern of Suckling, in which he took, though much more excusably, the same kind of ill-bred liberties; and similar things abound in his works. It is scarcely surprising that the good Macvey Napier (rather awkwardly, and giving Macaulay much trouble to patch things up) should have said that he would like a "gentleman-like" article from Mr. Hunt for the *Edinburgh;* and the taunt about the Cockney School undoubtedly derived its venom from this weakness of his. Lamb was not descended from the kings that long the Tuscan sceptre swayed, and had some homely ways; Keats had to do with livery-stables, Hazlitt with shady lodging-houses and lodging-house keepers. But Keats might have been, whatever his weaknesses, his own and Spenser's Sir Calidore for gentle feeling and conduct; the man who called Lamb vulgar would only prove his own vulgarity; and Hazlitt, though he had some darker stains on his character than any that rest on Hunt, was far too potent a spirit for the fire within him not to burn out mere vulgarity. Leigh Hunt I fear must be allowed to be now and then merely vulgar—a Pogson of talent, of genius, of immense amiability, of rather hard luck, but still of the Pogsons, Pogsonic.

LEIGH HUNT.

As I shall have plenty of good to say of him, I may as well despatch at once whatever else I have to say that is bad, which is little. The faults of taste which have just been noticed passed easily into occasional, though only occasional, faults of criticism. I do not recommend anybody who has not the faculty of critical adjustment, and who wants to like Leigh Hunt, to read his essay on Dante in the *Italian Poets.* For flashes of crass insensibility to great poetry it is difficult to match anywhere, and impossible to match in Leigh Hunt. His favourite theological doctrine, like that of Béranger's hero, was, *Ne damnons personne.* He did not like monarchy, and he did not understand metaphysics. So the great poet, who, more than any other great poet except Shakespeare, grows on those who read him, receives from Leigh Hunt not an honest confession, like Sir Walter's, that he does not like him, which is perhaps the first honest impression of the majority of Dante's readers, but tirade upon tirade of abuse and bad criticism. Further, Leigh Hunt's unfortunate necessity of preserving his own journalism has made him keep a thousand things that he ought to have left to the kindly shade of the newspaper files—a cemetery where, thank Heaven, the tombs are not open as in the other city of Dis. The book called *Table*

Talk, for instance, contains, with a little better matter, chiefly mere rubbish like this section :

LEIGH HUNT.

BEAUMARCHAIS

Beaumarchais, author of the celebrated comedy of "Figaro," an abridgment of which has been rendered more famous by the music of Mozart, made a large fortune by supplying the American republicans with arms and ammunition, and lost it by speculations in salt and printing. His comedy is one of those productions which are accounted dangerous, from developing the spirit of intrigue and gallantry with more gaiety than objection ; and they would be more unanimously so, if the good humour and self-examination to which they excite did not suggest a spirit of charity and inquiry beyond themselves.

Leigh Hunt tried almost every conceivable kind of literature, including a historical novel, *Sir Ralph Esher*, several dramas (one or two of which, the "Legend of Florence" being the chief, got acted), and at nearly the beginning and nearly the end of his career two religious works, or works on religion, an attack on Methodism and "The Religion of the Heart." All this we may not unkindly brush away, and consider him first as a poet, secondly as a critic, and thirdly as what can be best, though rather unphilosophically, called a miscellanist.

Few good judges nowadays, I think, would deny that Leigh Hunt had a certain faculty for poetry, and fewer still would rank it very high. To something like, but less than, the tunefulness of Moore, he joined a very much better taste in models and an infinitely wider and deeper study of them. There is no doubt that his versification in "Rimini" (which may be described as Chaucerian in basis with a strong admixture of Dryden, further crossed and dashed slightly with the peculiar music of the followers of Spenser, especially Browne and Wither) had a very strong influence both on Keats and on Shelley, and that it drew from them music much better than itself. This fluent, musical, many-coloured verse was a capital medium for tale-telling, and Leigh Hunt is always at his best when he employs it. The more varied measures and the more ambitious aim of "Captain Sword and Captain Pen" seem to me very much less successful. Not only was Leigh Hunt far from strong enough for a serious argument, but the cheery, sentimental optimism of which he was one of the most persevering exponents—the kind of thing which vehemently protests that in the good time coming nobody shall be damned, or starved, or put in prison, or subjected to the perils of villainous saltpetre, or prevented from doing just what he likes, and that all existence ought to be and shortly will be a vaguely refined beer and skittles—did not lend itself very well to verse. Nor are Hunt's lyrics particularly strong. His best thing by far is the charming trifle (the heroine being, it has been said and also denied, Mrs. Carlyle) which he called a "rondeau," though it is not one.

LEIGH HUNT.

Jenny kissed me when we met,
Jumping from the chair she sat in:
Time, you thief, who love to get
Sweets into your list, put *that* in!
Say I'm weary, say I'm sad,
Say that health and wealth have missed me,
Say I'm growing old—but add,
Jenny kissed me.

Even here it may be noticed that though the last four lines could hardly be bettered, the second couplet is rather weak. Some of Leigh Hunt's sonnets, especially that which he wrote on the Nile in rivalry with Shelley and Keats, are very good.

It flows through old hushed Egypt and its sands,
Like some grave mighty thought threading a dream;
And times and things, as in that vision, seem
Keeping along it their eternal stands;—
Caves, pillars, pyramids, the shepherd-bands
That roamed through the young earth, the glory extreme
Of high Sesostris, and that southern beam,
The laughing queen that caught the world's great hands.
Then comes a mightier silence, stern and strong,
As of a world left empty of its throng,
And the void weighs on us; and then we wake,
And hear the fruitful stream lapsing along
'Twixt villages, and think how we shall take
Our own calm journey on for human sake.

This was written in 1818, and I think it will be admitted that the italicised line is a rediscovery of a cadence which had been lost for centuries, and which has been constantly borrowed and imitated since.

Every now and then he had touches of something much above his usual style, as in the concluding lines of the whimsical "flyting," as the Scotch poets of the fifteenth century would have called it, between the Man and the Fish:

LEIGH HUNT.

> Man's life is warm, glad, sad, 'twixt loves and graves,
> Boundless in hope, honoured with pangs austere,
> Heaven-gazing; and his angel-wings he craves:
> The fish is swift, small-needing, vague yet clear,
> A cold, sweet, silver life, wrapped in round waves,
> Quickened with touches of transporting fear.

As a rule, however, his poetry has little or nothing of this kind, and he will hold his place in the English *corpus poetarum*, first, because he was an associate of better poets than himself; secondly, because he invented a medium for the poetic tale which was as poetical as Crabbe's was prosaic; thirdly, because of all persons perhaps who have ever attempted English verse on their own account, he had the most genuine affection for, and the most intimate and extensive acquaintance with, the triumphs of his predecessors in poetry. Of prose he was a much less trustworthy judge, as may be instanced once for all by his pronouncing Gibbon's style to be bad; but of poetry he could tell with an extraordinary mixture of sympathy and discretion. And this will introduce us to his second faculty, the faculty of literary criticism, in which he is, with all his drawbacks, on a level with Coleridge, with Lamb, and with Hazlitt, his defects as compared with them being in each case made up by compensatory, or more than compensatory, merits.

LEIGH HUNT.

How considerable a critic Leigh Hunt was, may be judged from the fact that he himself confesses the great critical fault of his principal poem—the selection, for amplification and paraphrase, of a subject which has once for all been treated with imperial and immortal brevity by a great poet. With equal ingenuousness and equal truth he further confesses that, at the time, he not only did not see this fault, but was critically incapable of seeing it. For there is that one comfort about this discomfortable and discredited art of ours, that age at any rate does not impair it. The first sprightly runnings of criticism are never the best; and in the case of all really great critics, from Dryden to Sainte-Beuve, the critical faculty has gone on constantly increasing. The chief examples of Leigh Hunt's critical accomplishment are to be found in the two books called respectively, *Wit and Humour*, and *Imagination and Fancy*, both being selections from the English poets, with critical remarks interspersed as a sort of running commentary. But hardly any book of his is quite barren of such examples; for he neither would, nor indeed apparently could, restrain his desultory fancy from this as from other indulgences. His criticism is very distinct in kind. It is almost purely and in the strict and proper sense æsthetic—that is to say, it does hardly anything but reproduce the sensations produced upon Hunt himself by the reading of his favourite passages. As his sense of poetry was extraordinarily keen and accurate, there is perhaps no body of "beauties" of English poetry to be found anywhere in the language which is selected with such uniform and unerring judgment as this or these. Even Lamb, in his own favourite subjects and authors, misses treasure-trove which Leigh Hunt unfailingly discovers, as in the now pretty generally acknowledged case of the character of De Flores in Middleton's "Changeling." And Lamb had a much less wide and a much more crotchety system of admissions and exclusions. Macaulay was perfectly right in fixing, at the beginning of his essay on the dramatists of the Restoration, upon this catholicity of Hunt's taste as the main merit in it; and it is really a great pity that the two volumes referred to were not, as they were intended to be, followed up by others respectively devoted to Action and Passion, Contemplation, and Song. But Leigh Hunt was sixty when he planned them, and age, infirmity, perhaps also the less pressing need which the comparative affluence of his later years brought, prevented the completion. It has also to be remarked that Hunt is much better as a taster than as a professor or expounder. He says indeed many happy things about his favourite passages, but they evidently represent rather afterthought than forethought. He is not good at generalities, and

LEIGH HUNT.

when he tries them is apt, instead of flying (as an Ariel of criticism should do), to sprawl. Yet it was impossible for a man who was so almost invariably right in particulars, to go very wrong in general; and the worst that can be said of Leigh Hunt's general critical axioms and conclusions is that they are much better than the reasons that support them. For instance, he is probably right in calling the famous "intellectual" and "henpecked you all" in "Don Juan," "the happiest triple rhyme ever written." But when he goes on to say that "the sweepingness of the assumption completes the flowing breadth of the effect," he goes very near to talking nonsense. For most people, however, a true opinion persuasively stated is of much more consequence than the most elaborate logical justification of it; and it is this that makes Leigh Hunt's criticism such excellent good reading. It is impossible not to feel that when a guide (which after all a critic should be) is recommended with cautions that, though an invaluable fellow for the most part, he is not unlikely in certain places to lead the traveller over a precipice, it is a very dubious kind of recommendation. Yet this is the way in which one has to speak of Jeffrey and Hazlitt, of Wilson and De Quincey. Of Leigh Hunt it need hardly ever be said; for in the unlucky diatribes on Dante above cited, the most unwary reader can see that his author has lost his temper and with it his head. As a rule he avoids

LEIGH HUNT.

the things that he is not qualified to judge, such as the rougher and sublimer parts of poetry. Of its sweetness and its music, of its grace and its wit, of its tenderness and its fancy, no better judge ever existed than Leigh Hunt. He jumped at such things, when he came near them, almost as involuntarily as a needle to a magnet.

LEIGH HUNT.

He was, however, perhaps most popular in his own time, and certainly he gained most of the not excessive share of pecuniary profit which fell to his lot, as what I have called a miscellanist. One of the things which have not yet been sufficiently done in the criticism of English literary history, is a careful review of the successive steps by which the periodical essay of Addison and his followers during the eighteenth century passed into the magazine-paper of our own days. The later examples of the eighteenth century, the "Observers" and "Connoisseurs," the "Loungers" and "Mirrors" and "Lookers-On," are fairly well worth reading in themselves, especially as the little volumes of the "British Essayists" go capitally in a travelling-bag; but the gap between them and the productions of Leigh Hunt, of Lamb, and of the *Blackwood* men, with Praed's schoolboy attempts not left out, is a very considerable one. Leigh Hunt is himself entitled to a high place in the new school so far as mere priority goes, and to one not low in actual merit. He relates himself, more than once, with the childishness which is the good side of his

Skimpolism, how not merely his literary friends but persons of quality had special favourites among the miscellaneous papers of the *Indicator*, like (he would certainly have used the parallel himself if he had known it or thought of it) the Court of France with Marot's Psalms. This miscellaneous work of his extends, as it ought to do, to all manner of subjects. The pleasantest example to my fancy is the book called *The Town*, a gossiping description of London from St. Paul's to St. James's, which he afterwards followed up with books on the West End and Kensington, and which, though of course second-hand as to its facts, is by no means uncritical, and by far the best reading of any book of its kind. Even the Autobiography might take rank in this class; and the same kind of stuff made up the staple of the numerous periodicals which Leigh Hunt edited or wrote, and of the still more numerous books which he compounded out of the dead periodicals. It may be that a severe criticism will declare that, here as well as elsewhere, he was more original than accomplished; and that his way of treating subjects was pursued with better success by his imitators than by himself. Such a paper, for instance, as "On Beds and Bedrooms" suggests (and is dwarfed by the suggestion) Lamb's "Convalescent" and other similar work. "Jack Abbott's Breakfast," which is, or was, exceedingly popular with Hunt's admirers, is an account of the misfortunes of a luckless young

LEIGH HUNT.

man who goes to breakfast with an absent-minded pedagogue, and, being turned away empty, orders successive refreshments at different coffee-houses, each of which proves a feast of Tantalus. The idea is not bad; but the carrying out suits the stage better than the study, and is certainly far below such things as Maginn's adventures of Jack Ginger and his friends, with the tale untold that Humphries told Harlow. "A Few Remarks on the Rare Vice called Lying" is a most promising title; he must be a very good-natured judge who finds appended to it a performing article. "The Old Lady" and "The Old Gentleman" were once great favourites; they seem to have been studied from Earle's *Microcosmography*, not the least excellent of the books that have proceeded from foster-children of Walter de Merton, but they are over-laboured in particulars. So too are "The Adventures of Carfington Blundell" and "Inside of an Omnibus." Leigh Hunt's humour is so devoid of bitterness that it sometimes becomes insipid; his narrative so fluent and gossiping that it sometimes becomes insignificant. His enemies called him immoral, which appears to have been a gross calumny so far as his private life was concerned, and is certainly a gross exaggeration as regards his writing. But he was rather too much given to dally about voluptuous subjects with a sort of chuckling epicene triviality. He is so far from being passionate that he sometimes becomes

LEIGH HUNT.

almost offensive. He is terribly apt to labour a conceit or a prettiness till it becomes vapid; and his "Criticism on Female Beauty," though it contains some extremely sensible remarks, also contains much which is suggestive of Mr. Tupman. Yet his miscellaneous writing has one great merit (besides its gentle playfulness and its untiring variety) which might procure pardon for worse faults. With no one perhaps are those literary memories which transform and vivify life so constantly present as with Leigh Hunt. Although the world was a perfectly real thing to him, and not by any means seen only through the windows of a library, he took everywhere with him the remembrances of what he had read, and they helped him to clothe and colour what he saw and what he wrote. Between him, therefore, and readers who themselves have read a good deal, and loved what they have read not a little, there is always something in common; and yet probably no bookish writer has been less resented by his unbookish readers as a thruster of the abominable things—superior knowledge and superior scholarship—upon them. Some vices of the snob Leigh Hunt undoubtedly had, but he was never in the least a pretentious snob. He quotes his books not in the spirit of a man who is looking down on his fellows from a proper elevation, but in the spirit of a kindly host who is anxious that his guests should enjoy the good things on his table.

LEIGH HUNT.

LEIGH HUNT.

It is this sincere and unostentatious love of letters, and anxiety to spread the love of letters, that is the redeeming point of Leigh Hunt throughout: he is saved *quia multum amavit.* It was this which prompted that rather grandiose but still admirable palinode of Christopher North, in August 1834,—"the Animosities are mortal: but the Humanities live for ever,"—an apology which naturally enough pleased Hunt very much. He is one of those persons with whom it is impossible to be angry, or at least to be angry long. "The bailiff who took him was fond of him," it is recorded of Captain Costigan; and in milder moments the same may be said of the critical bailiffs who are compelled to "take" Leigh Hunt. Even in his least happy books (such as the "Jar of Honey from Mount Hybla," where all sorts of matter, some of it by no means well known to the writer, have been hastily cobbled together) this love, and for the most part intelligent and animated love, for literature appears. If in another of his least happy attempts, the critical parts of the already mentioned *Stories from the Italian Poets*, he is miles below the great argument of Dante, and if he is even guilty to some extent of vulgarising the lesser but still great poets with whom he deals, he never comes, even in Dante, to any passage he can understand without exhibiting such a warmth of enthusiasm and enjoyment that it softens the stoniest readers. He can gravely call Dante's Hell "geologically speaking a most fantastical formation" (which it certainly is), and joke clumsily about the poet's putting Cunizza and Rahab in Paradise. He can write, in the true spirit of vulgarising, that "the Florentine is thought to have been less strict in his conduct in regard to the sex than might be supposed from his platonical aspirations," heedless of the great confessions implied in the swoon at Francesca's story, and the passage through the fire at the end of the seventh circle of Purgatory. But when he comes to things like "Dolce color d'oriental zaffiro," and "Era già l'ora," it is hardly possible to do more justice to the subject. The whole description of his Italian sojourn in the Autobiography is an example of the best kind of such writing. Again, of all the people who have rejoiced in Samuel Pepys, Leigh Hunt "does it most natural," being indeed a kind of nineteenth-century Pepys himself, whom the gods had made less comfortable in worldly circumstances and no man of business, but to whom as a compensation they had given the feeling for poetry which Samuel lacked. At different times Dryden, Spenser, and Chaucer were respectively his favourite English poets; and as there was nothing faithless in his inconstancy, he took up his new loves without ceasing to love the old. It is perhaps rather more surprising that he should have liked Spenser than that he should have liked the other two; and we must suppose that the profusion of beautiful pictures in the "Faerie Queen" enabled him, not to

LEIGH HUNT.

appreciate (for he never could have done that), but to tolerate or pass over the deep melancholy and the occasional philosophisings of the poet. But the attraction of Dryden and Chaucer for him is very easily understood. Both are eminently cheerful poets, Dryden with the cheerfulness born of manly sense, Chaucer with that of youth and abounding animal spirits. Leigh Hunt seems to have found this cheerfulness as akin to his own, as the vigour of both was complementary and satisfactory to his own, I shall not say weakness, but fragility. Add yet again to this that Hunt seems—a thing very rarely to be said of critics—never to have disliked a thing simply because he could not understand it. If he sometimes abused Dante, it was not merely because he could not understand him, though he certainly could not, but because Dante trod (and when Dante treads he treads heavily) on his most cherished prejudices. Now he had not very many prejudices, and so he had an advantage here also.

LEIGH HUNT.

Lastly, as he may be read with pleasure, so he may be skipped without shame. There are some writers whom to skip may seem to a conscientious devotee of letters both wicked and unwise—wicked because it is disrespectful to them, unwise because it is quite likely to inflict loss on the reader. Now nobody can ever think of respecting Leigh Hunt; he is not unfrequently amiable, but never in the least venerable. Even at his best he seldom or never affects the reader with admiration, only with a mild pleasure. It is at once a penalty for his sins and a compliment to his good qualities, that to make any kind of fuss over him would be absurd. Nor is there any selfish risk run by treating him, in the literary sense, in an unceremonious manner. His writing of all kinds carries desultoriness to the height, and may be begun at the beginning, or at the end, or in the middle, and left off at any place, without the least risk of serious loss. He is excellent good company for half an hour, sometimes for much longer ; but the reader rarely thinks very much of what he has said when the interview is over, and never experiences any violent hunger or thirst for its renewal, though such renewal is agreeable enough in its way. Such an author is a convenient possession on the shelves : a possession so convenient that occasionally a blush of shame may suggest itself at the thought that he should be treated so cavalierly. But this is quixotic. The very best things that he has done hardly deserve more respectful treatment, for they are little more than a faithful and fairly lively description of his own enjoyments ; the worst things deserve treatment much less respectful. Yet let us not leave him with a harsh mouth ; for, as has been said, he loved the good literature of others very much, and he wrote not a little that was good literature of his own.

LEIGH HUNT.

VIII

PEACOCK

IN the year 1875 Mr. Bentley conferred no small favour upon lovers of English literature by reprinting, in compact form and good print, the works of Thomas Love Peacock, up to that time scattered and in some cases not easily obtainable. So far as the publisher was concerned, nothing more could reasonably have been demanded; it is not easy to say quite so much of the editor, the late Sir Henry Cole. His editorial labours were indeed considerably lightened by assistance from other hands. Lord Houghton contributed a critical preface, which has the ease, point, and grasp of all his critical monographs. Miss Edith Nicolls, the novelist's granddaughter, supplied a short biography, written with much simplicity and excellent good taste. But as to editing in the proper sense—introduction, comment, illustration, explanation—there is next to none of it in the book. The principal thing, however, was to have Peacock's delightful work

PEACOCK.

conveniently accessible, and that the issue of 1875 accomplished. The author is still by no means universally or even generally known; though he has been something of a critic's favourite. Almost the only dissenter, as far as I know, among critics, is Mrs. Oliphant, who has not merely confessed herself, in her book on the literary history of Peacock's time, unable to comprehend the admiration expressed by certain critics for *Headlong Hall* and its fellows, but is even, if I do not mistake her, somewhat sceptical of the complete sincerity of that admiration. There is no need to argue the point with this agreeable practitioner of Peacock's own art. A certain well-known passage of Thackeray, about ladies and *Jonathan Wild*, will sufficiently explain her own inability to taste Peacock's persiflage. As for the genuineness of the relish of those who can taste him there is no way that I know to convince sceptics. For my own part I can only say that, putting aside scattered readings of his work in earlier days, I think I have read the novels through on an average once a year ever since their combined appearance. Indeed, with Scott, Thackeray, Borrow, and Christopher North, Peacock composes my own private Paradise of Dainty Devices, wherein I walk continually when I have need of rest and refreshment. This is a fact of no public importance, and is only mentioned as a kind of justification for recommending him to others.

PEACOCK.

PEACOCK.

Peacock was born at Weymouth on 18th October 1785. His father (who died a year or two after his birth) was a London merchant; his mother was the daughter of a naval officer. He seems during his childhood to have done very much what he pleased, though, as it happened, study always pleased him; and his gibes in later life at public schools and universities lose something of their point when it is remembered that he was at no university, at no school save a private one, and that he left even that private school when he was thirteen. He seems, however, to have been very well grounded there, and on leaving it he conducted his education and his life at his own pleasure for many years. He published poems before he was twenty, and he fell in love shortly after he was twenty-two. The course of this love did not run smooth, and the lady, marrying some one else, died shortly afterwards. She lived in Peacock's memory till his death, sixty years later, which event is said to have been heralded (in accordance with not the least poetical of the many poetical superstitions of dreaming) by frequent visions of this shadowy love of the past. Probably to distract himself, Peacock, who had hitherto attempted no profession, accepted the rather unpromising post of under-secretary to Admiral Sir Home Popham on board ship. His mother, in her widowhood, and he himself had lived much with his sailor grandfather, and he was always fond of naval matters. But it is not surprising to find that his occupation, though he kept it for something like a year, was not to his taste. He gave it up in the spring of 1809, and returned to leisure, poetry, and pedestrianism. The "Genius of the Thames," a sufficiently remarkable poem, was the result of the two latter fancies. A year later he went to Wales and met his future wife, Jane Griffith, though he did not marry her for ten years more. He returned frequently to the principality, and in 1812 made, at Nant Gwillt, the acquaintance of Shelley and his wife Harriet. This was the foundation of a well-known friendship, which has supplied by far the most solid and trustworthy materials existing for the poet's biography. It was Wales, too, that furnished the scene of his first and far from worst novel *Headlong Hall*, which was published in 1816. From 1815 to 1819 Peacock lived at Marlow, where his intercourse with Shelley was resumed, and where he produced not merely *Headlong Hall* but *Melincourt* (the most unequal, notwithstanding many charming sketches, of his works), the delightful *Nightmare Abbey* (with a caricature, as genius caricatures, of Shelley for the hero), and the long and remarkable poem of "Rhododaphne."

PEACOCK.

During the whole of this long time, that is to say up to his thirty-fourth year, with the exception of his year of secretaryship, Peacock had been his own master. He now, in 1819, owed curtailment of his liberty but considerable increase of fortune to a long-disused practice on the part of the managers of public institutions, of which Sir Henry Taylor gave another interesting example. The directors of the East India Company offered him a clerkship because he was a clever novelist and a good Greek scholar. He retained his place ("a precious good place too," as Thackeray with good-humoured envy says of it in "The Hoggarty Diamond") with due promotion for thirty-seven years, and retired from it in 1856 with a large pension. He had married Miss Griffith very shortly after his appointment; in 1822 *Maid Marian* appeared, and in 1823 Peacock took a cottage, which became after a time his chief and latterly his only residence, at Halliford, near his beloved river. For some years he published nothing, but 1829 and 1831 saw the production of perhaps his two best books, *The Misfortunes of Elphin* and *Crotchet Castle.* After *Crotchet Castle*, official duties and perhaps domestic troubles (for his wife was a helpless invalid) interrupted his literary work for more than twenty years, an almost unexampled break in the literary activity of a man so fond of letters. In 1852 he began to write again as a contributor to *Fraser's Magazine.* It is rather unfortunate that no complete republication, nor even any complete list of these articles, has been made. The papers on Shelley and the charming story of *Gryll Grange* were the chief of them. The author was an old man when he wrote this last, but he survived it six years, and died on 23d January 1866, having latterly lived very much alone. Indeed, after Shelley's death he seems never to have had any very intimate friend except Lord Broughton, with whose papers most of Peacock's correspondence is for the present locked up.

PEACOCK.

There is a passage in Shelley's "Letter to Maria Gisborne" which has been often quoted before, but which must necessarily be quoted again whenever Peacock's life and literary character are discussed:—

And there
Is English P——, with his mountain Fair
Turned into a flamingo, that shy bird
That gleams i' the Indian air. Have you not heard
When a man marries, dies, or turns Hindoo,
His best friends hear no more of him? But you
Will see him, and will like him too, I hope,
With his milk-white Snowdonian Antelope
Matched with his Camelopard. *His fine wit*
Makes such a wound, the knife is lost in it;
A strain too learnèd for a shallow age,
Too wise for selfish bigots; let his page
Which charms the chosen spirits of his time,
Fold itself up for a serener clime
Of years to come, and find its recompense
In that just expectation.

The enigmas in this passage (where it is undisputed that "English P——" is Peacock) have much exercised the commentators. That Miss Griffith, after her marriage, while still remaining a

Snowdonian antelope, should also have been a flamingo, is odd enough; but this as well as the "camelopard" (probably turning on some private jest then intelligible enough to the persons concerned, but dark to others) is not particularly worth illuminating. The italicised words describing Peacock's wit are more legitimate subjects of discussion. They seem to me, though not perhaps literally explicable after the fashion of the duller kind of commentator, to contain both a very happy description of Peacock's peculiar humour, and a very sufficient explanation of the causes which have, both then and since, made that humour palatable rather to the few than to the many. Not only is Peacock peculiarly liable to the charge of being too clever, but he uses his cleverness in a way peculiarly bewildering to those who like to have "This is a horse" writ large under the presentation of the animal. His "rascally comparative" fancy, and the abundant stores of material with which his reading provided it, lead him perpetually to widen "the wound," till it is not surprising that "the knife" (the particular satirical or polemical point that he is urging) gets "lost in it." This weakness, if it be one, has in its different ways of operation all sorts of curious results. One is, that his personal portraits are perhaps farther removed from faithful representations of the originals than the personal sketches of any other writer, even among the most deliberate misrepresenters. There is, indeed, a droll topsy-turvy resemblance to Shelley throughout the Scythrop of *Nightmare Abbey*, but there Peacock was hardly using the knife at all. When he satirises persons, he goes so far away from their real personalities that the libel ceases to be libellous. It is difficult to say whether Mr. Mystic, Mr. Flosky, or Mr. Skionar is least like Coleridge; and Southey, intensely sensitive as he was to criticism, need not have lost his equanimity over Mr. Feathernest. A single point suggested itself to Peacock, that point suggested another, and so on and so on, till he was miles away from the start. The inconsistency of his political views has been justly, if somewhat plaintively, reflected on by Lord Houghton in the words, "the intimate friends of Mr. Peacock may have understood his political sentiments, but it is extremely difficult to discover them from his works." I should, however, myself say that, though it may be extremely difficult to deduce any definite political sentiments from Peacock's works, it is very easy to see in them a general and not inconsistent political attitude—that of intolerance of the vulgar and the stupid. Stupidity and vulgarity not being (fortunately or unfortunately) monopolised by any political party, and being (no doubt unfortunately) often condescended to by both, it is not surprising to find Peacock — especially with his noble disregard of apparent consistency and the inveterate habit of pillar-to-post joking, which has been

PEACOCK.

PEACOCK.

commented on—distributing his shafts with great impartiality on Trojan and Greek; on the opponents of reform in his earlier manhood, and on the believers in progress during his later; on virtual representation and the telegraph; on barouche-driving as a gentleman's profession, and lecturing as a gentleman's profession. But this impartiality (or, if anybody prefers it, inconsistency) has naturally added to the difficulties of some readers with his works. It is time, however, to endeavour to give some idea of the gay variety of those works themselves.

Although there are few novelists who observe plot less than Peacock, there are few also who are more regular in the particular fashion in which they disdain plot. Peacock is in fiction what the dramatists of the school of Ben Jonson down to Shadwell are in comedy—he works in "humours." It ought not to be, but perhaps is, necessary to remind the reader that this is by no means the same thing in essence, though accidentally it very often is the same, as being a humourist. The dealer in humours takes some fad or craze in his characters, some minor ruling passion, and makes his profit out of it. Generally (and almost always in Peacock's case) he takes if he can one or more of these humours as a central point, and lets the others play and revolve in a more or less eccentric fashion round it. In almost every book of Peacock's there is a host who is possessed by the cheerful mania for collecting other maniacs round him. Harry Headlong of Headlong Hall, Esquire, PEACOCK. a young Welsh gentleman of means, and of generous though rather unchastened taste, finding, as Peacock says, in the earliest of his gibes at the universities, that there are no such things as men of taste and philosophy in Oxford, assembles a motley host in London, and asks them down to his place at Llanberis. The adventures of the visit (ending up with several weddings) form the scheme of the book, as indeed repetitions of something very little different form the scheme of all the other books, with the exception of *The Misfortunes of Elphin*, and perhaps *Maid Marian*. Of books so simple in one way, and so complex in others, it is impossible and unnecessary to give any detailed analysis. But each contains characteristics which contribute too much to the knowledge of Peacock's idiosyncrasy to pass altogether unnoticed. The contrasts in *Headlong Hall* between the pessimist Mr. Escot, the optimist Mr. Foster, and the happy-mean man Mr. Jenkison (who inclines to both in turn, but on the whole rather to optimism), are much less amusing than the sketches of Welsh scenery and habits, the passages of arms with representatives of the *Edinburgh* and *Quarterly Reviews* (which Peacock always hated), and the satire on "improving," craniology, and other passing fancies of the day. The book also contains the first and most unfriendly of those sketches of clergymen of the

PEACOCK.

Church of England which Peacock gradually softened till, in Dr. Folliott and Dr. Opimian, his curses became blessings altogether. The Reverend Dr. Gaster is an ignoble brute, though not quite life-like enough to be really offensive. But the most charming part of the book by far (for its women are mere lay figures) is to be found in the convivial scenes. *Headlong Hall* contains, besides other occasional verse of merit, two drinking-songs—"Hail to the Headlong," and the still better "A Heel-tap! a heel-tap! I never could bear it"—songs not quite so good as those in the subsequent books, but good enough to make any reader think with a gentle sigh of the departure of good fellowship from the earth. Undergraduates and Scotchmen (and even in their case the fashion is said to be dying) alone practise at the present day the full rites of Comus.

Melincourt, published, and indeed written, very soon after *Headlong Hall*, is a much more ambitious attempt. It is some three times the length of its predecessor, and is, though not much longer than a single volume of some three-volume novels, the longest book that Peacock ever wrote. It is also much more ambitiously planned; the twice attempted abduction of the heiress, Anthelia Melincourt, giving something like a regular plot, while the introduction of Sir Oran Haut-ton (an orang-outang whom the eccentric hero, Forester, has domesticated and intends to introduce to parliamentary life) can only be understood as aiming

PEACOCK.

at a regular satire on the whole of human life, conceived in a milder spirit than "Gulliver," but belonging in some degree to the same class. Forester himself, a disciple of Rousseau, a fervent anti-slavery man who goes to the length of refusing his guests sugar, and an ideologist in many other ways, is also an ambitious sketch; and Peacock has introduced episodes after the fashion of eighteenth-century fiction, besides a great number of satirical excursions dealing with his enemies of the Lake school, with paper money, and with many other things and persons. The whole, as a whole, has a certain heaviness. The enthusiastic Forester is a little of a prig, and a little of a bore; his friend the professorial Mr. Fax proses dreadfully; the Oran Haut-ton scenes, amusing enough of themselves, are overloaded (as is the whole book) with justificative selections from Buffon, Lord Monboddo, and other authorities. The portraits of Southey, Coleridge, Wordsworth, Canning, and others, are neither like, nor in themselves very happy, and the heroine Anthelia is sufficiently uninteresting to make us extremely indifferent whether the virtuous Forester or the *roué* Lord Anophel Achthar gets her. On the other hand, detached passages are in the author's very best vein; and there is a truly delightful scene between Lord Anophel and his chaplain Grovelgrub, when the athletic Sir Oran has not only foiled their attempt on Anthelia, but has mast-headed them on the top of a rock perpendicular. But the gem of the book is the election for the borough of One-Vote—a very amusing farce on the subject of rotten boroughs. Mr. Forester has bought one of the One-Vote seats for his friend the Orang, and, going to introduce him to the constituency, falls in with the purchaser of the other seat, Mr. Sarcastic, who is a practical humorist of the most accomplished kind. The satirical arguments with which Sarcastic combats Forester's enthusiastic views of life and politics, the elaborate spectacle which he gets up on the day of nomination, and the free fight which follows, are recounted with extraordinary spirit. Nor is the least of the attractions of the book an admirable drinking-song, superior to either of those in *Headlong Hall*, though perhaps better known to most people by certain Thackerayan reminiscences of it than in itself:—

PEACOCK.

THE GHOSTS

In life three ghostly friars were we,
And now three friendly ghosts we be.
Around our shadowy table placed,
The spectral bowl before us floats:
With wine that none but ghosts can taste
We wash our unsubstantial throats.
Three merry ghosts—three merry ghosts—three merry
ghosts are we:
Let the ocean be port and we'll think it good sport
To be laid in that Red Sea.

With songs that jovial spectres chaunt,
Our old refectory still we haunt.

The traveller hears our midnight mirth:
"Oh list," he cries, "the haunted choir!
The merriest ghost that walks the earth
Is now the ghost of a ghostly friar."
Three merry ghosts—three merry ghosts—three merry
ghosts are we:
Let the ocean be port and we'll think it good sport
To be laid in that Red Sea.

In the preface to a new edition of *Melincourt*, which Peacock wrote nearly thirty years later, and which contains a sort of promise of *Gryll Grange*, there is no sign of any dissatisfaction on the author's part with the plan of the earlier book; but in his next, which came quickly, he changed that plan very decidedly. *Nightmare Abbey* is the shortest, as *Melincourt* is the longest, of his tales; and as *Melincourt* is the most unequal and the most clogged with heavy matter, so *Nightmare Abbey* contains the most unbroken tissue of farcical, though not in the least coarsely farcical, incidents and conversations. The misanthropic Scythrop (whose habit of Madeira-drinking has made some exceedingly literal people sure that he really could not be intended for the water-drinking Shelley); his yet gloomier father, Mr. Glowry; his intricate entanglements with the lovely Marionetta and the still more beautiful Celinda; his fall between the two stools; his resolve to commit suicide; the solution of that awkward resolve—are all simply delightful. Extravagant as the thing is, its brevity and the throng of incidents and jokes prevent it from

PEACOCK.

becoming in the least tedious. The pessimist-fatalist Mr. Toobad, with his "innumerable proofs of the temporary supremacy of the devil," and his catchword "the devil has come among us, having great wrath," appears just enough, and not too much. The introduced sketch of Byron as Mr. Cypress would be the least happy thing of the piece if it did not give occasion for a capital serious burlesque of Byronic verse, the lines, "There is a fever of the spirit," which, as better known than most of Peacock's verse, need not be quoted. Mr. Flosky, a fresh caricature of Coleridge, is even less like the original than Mr. Mystic, but he is much more like a human being, and in himself is great fun. An approach to a more charitable view of the clergy is discoverable in the curate Mr. Larynx, who, if not extremely ghostly, is neither a sot nor a sloven. But the quarrels and reconciliations between Scythrop and Marionetta, his invincible inability to make up his mind, the mysterious advent of Marionetta's rival, and her residence in hidden chambers, the alternate sympathy and repulsion between Scythrop and those elder disciples of pessimism, his father and Mr. Toobad—all the contradictions of Shelley's character, in short, with a suspicion of the incidents of his life brought into the most ludicrous relief, must always form the great charm of the book. A tolerably rapid reader may get through it in an hour or so, and there is hardly a more delightful hour's reading of anything like the same kind in the English language, either for the incidental strokes of wit and humour, or for the easy mastery with which the whole is hit off. It contains, moreover, another drinking-catch, "Seamen Three," which, though it is, like its companion, better known than most of Peacock's songs, may perhaps find a place:—

PEACOCK.

Seamen three! What men be ye?
Gotham's three wise men we be.
Whither in your bowl so free?
To rake the moon from out the sea.
The bowl goes trim, the moon doth shine,
And our ballast is old wine;
And your ballast is old wine.

Who art thou so fast adrift?
I am he they call Old Care.
Here on board we will thee lift.
No: I may not enter there.
Wherefore so? 'Tis Jove's decree
In a bowl Care may not be;
In a bowl Care may not be.

Fear ye not the waves that roll?
No: in charmèd bowl we swim.
What the charm that floats the bowl?
Water may not pass the brim.
The bowl goes trim, the moon doth shine,
And our ballast is old wine;
And your ballast is old wine.

A third song sung by Marionetta, "Why are thy looks so blank, Grey Friar?" is as good in another way; nor should it be forgotten that the said Marionetta, who has been thought to have some features of the luckless Harriet Shelley, is

Peacock's first lifelike study of a girl, and one of his pleasantest.

PEACOCK.

The book which came out four years after, *Maid Marian*, has, I believe, been much the most popular and the best known of Peacock's short romances. It owed this popularity, in great part, doubtless, to the fact that the author has altered little in the well-known and delightful old story, and has not added very much to its facts, contenting himself with illustrating the whole in his own satirical fashion. But there is also no doubt that the dramatisation of *Maid Marian* by Planché and Bishop as an operetta helped, if it did not make, its fame. The snatches of song through the novel are more frequent than in any other of the books, so that Mr. Planché must have had but little trouble with it. Some of these snatches are among Peacock's best verse, such as the famous "Bramble Song," the great hit of the operetta, the equally well-known "Oh, bold Robin Hood," and the charming snatch :—

For the tender beech and the sapling oak,
 That grow by the shadowy rill,
You may cut down both at a single stroke,
 You may cut down which you will ;

But this you must know, that as long as they grow,
 Whatever change may be,
You never can teach either oak or beech
 To be aught but a greenwood tree.

This snatch, which, in its mixture of sentiment, truth, and what may be excusably called "rollick," is very characteristic of its author, and is put in the mouth of Brother Michael, practically the hero of the piece, and the happiest of the various workings up of Friar Tuck, despite his considerable indebtedness to a certain older friar, whom we must not call "of the funnels." That Peacock was a Pantagruelist to the heart's core is evident in all his work; but his following of Master Francis is nowhere clearer than in *Maid Marian*, and it no doubt helps us to understand why those who cannot relish Rabelais should look askance at Peacock. For the rest, no book of Peacock's requires such brief comment as this charming pastoral, which was probably little less in Thackeray's mind than *Ivanhoe* itself when he wrote *Rebecca and Rowena.* The author draws in (it would be hardly fair to say drags in) some of his stock satire on courts, the clergy, the landed gentry, and so forth; but the very nature of the subject excludes the somewhat tedious digressions which mar *Melincourt*, and which once or twice menace, though they never actually succeed in spoiling, the unbroken fun of *Nightmare Abbey.*

PEACOCK.

The Misfortunes of Elphin, which followed after an interval of seven years, is, I believe, the least generally popular of Peacock's works, though (not at all for that reason) it happens to be my own favourite. The most curious instance of this general unpopularity is the entire omission, as far as I am aware, of any reference to it in any of the popular guide-books to Wales. One piece of verse, indeed, the "War-song of Dinas Vawr," a triumph of easy verse and covert sarcasm, has had some vogue, but the rest is only known to Peacockians. The abundance of Welsh lore which, at any rate in appearance, it contains, may have had something to do with this; though the translations or adaptations, whether faithful or not, are the best literary renderings of Welsh known to me. Something also, and probably more, is due to the saturation of the whole from beginning to end with Peacock's driest humour. Not only is the account of the sapping and destruction of the embankment of Gwaelod an open and continuous satire on the opposition to Reform, but the whole book is written in the spirit and manner of *Candide*—a spirit and manner which Englishmen have generally been readier to relish, when they relish them at all, in another language than in their own. The respectable domestic virtues of Elphin and his wife Angharad, the blameless loves of Taliesin and the Princess Melanghel, hardly serve even as a foil to the satiric treatment of the other characters. The careless incompetence of the poetical King Gwythno, the coarser vices of other Welsh princes, the marital toleration or blindness of Arthur, the cynical frankness of the robber King Melvas, above all, the drunkenness of the immortal Seithenyn, give the humorist themes which he caresses with inexhaustible affection, but in a manner no doubt very puzzling, if not shocking, to matter-of-fact readers. Seithenyn, the drunken prince and dyke-warden, whose carelessness lets in the inundation, is by far Peacock's most original creation (for Scythrop, as has been said, is rather a humorous distortion of the actual than a creation). His complete self-satisfaction, his utter fearlessness of consequences, his ready adaptation to whatever part, be it prince or butler, presents itself to him, and above all, the splendid topsy-turviness of his fashion of argument, make Seithenyn one of the happiest, if not one of the greatest, results of whimsical imagination and study of human nature. "They have not"—says the somewhile prince, now King Melvas's butler, when Taliesin discovers him twenty years after his supposed death—"they have not made it [his death] known to me, for the best of all reasons, that one can only know the truth. For if that which we think we know is not truth, it is something which we do not know. A man cannot know his own death. For while he knows anything he is alive; at least, I never heard of a dead man who knew anything, or pretended to know anything: if he had so pretended I should have told him to his face that he was no dead man." How nobly consistent is this with his other argument in the days of his princedom and his neglect of the embankment! Elphin has just reproached him with the proverb, "Wine speaks in the silence of reason." "I am very sorry," said Seithenyn,

PEACOCK.

"that you see things in a wrong light. But we will not quarrel, for three reasons: first, because you are the son of the king, and may do and say what you please without any one having a right to be displeased; second, because I never quarrel with a guest, even if he grows riotous in his cups; third, because there is nothing to quarrel about. And perhaps that is the best reason of the three; or rather the first is the best, because you are the son of the king; and the third is the second, that is the second best, because there is nothing to quarrel about; and the second is nothing to the purpose, because, though guests will grow riotous in their cups in spite of my good orderly example, God forbid that I should say that is the case with you. And I completely agree in the truth of your remark that reason speaks in the silence of wine."

Crotchet Castle, the last but one of the series, which was published two years after *Elphin* and nearly thirty before *Gryll Grange*, has been already called the best; and the statement is not inconsistent with the description already given of *Nightmare Abbey* and of *Elphin*. For *Nightmare Abbey* is chiefly farce, and *The Misfortunes of Elphin* is chiefly sardonic persiflage. *Crotchet Castle* is comedy of a high and varied kind. Peacock has returned in it to the machinery of a country house with its visitors, each of whom is more or less of a crotcheteer; and has thrown in a little romantic interest in the suit of a certain unmoneyed

Captain Fitzchrome to a noble damsel who is expected to marry money, as well as in the desertion and subsequent rescue of Susannah Touchandgo, daughter of a levanting financier. The charm of the book, however, which distinguishes it from all its predecessors, is the introduction of characters neither ridiculous nor simply good in the persons of the Rev. Dr. Folliott and Lady Clarinda Bossnowl, Fitzchrome's beloved. "Lady Clarinda," says the captain, when the said Lady Clarinda has been playing off a certain not unladylike practical joke on him, "is a very pleasant young lady;" and most assuredly she is, a young lady (in the nineteenth century and in prose) of the tribe of Beatrice, if not even of Rosalind. As for Dr. Folliott, the author is said to have described him as his amends for his earlier clerical sketches, and the amends are ample. A stout Tory, a fellow of infinite jest, a lover of good living, an inveterate paradoxer, a pitiless exposer of current cants and fallacies, and, lastly, a tall man of his hands, Dr. Folliott is always delightful, whether he is knocking down thieves, or annihilating, in a rather Johnsonian manner, the economist, Mr McQuedy, and the journalist, Mr. Eavesdrop, or laying down the law as to the composition of breakfast and supper, or using strong language as to "the learned friend" (Brougham), or bringing out, partly by opposition and partly by irony, the follies of the transcendentalists, the fops the doctrinaires, and

PEACOCK.

the mediævalists of the party. The book, moreover, contains the last and not the least of Peacock's admirable drinking-songs:— PEACOCK.

> If I drink water while this doth last,
>   May I never again drink wine;
> For how can a man, in his life of a span,
>   Do anything better than dine?
> We'll dine and drink, and say if we think
>   That anything better can be;
> And when we have dined, wish all mankind
>   May dine as well as we.
>
> And though a good wish will fill no dish,
>   And brim no cup with sack,
> Yet thoughts will spring as the glasses ring
>   To illumine our studious track.
> O'er the brilliant dreams of our hopeful schemes
>   The light of the flask shall shine;
> And we'll sit till day, but we'll find the way
>   To drench the world with wine.

The song is good in itself, but it is even more interesting as being the last product of Peacock's Anacreontic vein. Almost a generation passed before the appearance of his next and last novel, and though there is plenty of good eating and drinking in *Gryll Grange*, the old fine rapture had disappeared in society meanwhile, and Peacock obediently took note of the disappearance. It is considered, I believe, a mark of barbarian tastes to lament the change. But I am not certain that the Age of Apollinaris and lectures has yet produced anything that can vie as literature with the products of the ages of Wine and Song.

PEACOCK.

Gryll Grange, however, in no way deserves the name of a dry stick. It is, next to *Melincourt*, the longest of Peacock's novels, and it is entirely free from the drawbacks of the forty-years-older book. Mr. Falconer, the hero, who lives in a tower alone with seven lovely and discreet foster-sisters, has some resemblances to Mr. Forester, but he is much less of a prig. The life and the conversation bear, instead of the marks of a young man's writing, the marks of the writing of one who has seen the manners and cities of many other men, and the personages throughout are singularly lifelike. The loves of the second hero and heroine, Lord Curryfin and Miss Niphet, are much more interesting than their names would suggest. And the most loquacious person of the book, the Rev. Dr. Opimian, if he is somewhat less racy than Dr. Folliott, is not less agreeable. One main charm of the novel lies in its vigorous criticism of modern society in phases which have not yet passed away. "Progress" is attacked with curious ardour; and the battle between literature and science, which in our days even Mr. Matthew Arnold waged but as one *cauponans bellum*, is fought with a vigour that is a joy to see. It would be rather interesting to know whether Peacock, in planning the central incident of the play (an "Aristophanic comedy," satirising modern ways), was aware of the existence of Mansel's delightful parody of the "Clouds." But "Phrontisterion" has never been widely known out of Oxford, and the bearing of Peacock's own performance is rather social than political. Not the least noteworthy thing in the book is the practical apology which is made in it to Scotchmen and political economists (two classes whom Peacock had earlier persecuted) in the personage of Mr. McBorrowdale, a candid friend of Liberalism, who is extremely refreshing. And besides the Aristophanic comedy, *Gryll Grange* contains some of Peacock's most delightful verse, notably the really exquisite stanzas on "Love and Age."

The book is the more valuable because of the material it supplies, in this and other places, for rebutting the charges that Peacock was a mere Epicurean, or a mere carper. Independently of the verses just named, and the hardly less perfect "Death of Philemon," the prose conversation shows how delicately and with how much feeling he could think on those points of life where satire and jollification are out of place. For the purely modern man, indeed, it might be well to begin the reading of Peacock with *Gryll Grange*, in order that he may not be set out of harmony with his author by the robuster but less familiar tones, as well as by the rawer though not less vigorous workmanship, of *Headlong Hall* and its immediate successors. The happy mean between the heart on the sleeve and the absence of heart has scarcely been better shown than in this latest novel.

I have no space here to go through the

miscellaneous work which completes Peacock's

PEACOCK.

literary baggage. His regular poems, all early, are very much better than the work of many men who have won a place among British poets. His criticism, though not great in amount, is good; and he is especially happy in the kind of miscellaneous trifle (such as his trilingual poem on a whitebait dinner), which is generally thought appropriate to "university wits." But the characteristics of these miscellanies are not very different from the characteristics of his prose fiction, and, for purposes of discussion, may be included with them.

Lord Houghton has defined and explained Peacock's literary idiosyncrasy as that of a man of the eighteenth century belated and strayed in the nineteenth. It is always easy to improve on a given pattern, but I certainly think that this definition of Lord Houghton's (which, it should be said, is not given in his own words) needs a little improvement. For the differences which strike us in Peacock—the easy joviality, the satirical view of life, the contempt of formulas and of science—though they certainly distinguish many chief literary men of the eighteenth century from most chief literary men of the nineteenth, are not specially characteristic of the eighteenth century itself. They are found in the seventeenth, in the Renaissance, in classical antiquity—wherever, in short, the art of letters and the art of life have had comparatively free play. The chief differentia of Peacock

PEACOCK.

is a differentia common among men of letters; that is to say, among men of letters who are accustomed to society, who take no sacerdotal or singing-robe view of literature, who appreciate the distinction which literary cultivation gives them over the herd of mankind, but who by no means take that distinction too seriously. Aristophanes, Horace, Lucian, Rabelais, Montaigne, Saint-Evremond, these are all Peacock's literary ancestors, each, of course, with his own difference in especial and in addition. Aristophanes was more of a politician and a patriot, Lucian more of a freethinker, Horace more of a simple *pococurante*. Rabelais may have had a little inclination to science itself (he would soon have found it out if he had lived a little later), Montaigne may have been more of a pure egotist, Saint-Evremond more of a man of society, and of the verse and prose of society. But they all had the same *ethos*, the same love of letters as letters, the same contempt of mere progress as progress, the same relish for the simpler and more human pleasures, the same good fellowship, the same tendency to escape from the labyrinth of life's riddles by what has been called the humour-gate, the same irreconcilable hatred of stupidity and vulgarity and cant. The eighteenth century has, no doubt, had its claim to be regarded as the special flourishing time of this mental state urged by many others besides Lord Houghton; but I doubt whether the claim can be sustained, at any

PEACOCK.

rate to the detriment of other times, and the men of other times. That century took itself too seriously—a fault fatal to the claim at once. Indeed, the truth is that while this attitude has in some periods been very rare, it cannot be said to be the peculiar, still less the universal, characteristic of any period. It is a personal not a periodic distinction; and there are persons who might make out a fair claim to it even in the depths of the Middle Ages or of the nineteenth century.

However this may be, Peacock certainly held the theory of those who take life easily, who do not love anything very much except old books, old wine, and a few other things, not all of which perhaps need be old, who are rather inclined to see the folly of it than the pity of it, and who have an invincible tendency, if they tilt at anything at all, to tilt at the prevailing cants and arrogances of the time. These cants and arrogances of course vary. The position occupied by monkery at one time may be occupied by physical science at another; and a belief in graven images may supply in the third century the target, which is supplied by a belief in the supreme wisdom of majorities in the nineteenth. But the general principles—the cult of the Muses and the Graces for their own sake, and the practice of satiric archery at the follies of the day—appear in all the elect of this particular election, and they certainly appear in Peacock. The results no doubt are distasteful, not to say shocking, to some excellent people. It is impossible to avoid a slight chuckle when one thinks of the horror with which some such people must read Peacock's calm statement, repeated I think more than once, that one of his most perfect heroes "found, as he had often found before, that the more his mind was troubled, the more madeira he could drink without disordering his head." I have no doubt that the United Kingdom Alliance, if it knew this dreadful sentence (but probably the study of the United Kingdom Alliance is not much in Peacock), would like to burn all the copies of *Gryll Grange* by the hands of Mr. Berry, and make the reprinting of it a misdemeanour, if not a felony. But it is not necessary to follow Sir Wilfrid Lawson, or to be a believer in education, or in telegraphs, or in majorities, in order to feel the repulsion which some people evidently feel for the manner of Peacock. With one sense absent and another strongly present it is impossible for any one to like him. The present sense is that which has been rather grandiosely called the sense of moral responsibility in literature. The absent sense is that sixth, seventh, or eighth sense, called a sense of humour, and about this there is no arguing. Those who have it, instead of being quietly and humbly thankful, are perhaps a little too apt to celebrate their joy in the face of the afflicted ones who have it not; the afflicted ones, who have it not, only follow a general law in protesting that

PEACOCK.

the sense of humour is a very worthless thing, if not a complete humbug. But there are others of whom it would be absurd to say that they have no sense of humour, and yet who cannot place themselves at the Peacockian point of view, or at the point of view of those who like Peacock. His humour is not their humour; his wit not their wit. Like one of his own characters (who did not show his usual wisdom in the remark), they "must take pleasure in the thing represented before they can take pleasure in the representation." And in the things that Peacock represents they do not take pleasure. That gentlemen should drink a great deal of burgundy and sing songs during the process, appears to them at the best childish, at the worst horribly wrong. The prince-butler Seithenyn is a reprobate old man, who was unfaithful to his trust and shamelessly given to sensual indulgence. Dr. Folliott, as a parish priest, should not have drunk so much wine; and it would have been much more satisfactory to hear more of Dr. Opimian's sermons and district visiting, and less of his dinners with Squire Gryll and Mr. Falconer. Peacock's irony on social and political arrangements is all sterile, all destructive, and the sentiment that "most opinions that have anything to be said for them are about two thousand years old" is a libel on mankind. They feel, in short, for Peacock the animosity, mingled with contempt, which the late M. Amiel felt for "clever mockers."

PEACOCK.

It is probably useless to argue with any such. It might, indeed, be urged in all seriousness that the Peacockian attitude is not in the least identical with the Mephistophelian; that it is based simply on the very sober and arguable ground that human nature is always very much the same, liable to the same delusions and the same weaknesses; and that the oldest things are likely to be best, not for any intrinsic or mystical virtue of antiquity, but because they have had most time to be found out in, and have not been found out. It may further be argued, as it has often been argued before, that the use of ridicule as a general criterion can do no harm, and may do much good. If the thing ridiculed be of God, it will stand; if it be not, the sooner it is laughed off the face of the earth the better. But there is probably little good in urging all this. Just as a lover of the greatest of Greek dramatists must recognise at once that it would be perfectly useless to attempt to argue Lord Coleridge out of the idea that Aristophanes, though a genius, was vulgar and base of soul, so to go a good deal lower in the scale of years, and somewhat lower in the scale of genius, everybody who rejoices in the author of "Aristophanes in London" must see that he has no chance of converting Mrs. Oliphant, or any other person who does not like Peacock. The middle term is not present, the disputants do not in fact use the same language. The only thing to do is to recommend this

PEACOCK.

particular pleasure to those who are capable of being pleased by it, and to whom, as no doubt it is to a great number, it is pleasure yet untried.

PEACOCK.

It is well to go about enjoying it with a certain caution. The reader must not expect always to agree with Peacock, who not only did not always agree with himself, but was also a man of almost ludicrously strong prejudices. He hated paper money; whereas the only feeling that most of us have on that subject is that we have not always as much of it as we should like. He hated Scotchmen, and there are many of his readers who without any claim to Scotch blood, but knowing the place and the people, will say,

> That better wine and better men
> We shall not meet in May,

or for the matter of that in any other month. Partly because he hated Scotchmen, and partly because in his earlier days Sir Walter was a pillar of Toryism, he hated Scott, and has been guilty not merely of an absurd and no doubt partly humorous comparison of the Waverley novels to pantomimes, but of more definite criticisms which will bear the test of examination as badly. His strictures on a famous verse of "The Dream of Fair Women" are indefensible, though there is perhaps more to be said for the accompanying gibe at Sir John Millais's endeavour to carry out the description of Cleopatra in black (chiefly black) and white. The reader of Peacock must never mind his author trampling on his, the reader's, favourite corns; or rather he must lay his account with the agreeable certainty that Peacock will shortly afterwards trample on other corns which are not at all his favourites. For my part I am quite willing to accept these conditions. And I do not find that my admiration for Coleridge, and my sympathy with those who opposed the first Reform Bill, and my inclination to dispute the fact that Oxford is only a place of "unread books," make me like Peacock one whit the less. It is the law of the game, and those who play the game must put up with its laws. And it must be remembered that, at any rate in his later and best books, Peacock never wholly "took a side." He has always provided some personage or other who reduces all the whimsies and prejudices of his characters, even including his own, under a kind of dry light. Such is Lady Clarinda, who regards all the crotcheteers of Crotchet Castle with the same benevolent amusement; such Mr. McBorrowdale, who, when he is requested to settle the question of the superiority or inferiority of Greek harmony and perspective to modern, replies, "I think ye may just buz that bottle before you." (Alas! to think that if a man used the word "buz" nowadays some wiseacre would accuse him of vulgarity or of false English.) The general criticism in his work is always sane and vigorous, even though there may be flaws in the particular censures; and it is very seldom that even in his utterances of most flagrant prejudice anything really illiberal can be found. He had read much too widely and with too much discrimination for that. His reading had been corrected by too much of the cheerful give-and-take of social discussion, his dry light was softened and coloured by too frequent rainbows, the Apollonian rays being reflected on Bacchic dew. Anything that might otherwise seem hard and harsh in Peacock's perpetual ridicule is softened and mellowed by this pervading good fellowship which, as it is never pushed to the somewhat extravagant limits of the *Noctes Ambrosianæ*, so it distinguishes Peacock himself from the authors to whom in pure style he is most akin, and to whom Lord Houghton has already compared him—the French tale-tellers from Anthony Hamilton to Voltaire. In these, perfect as their form often is, there is constantly a slight want of geniality, a perpetual clatter and glitter of intellectual rapier and dagger which sometimes becomes rather irritating and teasing to ear and eye. Even the objects of Peacock's severest sarcasm, his Galls and Vamps and Eavesdrops, are allowed to join in the choruses and the bumpers of his easy-going symposia. The sole nexus is not cash payment but something much more agreeable, and it is allowed that even Mr. Mystic had "some super-excellent madeira." Yet how far the wine is from getting above the wit in these merry books

PEACOCK.

is not likely to escape even the most unsympathetic reader. The mark may be selected recklessly or unjustly, but the arrows always fly straight to it.

Peacock, in short, has eminently that quality of literature which may be called recreation. It may be that he is not extraordinarily instructive, though there is a good deal of quaint and not despicable erudition wrapped up in his apparently careless pages. It may be that he does not prove much; that he has, in fact, very little concern to prove anything. But in one of the only two modes of refreshment and distraction possible in literature, he is a very great master. The first of these modes is that of creation—that in which the writer spirits his readers away into some scene and manner of life quite different from that with which they are ordinarily conversant. With this Peacock, even in his professed poetical work, has not very much to do; and in his novels, even in *Maid Marian*, he hardly attempts it. The other is the mode of satirical presentment of well-known and familiar things, and this is all his own. Even his remotest subjects are near enough to be in a manner familiar, and *Gryll Grange*, with a few insignificant changes of names and current follies, might have been written yesterday. He is, therefore, not likely for a long time to lose the freshness and point which, at any rate for the ordinary reader, are required in satirical handlings of ordinary life; while his purely literary merits, especially his grasp of the perennial follies and characters of humanity, of the *ludicrum humani generis* which never varies much in substance under its ever-varying dress, are such as to assure him life even after the immediate peculiarities which he satirised have ceased to be anything but history.

PEACOCK.

IX

WILSON

AMONG those judgments of his contemporaries which make a sort of Inferno of the posthumous writings of Thomas Carlyle, that passed upon "Christopher North" has always seemed to me the most interesting, and perhaps on the whole the fairest. There is enough and to spare of onesidedness in it, and of the harshness which comes from onesidedness. But it is hardly at all sour, and, when allowance is made for the point of view, by no means unjust. The whole is interesting from the literary side, but as it fills two large pages it is much too long to quote. The personal description, "the broad-shouldered stately bulk of the man struck me: his flashing eye, copious dishevelled head of hair, and rapid unconcerned progress like that of a plough through stubble," is characteristically graphic, and far the best of the numerous pen sketches of "the Professor." As for the criticism, the following is the kernel passage of it:—

WILSON.

WILSON.

Wilson had much nobleness of heart and many traits of noble genius, but the central tie-beam seemed wanting always; very long ago I perceived in him the most irreconcilable contradictions: Toryism with sansculottism; Methodism of a sort with total incredulity; a noble loyal and religious nature not strong enough to vanquish the perverse element it is born into. Hence a being all split into precipitous chasms and the wildest volcanic tumults; rocks overgrown indeed with tropical luxuriance of leaf and flower but knit together at the bottom—that was my old figure of speech—only by an ocean of whisky punch. On these terms nothing can be done. Wilson seems to me always by far the most *gifted* of our literary men either then or still. And yet intrinsically he has written nothing that can endure. The central gift was wanting.

Something in the unfavourable part of this must no doubt be set down to the critic's usual forgetfulness of his own admirable dictum, "he is not thou, but himself; other than thou." John was quite other than Thomas, and Thomas judged him somewhat summarily as if he were a failure of a Thomas. Yet the criticism, if partly harsh and as a whole somewhat incomplete, is true enough. Wilson has written "intrinsically nothing that can endure," if it be judged by any severe test. An English Diderot, he must bear a harder version of the judgment on Diderot, that he had written good pages but no good book. Only very rarely has he even written good pages, in the sense of pages good throughout. The almost inconceivable haste with which he wrote (he is credited with having on one occasion actually written fifty-six pages of print for *Blackwood* in two days, and in the years of its double numbers he often contributed from a hundred to a hundred and fifty pages in a single month)—this prodigious haste would not of itself account for the puerilities, the touches of bad taste, the false pathos, the tedious burlesque, the more tedious jactation which disfigure his work. A man writing against time may be driven to dulness, or commonplace, or inelegance of style; but he need never commit any of the faults just noticed. They were due beyond doubt, in Wilson's case, to a natural idiosyncrasy, the great characteristic of which Carlyle has happily hit off in the phrase, "want of a tie-beam," whether he has or has not been charitable in suggesting that the missing link was supplied by whisky punch. The least attractive point about Wilson's work is undoubtedly what his censor elsewhere describes as his habit of "giving a kick" to many men and things. There is no more unpleasant feature of the *Noctes* than the apparent inability of the writer to refrain from sly "kicks" even at the objects of his greatest veneration. A kind of mania of detraction seizes him at times, a mania which some of his admirers have more kindly than wisely endeavoured to shuffle off as a humorous dramatic touch intentionally administered to him by his Eidolon North. The most disgraceful, perhaps the only really disgraceful, instance of this is the carping and offensive criticism of Scott's *Demonology*, written and published at a time when

WILSON.

Sir Walter's known state of health and fortunes might have protected him even from an enemy, much more from a friend, and a deeply obliged friend such as Wilson. Nor is this the only fling at Scott. Wordsworth, much more vulnerable, is also much more frequently assailed; and even Shakespeare does not come off scot-free when Wilson is in his ugly moods.

WILSON.

It need hardly be said that I have no intention of saying that Scott or Wordsworth or Shakespeare may not be criticised. It is the way in which the criticism is done which is the crime; and for these acts of literary high treason, or at least leasing-making, as well as for all Wilson's other faults, nothing seems to me so much responsible as the want of bottom which Carlyle notes. I do not think that Wilson had any solid fund of principles, putting morals and religion aside, either in politics or in literature. He liked and he hated much and strongly, and being a healthy creature he on the whole liked the right things and hated the wrong ones; but it was for the most part a merely instinctive liking and hatred, quite un-coördinated, and by no means unlikely to pass the next moment into hatred or liking as the case might be.

These are grave faults. But for the purpose of providing that pleasure which is to be got from literature (and this, like one or two other chapters here, is partly an effort in literary hedonism) Wilson stands very high, indeed so high that he can be ranked only below the highest. He who will enjoy him must be an intelligent voluptuary, and especially well versed in the art of skipping. When Wilson begins to talk fine, when he begins to wax pathetic, and when he gets into many others of his numerous altitudes, it will behove the reader, according to his own tastes, to skip with discretion and vigour. If he cannot do this, if his eye is not wary enough, or if his conscience forbids him to obey his eyes' warnings, Wilson is not for him. It is true that Mr. Skelton has tried to make a "Comedy of the *Noctes Ambrosianæ*," in which the skipping is done ready to hand. But, with all the respect due to the author of *Thalatta*, the process is not, at least speaking according to my judgment, successful. No one can really taste that eccentric book unless he reads it as a whole; its humours arbitrarily separated and cut-and-dried are nearly unintelligible. Indeed Professor Ferrier's original attempt to give Wilson's work only, and not all of that work when it happened to be mixed with others, seems to me to have been a mistake. But of that further, when we come to speak of the *Noctes* themselves.

Wilson's life, for more than two-thirds of it a very happy one and not devoid of a certain eventfulness, can be summarised pretty briefly, especially as a full account of it is available in the very delightful work of his daughter Mrs. Gordon. Born in 1785, the son of a rich manufacturer of

Paisley and a mother who boasted gentle blood, he was brought up first in the house of a country minister (whose parish he has made famous in several sketches), then at the University of Glasgow, and then at Magdalen College, Oxford. He was early left possessor of a considerable fortune, and his first love, a certain "Margaret," having proved unkind, he established himself at Elleray on Windermere and entered into all the Lake society. Before very long (he was twenty-six at the time) he married Miss Jane Penny, daughter of a Liverpool merchant, and kept open house at Elleray for some years. Then his fortune disappeared in the keeping of a dishonest relation, and he had, in a way, his livelihood to make. I say "in a way," because the wind appears to have been considerably tempered to this shorn but robust lamb. He had not even to give up Elleray, though he could not live there in his old style. He had a mother who was able and willing to entertain him at Edinburgh, on the sole understanding that he did not "turn Whig," of which there was very little danger. He was enabled to keep not too exhausting or anxious terms as an advocate at the Scottish bar; and before long he was endowed, against the infinitely superior claims of Sir William Hamilton, and by sheer force of personal and political influence, with the lucrative Professorship of Moral Philosophy in the University of Edinburgh. But even before this he had

WILSON.

WILSON.

been exempted from the necessity of cultivating literature on a little oatmeal by his connexion with *Blackwood's Magazine.* The story of that magazine has often been told; never perhaps quite fully, but sufficiently. Wilson was not at any time, strictly speaking, editor; and a statement under his own hand avers that he never received any editorial pay, and was sometimes subject to that criticism which the publisher, as all men know from a famous letter of Scott's, was sometimes in the habit of exercising rather indiscreetly. But for a very great number of years, there is no doubt that he held a kind of quasi-editorial position, which included the censorship of other men's work and an almost, if not quite, unlimited right of printing his own. For some time the even more masterful spirit of Lockhart (against whom by the way Mrs. Gordon seems to have had a rather unreasonable prejudice) qualified his control over "Maga." But Lockhart's promotion to the *Quarterly* removed this influence, and from 1825 (speaking roughly) to 1835 Wilson was supreme. The death of William Blackwood and of the Ettrick Shepherd in the last-named year, and of his own wife in 1837 (the latter a blow from which he never recovered), strongly affected not his control over the publication but his desire to control it; and after 1839 his contributions (save in the years 1845 and 1848) were very few. Ill health and broken spirits disabled him, and in 1852 he had to resign his professorship, dying two years later after some months of almost total prostration.

WILSON.

Of the rest of the deeds of Christopher, and of his pugilism, and of his learning, and of his pedestrian exploits, and of his fishing, and of his cock-fighting, and of his hearty enjoyment of life generally, the books of the chronicles of Mrs. Gordon, and still more the twelve volumes of his works and the unreprinted contributions to *Blackwood*, shall tell.

It is with those works that our principal business is, and some of them I shall take the liberty of at once dismissing. His poems are now matters of interest to very few mortals. It is not that they are bad, for they are not; but that they are almost wholly without distinction. He came just late enough to have got the seed of the great romantic revival; and his verse work is rarely more than the work of a clever man who has partly learnt and partly divined the manner of Burns, Scott, Campbell, Coleridge, Wordsworth, Byron, and the rest. Nor, to my fancy, are his prose tales of much more value. I read them many years ago and cared little for them. I re-read, or attempted to re-read, them the other day and cared less. There seems, from the original prospectus of the edition of his works, to have been an intention of editing the course of moral philosophy which, with more or fewer variations, obtained him the agreeable income of a thousand a year or so for thirty years. But whether (as

Mrs. Gordon seems to hint) the notes were in too dilapidated and chaotic a condition for use, or whether Professor Ferrier, his son-in-law and editor (himself, with Dean Mansel, the last of the exact philosophers of Britain), revolted at the idea of printing anything so merely literary, or what it was, I know not—at any rate they do not now figure in the list. This leaves us ten volumes of collected works, to wit, four of the *Noctes Ambrosianæ*, four of *Essays Critical and Imaginative*, and two of *The Recreations of Christopher North*, all with a very few exceptions reprinted from *Blackwood*. Mrs. Gordon filially groans because the reprint was not more extensive, and without endorsing her own very high opinion of her father's work, it is possible to agree with her. It is especially noteworthy that from the essays are excluded three out of the four chief critical series which Wilson wrote—that on Spenser, praised by a writer so little given to reckless praise as Hallam, the *Specimens of British Critics*, and the *Dies Boreales*,—leaving only the series on Homer with its quasi-Appendix on the Greek dramatists, and the *Noctes* themselves.

WILSON.

It must be confessed that the *Noctes Ambrosianæ* are not easy things to commend to the modern reader, if I may use the word commend in its proper sense and with no air of patronage. Even Scotchmen (perhaps, indeed, Scotchmen most of all) are wont nowadays to praise them rather apologetically, as may be seen in the case of their editor and abridger Mr. Skelton. Like most other very original things they drew after them a flock of imbecile imitations; and up to the present day those who have lived in the remoter parts of Scotland must know, or recently remember, dreary compositions in corrupt following of the *Noctes*, with exaggerated attempts at Christopher's worst mannerisms, and invariably including a ghastly caricature of the Shepherd. Even in themselves they abound in stumbling-blocks, which are perhaps multiplied, at least at the threshold, by the arbitrary separation in Ferrier's edition of Wilson's part, and not all his part, from the whole series; eighteen numbers being excluded bodily to begin with, while many more and parts of more are omitted subsequently. The critical mistake of this is evident, for much of the machinery and all the characters of the *Noctes* were given to, not by, Wilson, and in all probability he accepted them not too willingly. The origin of the fantastic personages, the creation of which was a perfect mania with the early contributors to *Blackwood*, and who are, it is to be feared, too often a nuisance to modern readers, is rather dubious. Maginn's friends have claimed the origination of the *Noctes* proper, and of its well-known motto paraphrased from Phocylides, for "The Doctor," or, if his chief *Blackwood* designation be preferred, for the Ensign—Ensign O'Doherty. Professor Ferrier, on the other hand,

WILSON.

WILSON.

has shown a not unnatural but by no means critical or exact desire to hint that Wilson invented the whole. There is no doubt that the real original is to be found in the actual suppers at "Ambrose's." These Lockhart had described, in *Peter's Letters*, before the appearance of the first *Noctes* (the reader must not be shocked, the false concord is invariable in the book itself) and not long after the establishment of "Maga." As was the case with the magazine generally, the early numbers were extremely local and extremely personal. Wilson's glory is that he to a great extent, though not wholly, lifted them out of this rut, when he became the chief if not the sole writer after Lockhart's removal to London, and, with rare exceptions, reduced the personages to three strongly marked and very dramatic characters, Christopher North himself, the Ettrick Shepherd, and "Tickler." All these three were in a manner portraits, but no one is a mere photograph from a single person. On the whole, however, I suspect that Christopher North is a much closer likeness, if not of what Wilson himself was, yet at any rate of what he would have liked to be, than some of his apologists maintain. These charitable souls excuse the egotism, the personality, the violence, the inconsistency, the absurd assumption of omniscience and Admirable-Crichtonism, on the plea that "Christopher" is only the ideal Editor and not the actual Professor. It is quite true that Wilson, who, like all men of humour, must have known his own foibles, not unfrequently satirises them; but it is clear from his other work and from his private letters that they *were* his foibles. The figure of the Shepherd, who is the chief speaker and on the whole the most interesting, is a more debatable one. It is certain that many of Hogg's friends, and, in his touchy moments he himself, considered that great liberty was taken with him, if not that (as the *Quarterly* put it in a phrase which evidently made Wilson very angry) he was represented as a mere "boozing buffoon." On the other hand it is equally certain that the Shepherd never did anything that exhibited half the power over thought and language which is shown in the best passages of his *Noctes* eidolon. Some of the adventures described as having happened to him are historically known as having happened to Wilson himself, and his sentiments are much more the writer's than the speaker's. At the same time the admirably imitated patois and the subtle rendering of Hogg's very well known foibles—his inordinate and stupendous vanity, his proneness to take liberties with his betters, his irritable temper, and the rest—give a false air of identity which is very noteworthy. The third portrait is said to have been the farthest from life, except in some physical peculiarities, of the three. "Tickler," whose original was Wilson's maternal uncle Robert Sym, an

WILSON.

Edinburgh "writer," and something of a humorist in the flesh, is very skilfully made to hold the position of common-sense intermediary between the two originals, North and the Shepherd. He has his own peculiarities, but he has also a habit of bringing his friends down from their altitudes in a Voltairian fashion which is of great benefit to the dialogues, and may be compared to Peacock's similar use of some of his characters. The few occasional interlocutors are of little moment, with one exception; and the only female characters, Mrs. and Miss Gentle, would have been very much better away. They are not in the least lifelike, and usually exhibit the namby-pambiness into which Wilson too often fell when he wished to be refined and pathetic. The "English" or half-English characters, who come in sometimes as foils, are also rather of the stick, sticky. On the other hand, the interruptions of Ambrose, the host, and his household, though a little farcical, are well judged. And of the one exception above mentioned, the live Thomas De Quincey, who is brought in without disguise or excuse in some of the very best of the series, it can only be said that the imitation of his written style is extraordinary, and that men who knew his conversation say that the rendering of that is more extraordinary still.

WILSON.

The same designed exaggeration which some uncritical persons have called Rabelaisian (not noticing that the very fault of the *Noctes* is that, unlike Rabelais, their author mixes up probabilities and improbabilities so that there is a perpetual jarring) is maintained throughout the scenery and etceteras. The comfortable but modest accommodations of Ambrose's hotels in Gabriel's Road and Picardy Place are turned into abodes of not particularly tasteful luxury which put Lord Beaconsfield's famous upholstery to shame, and remind one of what they probably suggested, Edgar Poe's equally famous and much more terrible sketch of a model drawing-room. All the plate is carefully described as "silver"; if it had been gold there might have been some humour in it. The "wax" candles and "silken" curtains (if they had been *Arabian Nights* lamps and oriental drapery the same might be said) are always insisted on. If there is any joke here it seems to lie in the contrast with Wilson's actual habits, which were very simple. For instance, he gives us a gorgeous description of the apparatus of North's solitary confinement when writing for *Blackwood*; his daughter's unvarnished account of the same process agrees exactly as to time, rate of production, and so forth, but substitutes water for the old hock and "Scots pint" (magnum) of claret, a dirty little terra-cotta inkstand for the silver utensil of the *Noctes*, and a single large tallow candle for Christopher's "floods of light." He carried the whim so far as to construct for

WILSON.

himself—his *Noctes* self—an imaginary hall-by-the-sea on the Firth of Forth, which in the same way seems to have had an actual resemblance, half of likeness, half of contrast, to the actual Elleray, and to enlarge his own comfortable town house in Gloucester Place to a sort of fairy palace in Moray Place. But what has most puzzled and shocked readers lies in the specially Gargantuan passages relating to eating and drinking. The comments made on this seem (he was anything but patient of criticism) to have annoyed Wilson very much; and in some of the later *Noctes* he drops hints that the whole is mere Barmecide business. Unfortunately the same criticism applies to this as to the upholstery—the exaggeration is "done too natural." The Shepherd's consumption of oysters not by dozens but by fifties, the allowance of "six common kettles-full of water" for the night's toddy ration of the three, North's above-mentioned bottle of old hock at dinner and magnum of claret after, the dinners and suppers and "whets" which appear so often;—all these stop short of the actually incredible, and are nothing more than extremely convivial men of the time, who were also large eaters, would have actually consumed. Lord Alvanley's three hearty suppers, the exploits of the old member of Parliament in Boz's sketch of Bellamy's (I forget his real name, but he was not a myth), and other things might be quoted to show that there is a

WILSON.

fatal verisimilitude in the Ambrosian feasts which may, or may not, make them shocking (they don't shock me), but which certainly takes them out of the category of merely humorous exaggeration. The Shepherd's "jugs" numerous as they are (and by the way the Shepherd propounds two absolutely contradictory theories of toddy-making, one of which, according to the instructions of my preceptors in that art, who lived within sight of the hills that look down on Glenlivet, is a damnable heresy) are not in the least like the *seze muiz, deux bussars, et six tupins* of tripe that Gargamelle so rashly devoured. There are men now living, and honoured members of society in Scotland, who admit the soft impeachment of having drunk in their youth twelve or fourteen "double" tumblers at a sitting. Now a double tumbler, be it known to the Southron, is a jorum of toddy to which there go two wineglasses (of course of the old-fashioned size, not our modern goblets) of whisky. "Indeed," said a humorous and indulgent lady correspondent of Wilson's, "indeed, I really think you eat too many oysters at the *Noctes*;" and any one who believes in distributive justice must admit that they did.

WILSON.

If, therefore, the reader is of the modern cutlet-and-cup-of-coffee school of feeding, he will no doubt find the *Noctes* most grossly and palpably gluttonous. If he be a very superior person he will smile at the upholstery. If he objects to horseplay he will be horrified at finding the characters on one occasion engaging in a regular "mill," on more than one corking each other's faces during slumber, sometimes playing at pyramids like the bounding brothers of acrobatic fame, at others indulging in leap-frog with the servants, permitting themselves practical jokes of all kinds, affecting to be drowned by an explosive haggis, and so forth. Every now and then he will come to a passage at which, without being superfine at all, he may find his gorge rise; though there is nothing quite so bad in the *Noctes* as the picture of the ravens eating a dead Quaker in the *Recreations*, a picture for which Wilson offers a very lame defence elsewhere. He must put all sorts of prejudice, literary, political, and other, in his pocket. He must be prepared not only for constant and very scurrilous flings at "Cockneys" (Wilson extends the term far beyond the Hunt and Hazlitt school, an extension which to this day seems to give a strange delight to Edinburgh journalists), but for the wildest heterodoxies and inconsistencies of political, literary, and miscellaneous judgment, for much bastard verse-prose, for a good many quite uninteresting local and ephemeral allusions, and, of course, for any quantity of Scotch dialect. If all these allowances and provisos are too many for him to make, it is probably useless for him to attempt the *Noctes* at all. He will pretty certainly, with the *Quarterly* reviewer, set their characters down as boozing

WILSON.

buffoons, and decline the honour of an invitation to Ambrose's or The Lodge, to Southside or the tent in Ettrick Forest.

WILSON.

But any one who can accommodate himself to these little matters, much more any one who can enter into the spirit of days merrier, more leisurely, and if not less straitlaced than our own, yet lacing their laces in a different fashion, will find the *Noctes* very delightful indeed. The mere high jinks, when the secret of being in the vein with them has been mastered, are seldom unamusing, and sometimes (notably in the long swim out to sea of Tickler and the Shepherd) are quite admirable fooling. No one who has an eye for the literary-dramatic can help, after a few *Noctes* have been read, admiring the skill with which the characters are at once typified and individualised, the substance which they acquire in the reader's mind, the personal interest in them which is excited. And to all this, peculiarly suited for an alterative in these solemn days, has to be added the abundance of scattered and incomplete but remarkable gems of expression and thought that come at every few pages, sometimes at every page, of the series.

Some of the burlesque narratives (such as the Shepherd's Mazeppa-like ride on the Bonassus) are inimitably good, though they are too often spoilt by Wilson's great faults of prolixity and uncertainty of touch. The criticisms, of which there are many, are also extremely unequal, but not a few very fine passages may be found among them. The politics, it must be owned, are not good for much, even from the Tory point of view. But the greatest attraction of the whole, next to its sunshiny heartiness and humour, is to be found in innumerable and indescribable bits, phrases, sentences, short paragraphs, which have, more than anything out of the dialogues of the very best novels, the character and charm of actual conversation. To read a *Noctes* has, for those who have the happy gift of realising literature, not much less than the effect of actually taking part in one, with no danger of headache or indigestion after, and without the risk of being playfully corked, or required to leap the table for a wager, or forced to extemporise sixteen stanzas standing on the mantelpiece. There must be some peculiar virtue in this, for, as is very well known, the usual dialogue leaves the reader more outside of it than almost any other kind of literature.

WILSON.

This peculiar charm is of necessity wanting to the rest of Wilson's works, and in so far they are inferior to the *Noctes*; but they have compensatory merits of their own, while, considered merely as literature, there are better things in them than anything that is to be found in the colloquies of those men of great gormandising abilities —Christopher North, James Hogg, and Timothy Tickler. Of the four volumes of *Essays Critical and Imaginative*, the fourth, on Homer and his translators, with an unfinished companion piece on the Greek drama, stands by itself, and has indeed, I believe, been separately published. It is well worth reading through at a sitting, which cannot be said of every volume of criticism. What is more, it may, I think, be put almost first in its own division of the art, though whether that division of the art is a high or low one is another question. I should not myself rank it very high. With Wilson, criticism, at least here, is little more than the eloquent expression of likes and dislikes. The long passages in which he deals with the wrath of Achilles and with the love of Calypso, though subject to the general stricture already more than once passed, are really beautiful specimens of literary enthusiasm; nor is there anything in English more calculated to initiate the reader, especially the young reader, in the love at least, if not the understanding, of Homer. The same enthusiastic and obviously quite genuine appreciation appears in the essay on the "Agamemnon." But of criticism as criticism—of what has been called tracing of literary cause and effect, of any coherent and co-ordinated theory of the good and bad in verse and prose, and the reasons of their goodness or badness, it must be said of this, as of Wilson's other critical work, that it is to be found *nusquam nullibi nullimodis.* He can preach (though with too great volubility, and with occasional faults of taste) delightful sermons about

WILSON.

what he likes at the moment—for it is by no means always the same; and he can make formidable onslaughts with various weapons on what he dislikes at the moment—which again is not always the same. But a man so certain to go off at score whenever his likes or dislikes are excited, and so absolutely unable to check himself whenever he feels tempted thus to go off, lacks the very first qualifications of the critic:—lacks them, indeed, almost as much as the mere word-grinder who looks to see whether a plural substantive has a singular verb, and is satisfied if it has not, and horrified if it has. His most famous sentence "The Animosities are mortal, but the Humanities live for ever" is certainly noble. But it would have been better if the Humanities had oftener choked the Animosities at their birth.

WILSON.

Wilson's criticism is to be found more or less everywhere in his collected writings. I have said that I think it a pity that, of his longest critical attempts, only one has been republished; and the reason is simple. For with an unequal writer (and Wilson is a writer unequalled in his inequality) his best work is as likely to be found in his worst book as his worst work in his best book; while the constant contemplation for a considerable period of one subject is more likely than anything else to dispel his habits of digression and padding. But the ubiquity of his criticism through the ten volumes was, in the circumstances of their editing, simply unavoidable. He had himself superintended a selection of all kinds, which he called *The Recreations of Christopher North*, and this had to be reprinted entire. It followed that, in the *Essays Critical and Imaginative*, an equally miscellaneous character should be observed. Almost everything given, and much not given, in the Works is worth consideration, but for critical purposes a choice is necessary. Let us take the consolidated essay on Wordsworth (most of which dates before 1822), the famous paper on Lord, then Mr., Tennyson's poems in 1832, and the generous palinode on Macaulay's "Lays" of 1842. No three papers could better show Wilson in his three literary stages, that of rather cautious tentative (for though he was not a very young man in 1818, the date of the earliest of the Wordsworth papers, he was a young writer), that of practised and unrestrained vigour (for 1832 represents about his literary zenith), and that of reflective decadence, for by 1842 he had ceased to write habitually, and was already bowed down by mental sorrows and physical ailments.

WILSON.

In the first paper, or set of papers, it is evident that he is ambitiously groping after a more systematic style of criticism than he found in practice to be possible for him. Although he elsewhere scoffs at definitions, he tries to formulate very precisely the genius of Scott, of Byron, and of Wordsworth; he does his best to connect his individual judgments with these formulas; he shuns mere verbal criticism, and (to some extent) mere exaltation or depreciation of particular passages. But it is quite evident that he is ill at ease; and I do not think that any one now reading the essay can call it a successful one, or can attempt to rank it with those which, from different points of view, Hazlitt and De Quincey (Hazlitt nearly at the same time) wrote about Wordsworth. Indeed, Hazlitt is the most valuable of all examples for a critical comparison with Wilson; both being violent partisans and crotcheteers, both being animated with the truest love of poetry, but the one possessing and the other lacking the "tie-beam" of a consistent critical theory.

WILSON.

A dozen years later Wilson had cast his slough, and had become the autocratic, freespoken, self-constituted dictator, Christopher North. He was confronted with the very difficult problem of Mr. Tennyson's poems. He knew they were poetry; that he could not help seeing and knowing. But they seemed to him to be the work of a "cockney" (it would be interesting to know whether there ever was any one less of a cockney than the author of "Mariana"), and he was irritated by some silly praise which had been given to them. So he set to work, and perpetrated the queerest jumble of sound and unsound criticism that exists in the archives of that art, so far as a humble but laborious student and practitioner thereof knoweth.

He could not for the life of him help admiring "Adeline," "Oriana," "Mariana," "The Ode to Memory." Yet he had nothing but scorn for the scarcely less exquisite "Mermaid" and "Sea Fairies"—though the first few lines of the latter, excluded by this and other pseudo-criticism from the knowledge of half a generation of English readers, equal almost anything that the poet has ever done. And only the lucky memory of a remark of Hartley Coleridge's (who never went wrong in criticism, whatever he did in life) saved him from explicitly damning "The Dying Swan," which stands at the very head of a whole class of poetry. In all this essay, to borrow one of his own favourite words, he simply "plouters"—splashes and flounders about without any guidance of critical theory. Compare, to keep up the comparative method, the paper with the still more famous and far more deadly attack which Lockhart made a little later in the *Quarterly*. There one finds little, if any, generosity; an infinitely more cold-blooded and deliberate determination to "cut up." But the critic (and how quaint and pathetic it is to think that the said critic was the author of "I ride from land to land" and "When youthful hope is fled") sees his theory of poetry straight before him, and never takes his eye off it. The individual censures may be just or unjust, but they fit together like the propositions of a masterpiece of legal judgment. The poet is condemned

WILSON.

under the statute,—so much the worse for the statute perhaps, but that does not matter —and he can only plead No jurisdiction; whereas with Christopher it is quite different. If he does not exactly blunder right (and he sometimes does that), he constantly blunders wrong—goes wrong, that is to say, without any excuse of theory or general view. That is not criticism.

WILSON.

We shall not find matters much mended from the strictly critical point of view, when we come, ten years later, to the article on the "Lays." Here Christopher, as I hold with all respect to persons of distinction, is absolutely right. He does not say one word too much of the fire and life of those wonderful verses, of that fight of all fights—as far as English verse goes, except Drayton's "Agincourt" and the last canto of "Marmion"; as far as English prose goes, except some passages of Mallory and two or three pages of Kingsley's—the Battle of the Lake Regillus. The subject and the swing attracted him; he liked the fight, and he liked the ring as of Sir Walter at his very best. But he goes appallingly wrong all through on general critical points.

Yet, according to his own perverse fashion, he never goes wrong without going right. Throughout his critical work there are scattered the most intelligent ideas, the neatest phrases, the most appreciative judgments. How good is it to say that "the battle of Trafalgar, though in some sort it neither began nor ended anything, was a kind of consummation of national prowess."

WILSON.

How good again in its very straightforwardness and simplicity is the dictum "it is not necessary that we should understand fine poetry in order to feel and enjoy it, any more than fine music." Hundreds and thousands of these things lie about the pages. And in the next page to each the critic probably goes and says something which shows that he had entirely forgotten them. An intelligent man may be angry with Christopher—I should doubt whether any one who is not occasionally both angry and disgusted with him can be an intelligent man. But it is impossible to dislike him or fail to admire him as a whole.

There is a third and very extensive division of Wilson's work which may not improbably be more popular, or might be if it were accessible separately, with the public of to-day, than either of those which have been surveyed. His "drunken *Noctes*," as Carlyle unkindly calls them, require a certain peculiar attitude of mind to appreciate them. As for his criticisms, it is frequently said, and it certainly would not become me to deny it, that nobody reads criticism but critics. But Wilson's renown as an athlete, a sportsman, and a lover of nature, who had a singular gift in expressing his love, has not yet died ; and there is an ample audience now for men who can write about athletics, about sport, and about scenery. Nor is it questionable that on these subjects he is seen, on the whole, at his best. True, his faults pursue him even here, and are aggravated by a sort of fashion of the time which made him elaborately digress into politics, into literature, even (God rest his soul!) into a kind of quasi-professional and professorial sermonising on morals and theology, in the midst of his sporting articles. But the metal more attractive of the main subject would probably recommend these papers widely, if they were not scattered pell-mell about the *Essays Critical and Imaginative*, and the *Recreations of Christopher North*. Speaking generally they fall into three divisions—essays on sport in general, essays on the English Lakes, and essays on the Scottish Highlands. The best of the first class are the famous papers called "Christopher North in his Sporting Jacket," and the scattered reviews and articles redacted in the *Recreations* under the general title of "Anglimania." In the second class all are good; and a volume composed of "Christopher at the Lakes," "A Day at Windermere," "Christopher on Colonsay" (a wild extravaganza which had a sort of basis of fact in a trotting-match won on a pony which Wilson afterwards sold for four pounds), and "A Saunter at Grasmere," with one or two more, would be a thing of price. The best of the third class beyond all question is the collection, also redacted by the author for the *Recreations*, entitled "The Moors." This last is

WILSON.

perhaps the best of all the sporting and descriptive pieces, though not the least exemplary of its author's vagaries ; for before he can get to the Moors, he gives us heaven knows how many pages of a criticism on Wordsworth, which, in that place at any rate, we do not in the least want ; and in the very middle of his wonderful and sanguinary exploits on and near Ben Cruachan, he "interrupts the muffins" in order to deliver to a most farcical and impertinent assemblage a quite serious and still more impertinent sermon. But all these papers are more or less delightful. For the glowing description of, and the sneaking apology for, cat-worrying which the "Sporting Jacket" contains, nothing can be said. Wilson deliberately overlooks the fact that the whole fun of that nefarious amusement consists in the pitting of a plucky but weak animal against something much more strongly built and armed than itself. One may regret the P.R., and indulge in a not wholly sneaking affection for cock-fighting, dog-fighting, and anything in which there is a fair match, without having the slightest weakness for this kind of brutality. But, generally speaking, Wilson is a thoroughly fair sportsman, and how enthusiastic he is, no one who has read him can fail to know. Of the scenery of loch or lake, of hill or mountain, he was at once an ardent lover and a describer who has never been equalled. His accustomed exaggeration and false emphasis are nowhere so little perceptible as when

WILSON.

WILSON.

he deals with Ben Cruachan or the Old Man of Coniston, with the Four Great Lakes of Britain, East and West (one of his finest passages), or with the glens of Etive and Borrowdale. The accursed influence of an unchastened taste is indeed observable in the before-mentioned "Dead Quaker of Helvellyn," a piece of unrelieved nastiness which he has in vain tried to excuse. But the whole of the series from which this is taken ("Christopher in his Aviary") is in his least happy style, alternately grandiose and low, relieved indeed by touches of observation and feeling, as all his work is, but hardly redeemed by them. The depths of his possible fall may also be seen from a short piece which Professor Ferrier, obligingly describing it as "too lively to be omitted," has adjoined to "Christopher at the Lakes." But, on the whole, all the articles mentioned in the list at the beginning of this paragraph, with the capital "Streams" as an addition, with the soliloquies on "The Seasons," and with part (*not* the narrative part) of "Highland Storms," are delightful reading. The progress of the sportsman has never been better given than in "Christopher North in his Sporting Jacket." In "The Moors" the actual sporting part is perhaps a little spoilt by the affectation of infallibility, qualified it is true by an aside or two, which so often mars the Christopherian utterances. But Wilson's description has never been bettered. The thunderstorm on the hill, the rough conviviality at the illicit distillery, the evening voyage on the loch, match, if they do not beat, anything of the kind in much more recent books far better known to the present generation. A special favourite of mine is the rather unceremonious review of Sir Humphry Davy's strangely over-praised "Salmonia." The passage of utter scorn and indignation at the preposterous statement of the chief personage in the dialogues, that after an exceptionally hard day's walking and fishing "half a pint of claret per man is enough," is sublime. Nearly the earliest, and certainly the best, protest against some modern fashions in shooting is to be found in "The Moors." In the same series, the visit to the hill cottage, preceding that to the still, has what it has since become the fashion to call the idyllic flavour, without too much of the rather mawkish pathos with which, in imitation of Mackenzie and the sensibility-writers of the last century, Wilson is apt to daub his pictures of rural and humble life. The passages on Oxford, to go to a slightly different but allied subject, in "Old North and Young North" (a paper not yet mentioned), make their fullest appeal to Oxford men, but I can hardly be mistaken in thinking that outsiders must see at least some of the beauty of them. But the list of specially desirable things in these articles is endless; hardly one of them can be taken up without discovering many such, not one of them without discovering some.[1]

WILSON.

And, throughout the whole collection, there is the additional satisfaction that the author is writing only of what he thoroughly knows and understands. At the Lakes Wilson lived for years, and was familiar with every cranny of the hills, from the Pillar to Hawes Water, and from Newby Bridge to Saddleback. He began marching and fishing through the Highlands when he was a boy, enticed even his wife into perilous pedestrian enterprises with him, and, though the extent of his knowledge was perhaps not quite so large as he pretends, he certainly knew great tracts as well as he knew Edinburgh. Nor were his qualifications as a sportsman less authentic, despite the somewhat Munchausenish appearance which some of the feats narrated in the *Noctes* and the *Recreations* wear, and are indeed intended to wear. His enormous baskets of trout seem to have been, if not quite so regular as he sometimes makes them out, at any rate fully historical as occasional feats. As has been hinted, he really did win the trotting-match on the pony, Colonsay, against a thoroughbred, though it was only on the technical point of the thoroughbred breaking his pace. His walk from

1 If I accepted (a rash acceptance) the challenge to name the three very best things in Wilson I should, I think, choose the famous Fairy's Funeral in the *Recreations*, the Shepherd's account of his recovery from illness in the *Noctes*, and, in a lighter vein, the picture of girls bathing in "Streams."

London to Oxford in a night seems to have been a fact, and indeed there is nothing at all impossible in it, for the distance through Wycombe is not more than fifty-three miles; while the less certainly authenticated feat of walking from Liverpool to Elleray (eighty miles at least), without more than a short rest, also appears to be genuine. Like the heroes of a song that he loved, though he seems to have sung it in a corrupt text, he could wrestle and fight and jump out anywhere; and, until he was thoroughly broken by illness, he appears to have made the very most of the not inconsiderable spare time of a Scotch professor who has once got his long series of lectures committed to paper, and has nothing to do for the rest of his life but collect bundles of pound notes at the beginning of each session. All this, joined to his literary gifts, gives a reality to his out-of-door papers which is hardly to be found elsewhere except in some passages of Kingsley, between whom and Wilson there are many and most curious resemblances, chequered by national and personal differences only less curious.

WILSON.

I do not think he was a good reviewer, even after making allowance for the prejudices and partisanships of the time, and for the monkey tricks of mannerism, which, at any rate in his earlier days, were incumbent on a reviewer in "Maga." He is too prone to the besetting sins of reviewing—the right hand defections and left hand fallings off, which, being interpreted, consist first in expressing agreement or disagreement with the author's views, and secondly in digressing into personal statements of one's own views of things connected with them instead of expounding more or less clearly what the book is, and addressing oneself to the great question, Is it a good or a bad piece of work according to the standard which the author himself strove to reach? I have said that I do not think he was on the whole a good critic (for a man may be a good critic and a bad reviewer, though the reverse will hardly stand), and I have given my reasons. That he was neither a great, nor even a very good poet or tale-teller, I have no doubt whatever. But this leaves untouched the attraction of his miscellaneous work, and its suitableness for the purpose of recreation. For that purpose I think it to be among the very best work in all literature. Its unfailing life and vigour, its vast variety, the healthy and inspiriting character of the subjects with which in the main it deals, are the characteristics which make its volumes easy-chair books of the best order. Its beauty no doubt is irregular, faulty, engaging rather than exquisite, attractive rather than artistically or scientifically perfect. I do not know that there is even any reason to join in the general lament over Wilson as being a gigantic failure, a monument of wasted energies and half-developed faculty. I do not at all think that there was anything in him much better than he actually did, or

WILSON.

that he ever could have polished and sand-papered the faults out of his work. It would pretty certainly have lost freshness and vigour; it would quite certainly have been less in bulk, and bulk is a very important point in literature that is to serve as recreation. It is to me not much less certain that it never would have attained the first rank in symmetry and order. I am quite content with it as it is, and I only wish that still more of it were easily accessible.

WILSON.

X

DE QUINCEY[1]

IN not a few respects the literary lot of Thomas De Quincey, both during his life and after it, has been exceedingly peculiar. In one respect it has been unique. I do not know that any other author of anything like his merit, during our time, has had a piece of work published for fully twenty years as his, only for it to be excluded as somebody else's at the end of that time. Certainly *The Traditions of the Rabbins* was very De Quinceyish; indeed, it was so De Quinceyish that the discovery, after such a length of time, that it was not De Quincey's at all, but "Salathiel" Croly's, must have given unpleasant qualms to more than one critic accustomed to be positive on internal evidence. But if De Quincey had thus attributed to him work that was not his, he has also had the utmost difficulty in getting attributed to him, in any accessible form, work that was his own. Three, or

DE QUINCEY.

[1] See Appendix A—De Quincey.

nominally four, editions—one in the decade of his death, superintended for the most part DE QUINCEY. by himself; another in 1862, whose blue coat and white labels dwell in the fond memory; and another in 1878 (reprinted in 1880) a little altered and enlarged, with the Rabbins turned out and more soberly clad, but identical in the main —put before the British public for some thirty-five years a certain portion of his strange, long-delayed, but voluminous work. This work had occupied him for about the same period, that is to say for the last and shorter half of his extraordinary and yet uneventful life. Now, after much praying of readers, and grumbling of critics, we have a fifth and definitive edition from the English critic who has given most attention to De Quincey, Professor Masson.[1] I may say, with hearty acknowledgment of Mr. Masson's services to English literature, that I do not very much like this last edition. De Quincey, never much favoured by the mechanical producers of books, has had his sizings, as Byron would say, still further stinted in the matter of print, margins, and the like; and what I cannot but regard as a rather unceremonious tampering with his own arrangement has taken place, the new matter being not added in supplementary volumes or in appendices to the reprinted volumes, but thrust into or between the separate essays, sometimes to the destruction of

[1] *The Collected Writings of Thomas de Quincey;* edited by David Masson. In fourteen volumes; Edinburgh, 1889-90.

De Quincey's "redaction" altogether, and always to the confusion and dislocation of his arrangement, which has also been neglected in other ways. Still the actual generation of readers will undoubtedly have before them a fuller and completer edition of De Quincey than even Americans have yet had; and they will have it edited by an accomplished scholar who has taken a great deal of pains to acquaint himself thoroughly with the subject.

Will they form a different estimate from that which those of us who have known the older editions for a quarter of a century have formed, and will that estimate, if it is different, be higher or lower? To answer such questions is always difficult; but it is especially difficult here, for a certain reason which I had chiefly in mind when I said just now that De Quincey's literary lot has been very peculiar. I believe that I am not speaking for myself only; I am quite sure that I am speaking my own deliberate opinion when I say that on scarcely any English writer is it so hard to strike a critical balance—to get a clear definite opinion that you can put on the shelf and need merely take down now and then to be dusted and polished up by a fresh reading—as on De Quincey. This is partly due to the fact that his merits are of the class that appeals to, while his faults are of the class that is excused by, the average boy who has some interest in literature.

To read the *Essay on Murder*, the *English Mail Coach*, *The Spanish Nun*, *The Cæsars*, and half a score other things at the age of about fifteen or sixteen is, or ought to be, to fall in love with them. And there is nothing more unpleasant for *les âmes bien nées*, as the famous distich has it, than to find fault in after life with that with which you have fallen in love at fifteen or sixteen. Yet most unfortunately, just as De Quincey's merits, or some of them, appeal specially to youth, and his defects specially escape the notice of youth, so age with stealing steps especially claws those merits into his clutch and leaves the defects exposed to derision. The most gracious state of authors is that they shall charm at all ages those whom they do charm. There are others—Dante, Cervantes, Goethe are instances—as to whom you may even begin with a little aversion, and go on to love them more and more. De Quincey, I fear, belongs to a third class, with whom it is difficult to keep up the first love, or rather whose defects begin before long to urge themselves upon the critical lover (some would say there are no critical lovers, but that I deny) with an even less happy result than is recorded in one of Catullus's finest lines. This kind of discovery

DE QUINCEY.

Cogit amare *minus*, *nec* bene velle *magis*.

How and to what extent this is the case, it must be the business of this paper to attempt to show. But first it is desirable to give, as usual, a brief sketch of De Quincey's life. It need only be a brief one, for the external events of that life were few and meagre; nor can they be said to be, even after the researches of Mr. Page and Professor Masson, very accurately or exhaustively known. Before those researches "all was mist and myth" about De Quincey. I remember as a boy, a year or two after his death, hearing a piece of scandal about his domestic relations, which seems to have had no foundation whatever, but which pretty evidently was an echo of the "libel" (published in a short-lived newspaper of the kind which after many years has again risen to infest London) whereof he complains with perhaps more acrimony than dignity in a paper for the first time exhumed and reprinted in Professor Masson's edition. Many of the details of the *Confessions* and the *Autobiography* have a singular unbelievableness as one reads them; and though the tendency of recent biographers has been to accept them as on the whole genuine, I own that I am rather sceptical about many of them still. Was the ever-famous Malay a real Malay, or a thing of shreds and patches? Did De Quincey actually call upon the awful Dean Cyril Jackson and affably discuss with him the propriety of entering himself at Christ-church? Did he really journey pennilessly down to Eton on the chance of finding a casual peer of the realm of tender years who

DE QUINCEY.

would back a bill for him? These are but a few out of a large number of questions which in idle moods (for the answer to hardly one of them is of the least importance) suggest themselves; and which have been very partially answered hitherto even of late years, though they have been much discussed. The plain and tolerably certain facts which are important in connection with his work may be pretty rapidly summed up.

DE QUINCEY.

Thomas de Quincey, or Quincey, was born in Manchester—but apparently not, as he himself thought, at the country house of Greenhay which his parents afterwards inhabited—on 15th August 1785. His father was a merchant, well to do but of weak health, who died when Thomas was seven years old. Of his childhood he has left very copious reminiscences, and there is no doubt that reminiscences of childhood do linger long after later memories have disappeared. But to what extent De Quincey gave "cocked hats and canes" to his childish thoughts and to his relations with his brothers and sisters, individual judgment must decide. I should say, for my part, that the extent was considerable. It seems, however, pretty clear that he was as a child, very much what he was all his life—emphatically "old-fashioned," retiring without being exactly shy, full of far-brought fancies and yet intensely concentrated upon himself. In 1796 his mother moved to Bath, and Thomas was educated first at the

DE QUINCEY.

Grammar School there and then at a private school in Wiltshire. It was at Bath, his headquarters being there, that he met various persons of distinction—Lord Westport, Lord and Lady Carbery, and others—who figure largely in the *Autobiography*, but are never heard of afterwards. It was with Lord Westport, a boy somewhat younger than himself, that he took a trip to Ireland, the only country beyond Great Britain that he visited. In 1800 he was sent by his guardians to the Manchester Grammar School in order to obtain, by three years' boarding there, one of the Somerset Exhibitions to Brasenose. As a separate income of £150 had been left by De Quincey's father to each of his sons, as this income, or part of it, must have been accumulating, and as the mother was very well off, this roundabout way of securing for him a miserable forty or fifty pounds a year seems strange enough. But it has to be remembered that for all these details we have little security but De Quincey himself. However, that he did go to Manchester, and did, after rather more than half of his three years' probation, run away is indisputable. His mother was living at Chester, and the calf was not killed for this prodigal son; but he had liberty given him to wander about Wales on an allowance of a guinea a week. That there is some mystery, or mystification, about all this is nearly certain. If things really went as he represents them, his mother ought to have been ashamed

DE QUINCEY.

of herself, and his guardians ought to have had, to say the least, an experience of the roughest side of Lord Eldon's tongue. The wanderings in Wales were followed by the famous sojourn in Soho, with its waitings at money-lenders' doors, and its perambulations of Oxford Street. Then, by another sudden revolution, we find De Quincey with two-thirds of his allowance handed over to him and permission to go to Oxford as he wished, but abandoned to his own devices by his mother and his guardians, as surely no mother and no guardians ever abandoned an exceptionally unworldly boy of eighteen before. They seem to have put fifty guineas in his pocket and sent him up to Oxford, without even recommending him a college, and with an income which made it practically certain that he would once more seek the Jews. When he had spent so much of his fifty guineas that there was not enough left to pay caution-money at most colleges, he went to Worcester, where it happened to be low. He seems to have stayed there, on and off, for nearly six years. But he took no degree, his eternal caprices making him shun *vivâ voce* (then a much more important part of the examination than it is now) after sending in unusually good written papers. Instead of taking a degree, he began to take opium, and to make acquaintance with the "Lakers" in both their haunts of Somerset and Westmoreland. He entered himself at the Middle

Temple, he may have eaten some dinners, and somehow or other he "came into his property," though there are dire surmises that it was by the Hebrew door. At any rate in November 1809 he gave up both Oxford and London (which he had frequented a good deal, chiefly, he says, for the sake of the opera of which he was very fond), and established himself at Grasmere. One of the most singular things about his singular life—an oddity due, no doubt, in part to the fact that he outlived his more literary associates instead of being outlived by them—is that though we hear much from De Quincey of other people we hear extremely little from other people about De Quincey. Indeed what we do so hear dates almost entirely from the last days of his life.

DE QUINCEY.

As for the autobiographic details in his *Confessions* and elsewhere, anybody who chooses may put those Sibylline leaves together for himself. It would only appear certain that for ten years he led the life of a recluse student and a hard laudanum-drinker, varied by a little society now and then; that in 1816 he married Margaret Simpson, a dalesman's daughter, of whom we have hardly any personal notices save to the effect that she was very beautiful, and who seems to have been almost the most exemplary of wives to almost the most eccentric of husbands; that for most of the time he was in more or less ease and affluence (ease and affluence still, it would seem, of a treacherous Hebraic origin); and that about 1819 he found himself in great pecuniary difficulties. Then at length he turned to literature, started as editor of a little Tory paper at Kendal, went to London, and took rank, never to be cancelled, as a man of letters by the first part of *The Confessions of an Opium-Eater*, published in the *London Magazine* for 1821. He began as a magazine-writer, and he continued as such till the end of his life; his publications in book-form being, till he was induced to collect his articles, quite insignificant. Between 1821 and 1825 he seems to have been chiefly in London, though sometimes at Grasmere; between 1825 and 1830 chiefly at Grasmere, but much in Edinburgh, where Wilson (whose friendship he had secured, not at Oxford, though they were contemporaries, but at the Lakes) was now residing, and where he was introduced to Blackwood. In 1830 he moved his household to the Scotch capital, and lived there, and (after his wife's death in 1837) at Lasswade, or rather Polton, for the rest of his life. His affairs had come to their worst before he lost his wife, and it is now known that for some considerable time he lived, like Mr. Chrystal Croftangry, in the sanctuary of Holyrood. But De Quincey's way of "living" at any place was as mysterious as most of his other ways; and, though he seems to have been very fond of his family and not at all put out by them, it was his constant habit to establish himself in separate lodgings. These he as constantly shifted (sometimes as far as Glasgow) for no intelligible reason that has ever been discovered or surmised, his pecuniary troubles having long ceased. It was in the latest and most permanent of these lodgings, 42 Lothian Street, Edinburgh, not at Lasswade, that he died on the 8th of December 1859. He had latterly written mainly, though not solely, for *Tait's Magazine* and *Hogg's Instructor*. But his chief literary employment for at least seven years before this, had been the arrangement of the authorised edition of his works, the last or fourteenth volume of which was in the press at the time of his death.

DE QUINCEY.

So meagre are the known facts in a life of seventy-four years, during nearly forty of which De Quincey, though never popular, was still recognised as a great name in English letters, while during the same period he knew, and was known to, not a few distinguished men. But little as is recorded of the facts of his life, even less is recorded of his character, and for once it is almost impossible to discover that character from his works. The few persons who met him all agree as to his impenetrability,—an impenetrability not in the least due to posing, but apparently natural and fated. De Quincey was at once egotistic and impersonal, at once delighted to talk and resolutely shunning society. To him, one is tempted to say, reading and writing did come by nature, and nothing else was natural at all. With books he is always at home. A De Quincey in a world where there was neither reading nor writing of books, would certainly either have committed suicide or gone mad. Pope's theory of the master-passion, so often abused, justified itself here.

DE QUINCEY.

The quantity of work produced during this singular existence, from the time when De Quincey first began, unusually late, to write for publication, was very large. As collected by the author, it filled fourteen volumes; the collection was subsequently enlarged to sixteen, and though the new edition promises to restrict itself to the older and lesser number, the contents of each volume have been very considerably increased. But this printed and reprinted total, so far as can be judged from De Quincey's own assertions and from the observations of those who were acquainted with him during his later years, must have been but the smaller part of what he actually wrote. He was always writing, and always leaving deposits of his manuscripts in the various lodgings where it was his habit to bestow himself. The greater part of De Quincey's writing was of a kind almost as easily written by so full a reader and so logical a thinker as an ordinary newspaper article by an ordinary man; and except when he was sleeping, wandering about, or reading, he was always writing. It is, of course, true that he spent a great deal of time, especially in his last years of all, in re-writing and re-fashioning previously executed work; and also that illness and opium made considerable inroads on his leisure. But I should imagine that if we had all that he actually wrote during these nearly forty years, forty or sixty printed volumes would more nearly express its amount than fourteen or sixteen.

DE QUINCEY.

Still what we have is no mean bulk of work for any man to have accomplished, especially when it is considered how extraordinarily good much of it is. To classify it is not particularly easy; and I doubt, myself, whether any classification is necessary. De Quincey himself tried, and made rather a muddle of it. Professor Masson is trying also. But, in truth, except those wonderful purple patches of "numerous" prose, which are stuck all about the work, and perhaps in strictness not excepting them, everything that De Quincey wrote, whether it was dream or reminiscence, literary criticism or historical study, politics or political economy, had one characteristic so strongly impressed on it as to dwarf and obscure the differences of subject. It is not very easy to find a description at once accurate and fair, brief and adequate, of this peculiarity; it is best hinted at in a remark on De Quincey's conversation which I have seen quoted somewhere (whether by Professor Masson or not I hardly know), that it was, with many interesting and delightful qualities, a kind of "rigmarole." So far as I remember, the remark was not applied in any unfriendly spirit, nor is it adduced here in any such. But both in the printed works, in the remembrances of De Quincey's conversation which have been printed, in his letters which are exactly like his articles, and in those astonishing imaginary conversations attributed to him in the *Noctes Ambrosianæ*, which are said, by good authorities, exactly to represent his way of talk, this quality of rigmarole appears. It is absolutely impossible for him to keep to his subject, or any subject. It is as impossible for him to pull himself up briefly in any digression from that subject. In his finest passages, as in his most trivial, he is at the mercy of the will-o'-the-wisp of divagation. In his later re-handlings of his work, he did to some extent limit his followings of this will-o'-the-wisp to notes, but by no means always; and both in his later and in his earlier work, as it was written for the first time, he indulged them freely in the text.

DE QUINCEY.

For pure rigmarole, for stories, as Mr. Chadband has it, "of a cock and of a bull, and of a lady and of a half-crown," few things, even in De Quincey, can exceed, and nothing out of De Quincey can approach, the passages about the woman he met on the "cop" at Chester, and about the Greek letter that he did not send to the Bishop of Bangor, in the preliminary part of the *Confessions*. The first is the more teasing, because with a quite elvish superfluity of naughtiness he has here indulged in a kind of double rigmarole

DE QUINCEY.

about the woman and the "bore" in the river, and flits from one to the other, and from the other to the one (his main story standing still the while), for half a dozen pages, till the reader feels as Coleridge's auditors must have felt when he talked about "Ball and Bell, Bell and Ball." But the Greek letter episode, or rather, the episode about the Greek letter which never was written, is, if possible, more flagrantly rigmarolish. The-cop-and-bore-and-woman digression contains some remarkable description as a kind of solace to the Puck-led traveller; the other is bare of any such comfort. The Bishop's old housekeeper, who was De Quincey's landlady, told him, it seems, that the Bishop had cautioned her against taking in lodgers whom she did not know, and De Quincey was very angry. As he thought he could write Greek much better than the Bishop, he meditated expostulation in that language. He did not expostulate, but he proceeds instead to consider the possible effect on the Bishop if he had. There was a contemporary writer whom we can imagine struck by a similar whimsy: but Charles Lamb would have given us the Bishop and himself "quite natural and distinct" in a dozen lines, and then have dropped the subject, leaving our sides aching with laughter, and our appetites longing for more. De Quincey tells us at great length who the Bishop was, and how he was the Head of Brasenose, with some remarks on the relative status of

Oxford Colleges. Then he debates the pros and cons on the question whether the Bishop would have answered the letter or not, with some remarks on the difference between strict scholarship and the power of composing in a dead language. He rises to real humour in the remark, that as "Methodists swarmed in Carnarvonshire," he "could in no case have found pleasure in causing mortification" to the Bishop, even if he had vanquished him. By this time we have had some three pages of it, and could well, especially with this lively touch to finish, accept them, though they be something tedious, supposing the incident to be closed. The treacherous author leads us to suppose that it is closed; telling us how he left Bangor, and went to Carnarvon, which change gradually drew his thoughts away from the Bishop. So far is this from being the case, that he goes back to that Reverend Father, and for two mortal pages more, speculates further what would happen if he had written to the Bishop, what the Bishop would have said, whether he would not have asked him (De Quincey) to the Palace, whether, in his capacity of Head of a House, he would not have welcomed him to that seat of learning, and finally smoothed his way to a fellowship. By which time, one is perfectly sick of the Bishop, and of these speculations on the might-have-been, which are indeed by no means unnatural, being exactly what every man indulges in now and then in his

DE QUINCEY.

own case, which, in conversation, would not be unpleasant, but which, gradually and diffusely set down in a book, and interrupting a narrative, are most certainly "rigmarole."

DE QUINCEY.

Rigmarole, however, can be a very agreeable thing in its way, and De Quincey has carried it to a point of perfection never reached by any other rigmaroler. Despite his undoubted possession of a kind of humour, it is a very remarkable thing that he rigmaroles, so far as can be made out by the application of the most sensitive tests, quite seriously, and almost, if not quite, unconsciously. These digressions or deviations are studded with quips and jests, good, bad, and indifferent. But the writer never seems to suspect that his own general attitude is at least susceptible of being made fun of. It is said, and we can very well believe it, that he was excessively annoyed at Lamb's delightful parody of his *Letters to a Young Man whose Education has been Neglected*; and, on the whole, I should say that no great man of letters in this century, except Balzac and Victor Hugo, was so insensible to the ludicrous aspect of his own performances. This in the author of the *Essay on Murder* may seem surprising, but, in fact, there are few things of which there are so many subdivisions, or in which the subdivisions are marked off from each other by such apparently impermeable lines, as humour. If I may refine a little I should say that there was very frequently, if not generally, a humorous basis for these divagations of De Quincey's; but that he almost invariably lost sight of that basis, and proceeded to reason quite gravely away from it, in what is (not entirely with justice) called the scholastic manner. How much of this was due to the influence of Jean Paul and the other German humorists of the last century, with whom he became acquainted very early, I should not like to say. I confess that my own enjoyment of Richter, which has nevertheless been considerable, has always been lessened by the presence in him, to a still greater degree, of this same habit of quasi-serious divagation. To appreciate the mistake of it, it is only necessary to compare the manner of Swift. The *Tale of a Tub* is in appearance as daringly discursive as anything can be, but the author in the first place never loses his way, and in the second never fails to keep a watchful eye on himself, lest he should be getting too serious or too tedious. That is what Richter and De Quincey fail to do.

DE QUINCEY.

Yet though these drawbacks are grave, and though they are (to judge from my own experience) felt more seriously at each successive reading, most assuredly no man who loves English literature could spare De Quincey from it; most assuredly all who love English literature would sooner spare some much more faultless writers. Even that quality of his which has been already noted, his extraordinary attraction for youth, is a singular and priceless one. The Master of the Court of the Gentiles, or the Instructor of the Sons of the Prophets, he might be called in a fantastic nomenclature, which he would have himself appreciated, if it had been applied to any one but himself. What he somewhere calls his "extraordinary ignorance of daily life" does not revolt youth. His little pedantries, which to the day of his death were like those of a clever schoolboy, appeal directly to it. His best fun is quite intelligible; his worst not wholly uncongenial. His habit (a certain most respected professor in a northern university may recognise the words) of "getting into logical coaches and letting himself be carried on without minding where he is going" is anything but repugnant to brisk minds of seventeen. They are quite able to comprehend the great if mannered beauty of his finest style—the style, to quote his own words once more, as of "an elaborate and pompous sunset." Such a schoolmaster to bring youths of promise, not merely to good literature but to the best, nowhere else exists. But he is much more than a mere schoolmaster, and in order that we may see what he is, it is desirable first of all to despatch two other objections made to him from different quarters, and on different lines of thought. The one objection (I should say that I do not fully espouse either of them) is that he is an untrustworthy critic

DE QUINCEY.

of books; the other is that he is a very spiteful commentator on men.

DE QUINCEY.

This latter charge has found wide acceptance and has been practically corroborated and endorsed by persons as different as Southey and Carlyle. It would not in any case concern us much, for when a man is once dead it matters uncommonly little whether he was personally unamiable or not. But I think that De Quincey has in this respect been hardly treated. He led such a wholly unnatural life, he was at all times and in all places so thoroughly excluded from the natural contact and friction of society, that his utterances hardly partake of the ordinary character of men's speech. In the "vacant interlunar caves" where he hid himself, he could hardly feel the restraints that press on those who move within ear-shot and jostle of their fellows on this actual earth. This is not a triumphant defence, no doubt; but I think it is a defence. And further, it has yet to be proved that De Quincey set down anything in malice. He called his literary idol, Wordsworth, "inhumanly arrogant." Does anybody—not being a Wordsworthian and therefore out of reach of reason—doubt that Wordsworth's arrogance was inhuman? He, not unprovoked by scant gratitude on Coleridge's part for very solid services, and by a doubtless sincere but rather unctuous protest of his brother in opium-eating against the *Confessions*, told some home truths against that magnificent genius but most unsatisfactory man. A sort of foolish folk has recently arisen which tells us that because Coleridge wrote "The Ancient Mariner" and "Kubla Khan," he was quite entitled to leave his wife and children to be looked after by anybody who chose, to take stipends from casual benefactors, and to scold, by himself or by his next friend Mr. Wordsworth, other benefactors, like Thomas Poole, who were not prepared at a moment's notice to give him a hundred pounds for a trip to the Azores. The rest of us, though we may feel no call to denounce Coleridge for these proceedings, may surely hold that "The Ancient Mariner" and "Kubla Khan" are no defence to the particular charges. I do not see that De Quincey said anything worse of Coleridge than any man who knew the then little, but now well-known facts of Coleridge's life, was entitled to say if he chose. And so in other cases. That he was what is called a thoughtful person—that is to say that he ever said to himself, "Will what I am writing give pain, and ought I to give that pain?"—I do not allege. In fact, the very excuse which has been made for him above is inconsistent with it. He always wrote far too much as one in another planet for anything of the kind to occur to him, and he was perhaps for a very similar reason rather too fond of the "personal talk" which Wordsworth wisely disdained. But that he was in any proper sense spiteful, that is to say that he ever wrote either with a deliberate intention to wound or with a deliberate indifference whether he wounded or not, I do not believe.

DE QUINCEY.

The other charge, that he was a bad or rather a very untrustworthy critic of books, cannot be met quite so directly. He is indeed responsible for a singularly large number of singularly grave critical blunders—by which I mean of course not critical opinions disagreeing with my own, but critical opinions which the general consent of competent critics, on the whole, negatives. The minor classical writers are not much read now, but there must be a sufficient jury to whom I can appeal to know what is to be done with a professed critic of style—at least asserting himself to be no mean classical scholar—who declares that "Paganism had no more brilliant master of composition to show than"—Velleius Paterculus! Suppose this to be a mere fling or freak, what is to be thought of a man who evidently sets Cicero, as a writer, if not as a thinker, above Plato? It would be not only possible but easy to follow this up with a long list of critical enormities on De Quincey's part, enormities due not to accidental and casual crotchet or prejudice, as in Hazlitt's case, but apparently to some perverse idiosyncrasy. I doubt very much, though the doubt may seem horribly heretical to some people, whether De Quincey really cared much for poetry as poetry. He liked philosophical poets:—Milton,

Wordsworth, Shakespeare (inasmuch as he perceived Shakespeare to be the greatest of philosophical poets), Pope even in a certain way. But read the interesting paper which late in life he devoted to Shelley. He treats Shelley as a man admirably, with freedom alike from the maudlin sentiment of our modern chatterers and from Puritanical preciseness. He is not too hard on him in any way, he thinks him a pleasing personality and a thinker distorted but interesting. Of Shelley's strictly poetical quality he says nothing, if he knew or felt anything. In fact, of lyrical poetry generally, that is to say of poetry in its most purely poetical condition, he speaks very little in all his extensive critical dissertations. His want of appreciation of it may supply explanation of his unpardonable treatment of Goethe. That he should have maltreated *Wilhelm Meister* is quite excusable. There are fervent admirers of Goethe at his best who acknowledge most fully the presence in *Wilhelm* of the two worst characteristics of German life and literature, bad taste and tediousness. But it is not excusable that much later, and indeed at the very height of his literary powers and practice, he should have written the article in the *Encyclopædia Britannica* on the author of *Faust*, of *Egmont*, and above all of the shorter poems. Here he deliberately assents to the opinion that *Werther* is "superior to everything that came after it, and for mere power, Goethe's paramount work," dismisses *Faust* as something that "no two people have ever agreed about," sentences *Egmont* as "violating the historic truth of character," and mentions not a single one of those lyrics, unmatched, or rather only matched by Heine, in the language, by which Goethe first gave German rank with the great poetic tongues. His severity on Swift is connected with his special "will-worship" of ornate style, of which more presently, and in general it may be said that De Quincey's extremely logical disposition of mind was rather a snare to him in his criticism. He was constantly constructing general principles and then arguing downwards from them; in which case woe to any individual fact or person that happened to get in the way. Where Wilson, the "only intimate male friend I have had" (as he somewhere says with a half-pathetic touch of self-illumination more instructive than reams of imaginative autobiography), went wrong from not having enough of general principle, where Hazlitt went wrong from letting prejudices unconnected with the literary side of the matter blind his otherwise piercing literary sight, De Quincey fell through an unswervingness of deduction more French than English. Your ornate writer must be better than your plain one, *ergo*, let us say, Cicero must be better than Swift.

DE QUINCEY.

One other curious weakness of his (which has been glanced at already) remains to be noticed. This is the altogether deplorable notion of

DE QUINCEY.

jocularity which he only too often exhibits. Mr. Masson, trying to propitiate the enemy, admits that "to address the historian Josephus as 'Joe,' through a whole article, and give him a black eye into the bargain, is positively profane." I am not sure as to the profanity, knowing nothing particularly sacred about Josephus. But if Mr. Masson had called it excessively silly, I should have agreed heartily; and if any one else denounced it as a breach of good literary manners, I do not know that I should protest. The habit is the more curious in that all authorities agree as to the exceptional combination of scholarliness and courtliness which marked De Quincey's colloquial style and expression. Wilson's daughter, Mrs. Gordon, says that he used to address her father's cook "as if she had been a duchess"; and that the cook, though much flattered, was somewhat aghast at his *punctilio*. That a man of this kind should think it both allowable and funny to talk of Josephus as "Joe," and of Magliabecchi as "Mag," may be only a new example of that odd law of human nature which constantly prompts people in various relations of life, and not least in literature, to assume most the particular qualities (not always virtues or graces) that they have not. Yet it is fair to remember that Wilson and the *Blackwood* set, together with not a few writers in the *London Magazine*—the two literary coteries in connexion with whom De Quincey started as

DE QUINCEY.

a writer—had deliberately imported this element of horse-play into literature, that it at least did not seem to interfere with their popularity, and that De Quincey himself, after 1830, lived too little in touch with actual life to be aware that the style was becoming as unfashionable as it had always, save on very exceptional subjects, been ungraceful. Even on Wilson, who was to the manner born of riotous spirits, it often sits awkwardly; in De Quincey's case it is, to borrow Sir Walter's admirable simile in another case, like "the forced impudence of a bashful man." Grim humour he can manage admirably, and he also—as in the passage about the fate which waited upon all who possessed anything which might be convenient to Wordsworth, if they died—can manage a certain kind of sly humour not much less admirably. But "Joe" and "Mag," and, to take another example, the stuff about Catalina's "crocodile papa" in *The Spanish Nun*, are neither grim nor sly, they are only puerile. His stanchest defender asks, "why De Quincey should not have the same license as Swift and Thackeray?" The answer is quick and crushing. Swift and Thackeray justify their license by their use of it; De Quincey does not. After which it is hardly necessary to add, though this is almost final in itself, that neither Swift nor Thackeray interlards perfectly and unaffectedly serious work with mere fooling of the "Joe" and "Mag" kind. Swift did not put *mollis abuti* in the *Four last years of Queen Anne*, nor Thackeray his *Punch* jokes in the death-scene of Colonel Newcome. I can quite conceive De Quincey doing both.

DE QUINCEY.

And now I have done enough in the fault-finding way, and nothing shall induce me to say another word of De Quincey in this article save in praise. For praise he himself gives the amplest occasion; he might almost remain un-blamed altogether if his praisers had not been frequently unwise, and if his *exemplar* were not specially *vitiis imitabile.* Few English writers have touched so large a number of subjects with such competence both in information and in power of handling. Still fewer have exhibited such remarkable logical faculty. One main reason why one is sometimes tempted to quarrel with him is that his play of fence is so excellent that one longs to cross swords. For this and for other reasons no writer has a more stimulating effect, or is more likely to lead his readers on to explore and to think for themselves. In none is that incurable curiosity, that infinite variety of desire for knowledge and for argument which age can-not quench, more observable. Few if any have the indefinable quality of freshness in so large a measure. You never quite know, though you may have a shrewd suspicion, what De Quincey will say on any subject; his gift of sighting and approaching new facets of it is so immense.

Whether he was in truth as accomplished a classical scholar as he claimed to be I do not know; he has left few positive documents to tell us. But I should think that he was, for he has all the characteristics of a scholar of the best and rarest kind — the scholar who is exact as to language without failing to comprehend literature, and competent in literature without being slipshod as to language. His historical insight, of which the famous *Cæsars* is the best example, was, though sometimes coloured by his fancy, and at other times distorted by a slight tendency to *supercherie* as in *The Tartars* and *The Spanish Nun*, wonderfully powerful and acute. He was not exactly as Southey was, "omnilegent"; but in his own departments, and they were numerous, he went farther below the surface and connected his readings together better than Southey did. Of the two classes of severer study to which he specially addicted himself, his political economy suffered perhaps a little, acute as his views in it often are, from the fact that in his time it was practically a new study, and that he had neither sufficient facts nor sufficient literature to go upon. In metaphysics, to which he gave himself up for years, and in which he seems really to have known whatever there was to know, I fear that the opium fiend cheated the world of something like masterpieces. Only three men during De Quincey's lifetime had anything like his powers in this

DE QUINCEY.

department. Of these three men, Sir William Hamilton either could not or would not write English. Ferrier could and did write English; but he could not, as De Quincey could, throw upon philosophy the play of literary and miscellaneous illustration which of all the sciences it most requires, and which all its really supreme exponents have been able to give it. Mansel could do both these things; but he was somewhat indolent, and had many avocations. De Quincey could write perfect English, he had every resource of illustration and relief at command, he was in his way as "brazen-bowelled" at work as he was "golden-mouthed" at expression, and he had ample leisure. But the inability to undertake sustained labour, which he himself recognises as the one unquestionable curse of opium, deprived us of an English philosopher who would have stood as far above Kant in exoteric graces, as he would have stood above Bacon in esoteric value. It was not entirely De Quincey's fault. It seems to be generally recognised now that whatever occasional excesses he may have committed, opium was really required in his case, and gave us what we have as much as it took away what we have not. But if any one chose to write in the antique style a debate between Philosophy, Tar-water, and Laudanum, it would be almost enough to put in the mouth of Philosophy, "This gave me Berkeley and that deprived me of De Quincey."

DE QUINCEY.

De Quincey is, however, first of all a writer of ornate English, which was never, with him, a mere cover to bare thought. Overpraise and mispraise him as anybody may, he cannot be overpraised for this. Mistake as he chose to do, and as others have chosen to do, the relative value of his gift, the absolute value of it is unmistakable. What other Englishman, from Sir Thomas Browne downwards, has written a sentence surpassing in melody that on Our Lady of Sighs: "And her eyes, if they were ever seen, would be neither sweet nor subtle; no man could read their story; they would be found filled with perishing dreams and with wrecks of forgotten delirium"? Compare that with the masterpieces of some later practitioners. There are no out-of-the-way words; there is no needless expense of adjectives; the sense is quite adequate to the sound; the sound is only what is required as accompaniment to the sense. And though I do not know that in a single instance of equal length—even in the still more famous, and as a whole justly more famous, *tour de force* on Our Lady of Darkness—De Quincey ever quite equalled the combined simplicity and majesty of this phrase, he has constantly come close to it. The *Suspiria* are full of such passages—there are even some who prefer *Savannah la Mar* to the *Ladies of Sorrow.* Beautiful as it is I do not, because the accursed superfluous adjective appears there. The famous passages of the *Confessions* are in every one's

DE QUINCEY.

memory ; and so I suppose is the *Vision of Sudden Death.* Many passages in *The Cæsars,* though somewhat less florid, are hardly less good ; and the close of *Joan of Arc* is as famous as the most ambitious attempts of the *Confessions* and the *Mail Coach.* Moreover, in all the sixteen volumes, specimens of the same kind may be found here and there, alternating with very different matter ; so much so, that it has no doubt often occurred to readers that the author's occasional divergence into questionable quips and cranks is a deliberate attempt to set off his rhetoric, as dramatists of the noblest school have often set off their tragedy, with comedy, if not with farce. That such a principle would imply confusion of the study and the stage is arguable enough, but it does not follow that it was not present. At any rate the contrast, deliberate or not, is very strong indeed in De Quincey—stronger than in any other prose author except his friend, and pupil rather than master, Wilson.

The great advantage that De Quincey has, not only over this friend of his but over all practitioners of the ornate style in this century, lies in his sureness of hand in the first place, and secondly in the comparative frugality of means which perhaps is an inseparable accompaniment of sureness of hand. To mention living persons would be invidious ; but Wilson and Landor are within the most scrupulous critic's right of comparison. All three were contemporaries ; all three were Oxford men—Landor about ten years senior to the other two—and all three in their different ways set themselves deliberately to reverse the practice of English prose for nearly a century and a half. They did great things, but De Quincey did, I think, the greatest and certainly the most classical in the proper sense, for all Landor's superior air of Hellenism. Voluble as De Quincey often is, he seems always to have felt that when you are in your altitudes it is well not to stay there too long. And his flights, while they are far more uniformly high than Wilson's, which alternately soar and drag, are much more merciful in regard of length than Landor's, as well as for the most part much more closely connected with the sense of his subjects. There is scarcely one of the *Imaginary Conversations* which would not be the better for very considerable thinning, while, with the exception perhaps of *The English Mail Coach*, De Quincey's surplusage, obvious enough in many cases, is scarcely ever found in his most elaborate and ornate passages. The total amount of such passages in the *Confessions* is by no means large, and the more ambitious parts of the *Suspiria* do not much exceed a dozen pages. De Quincey was certainly justified by his own practice in adopting and urging as he did the distinction, due, he says, to Wordsworth, between the common and erroneous idea of style as the *dress* of thought,

DE QUINCEY.

and the true definition of it as the *incarnation* of thought. The most wizened of coxcombs may spend days and years in dressing up his meagre and ugly carcass; but few are the sons of men who have sufficient thought to provide the soul of any considerable series of avatars. De Quincey had; and therefore, though the manner (with certain exceptions heretofore taken) in him is always worth attention, it never need or should divert attention from the matter. And thus he was not driven to make a little thought do tyrannous duty as lay-figure for an infinite amount of dress, or to hang out frippery on a clothes-line with not so much as a lay-figure inside it. Even when he is most conspicuously "fighting a prize," there is always solid stuff in him.

DE QUINCEY.

Few indeed are the writers of whom so much can be said, and fewer still the miscellaneous writers, among whom De Quincey must be classed. On almost any subject that interested him—and the number of such subjects was astonishing, curious as are the gaps between the different groups of them—what he has to say is pretty sure, even if it be the wildest paradox in appearance, to be worth attending to. And in regard to most things that he has to say, the reader may be pretty sure also that he will not find them better said elsewhere. It has sometimes been complained by students, both of De Quincey the man and of De Quincey the writer, that there is something not exactly human in him. There is certainly much in him of the dæmonic, to use a word which was a very good word and really required in the language, and which ought not to be exiled because it has been foolishly abused. Sometimes, as has also been complained, the demon is a mere familiar with the tricksiness of Puck rather than the lightness of Ariel. But far oftener he is a more potent spirit than any Robin Goodfellow, and as powerful as Ariel and Ariel's master. Trust him wholly you may not; a characteristic often noted in intelligences that are neither exactly human, nor exactly diabolic, nor exactly divine. But he will do great things for you, and a little wit and courage on your part will prevent his doing anything serious against you. To him, with much greater justice than to Hogg, might Wilson have applied the nickname of Brownie, which he was so fond of bestowing upon the author of "Kilmeny." He will do solid work, conjure up a concert of aerial music, play a shrewd trick now and then, and all this with a curious air of irresponsibility and of remoteness of nature. In ancient days when kings played experiments to ascertain the universal or original language, some monarch might have been tempted to take a very clever child, interest him so far as possible in nothing but books and opium, and see whether he would turn out anything like De Quincey. But it is in the highest degree

DE QUINCEY.

improbable that he would. Therefore let us rejoice, though according to the precepts of wisdom and not too indiscriminately, in our De Quincey as we once, and probably once for all, received him.[1]

[1] *Note to Second Edition.*—The promised letters, etc., of De Quincey (see Appendix A) have now (May 1891) appeared under the title of *De Quincey Memorials* (two vols. London). I cannot say that they alter in any very material respect the views which I have expressed in the text and Appendix. But they contain a great deal of interesting matter, some of which undoubtedly corroborates and illustrates De Quincey's statements as to the friends of his youth and the like, and shows the *Confessions* and *Autobiography* to have a more solid basis of fact than has sometimes been supposed. The most interesting thing, however, which they disclose is not so much that De Quincey was right as that he was wrong in one point—his own idea of his mother's behaviour. The numerous letters from Mrs. De Quincey show that if she was not wholly wise in the conduct on which, following her son, I have made some rather severe strictures at p. 310 *sq.*, it was on her part due neither to neglect of duty nor to want of affection; but that she was on the contrary both then and always an affectionate, an anxiously thoughtful, and a very generous mother.

XI

LOCKHART

LOCKHART.

IN every age there are certain writers who seem to miss their due meed of fame, and this is most naturally and unavoidably the case in ages which see a great deal of what may be called occasional literature. There is, as it seems to me, a special example of this general proposition in the present century, and that example is the writer whose name stands at the head of this chapter. No one, perhaps, who speaks with any competence either of knowledge or judgment, would say that Lockhart made an inconsiderable figure in English literature. He wrote what some men consider the best biography on a large scale, and what almost every one considers the second best biography on a large scale, in English. His *Spanish Ballads* are admitted, by those who know the originals, to have done them almost more than justice ; and by those who do not know those originals, to be charming in themselves. His novels, if not masterpieces, have kept the field

LOCKHART.

better than most: I saw a very badly printed and flaringly-covered copy of *Reginald Dalton* for sale at the bookstall at Victoria Station the day before writing these words. He was a pillar of the *Quarterly*, of *Blackwood*, of *Fraser*, at a time when quarterly and monthly magazines played a greater part in literature than they have played since or are likely to play again. He edited one of these periodicals for thirty years. "Nobody," as Mr. Browning has it, "calls him a dunce." Yet there is no collected edition of his works; his sober, sound, scholarly, admirably witty, and, with some very few exceptions, admirably catholic literary criticism, is rarely quoted; and to add to this, there is a curious prepossession against him, which, though nearly a generation has passed since his death, has by no means disappeared.[1] Some years ago, in a periodical where I was, for the most part, allowed to say exactly what I liked in matters literary, I found a sentence laudatory of Lockhart, from the purely literary point of view, omitted between proof and publication. It so happened that the editor of this periodical could not even have known Lockhart personally, or have been offended by his management of the *Quarterly*, much less by his early *fredaines* in *Blackwood* and *Fraser*. It was this circumstance that first suggested to me the notion of trying to supply something like a criticism of this remarkable critic, which nobody has yet

[1] See Appendix B—Lockhart.

(1884) done, and which seems worth doing. For while the work of many of Lockhart's contemporaries, famous at the time, distinctly loses by re-reading, his for the most part does not; and it happens to display exactly the characteristics which are most wanting in criticism, biographical and literary, at the present day. If any one at the outset desires a definition, or at least an enumeration of those characteristics, I should say that they are sobriety of style and reserve of feeling, coupled with delicacy of intellectual appreciation and æsthetic sympathy, a strong and firm creed in matters political and literary, not excluding that catholicity of judgment which men of strong belief frequently lack, and, above all, the faculty of writing like a gentleman without writing like a mere gentleman. No one can charge Lockhart with dilettantism: no one certainly can charge him with feebleness of intellect, or insufficient equipment of culture, or lack of humour and wit.

LOCKHART.

His life was, except for the domestic misfortunes which marked its close, by no means eventful; and the present writer, if he had access to any special sources of information (which he has not), would abstain very carefully from using them. John Gibson Lockhart was born at the Manse of Cambusnethan on 14th July 1794, went to school early, was matriculated at Glasgow at twelve years old, transferred himself by means of a Snell exhibition to Balliol at fifteen, and took a first class in 1813. They said he caricatured the examiners: this was, perhaps, not the unparalleled audacity which admiring commentators have described it as being. Very many very odd things have been done in the Schools. But if there was nothing extraordinary in his Oxford life except what was, even for those days, the early age at which he began it, his next step was something out of the common; for he went to Germany, was introduced to Goethe, and spent some time there. An odd coincidence in the literary history of the nineteenth century is that both Lockhart and Quinet practically began literature by translating a German book, and that both had the remarkably good luck to find publishers who paid them beforehand. There are few such publishers now. Lockhart's book was Schlegel's *Lectures on History*, and his publisher was Mr. Blackwood. Then he came back to Scotland and to Edinburgh, and was called to the bar, and "swept the outer house with his gown," after the fashion admirably described in *Peter's Letters*, and referred to by Scott in not the least delightful though one of the most melancholy of his works, the Introduction to the *Chronicles of the Canongate*. Lockhart, one of whose distinguishing characteristics throughout life was shyness and reserve, was no speaker. Indeed, as he happily enough remarked in reply to the toast of his health at the farewell dinner given to celebrate his removal to London, "I cannot speak; if I could, I should not have left you." But if he could not speak he

LOCKHART.

could write, and the establishment of *Blackwood's Magazine*, after its first abortive numbers, gave him scope. "The scorpion which delighteth to sting the faces of men," as he or Wilson describes himself in the *Chaldee Manuscript* (for the passage is beyond Hogg's part), certainly justified the description. As to this famous *Manuscript*, the late Professor Ferrier undoubtedly made a blunder (in the same key as those that he made in describing the *Noctes*, in company with which he reprinted it) as "in its way as good as *The Battle of the Books*." *The Battle of the Books*, full of mistakes as it is, is literature, and the *Chaldee Manuscript* is only capital journalism. But it is capital journalism; and the exuberance of its wit, if it be only wit of the undergraduate kind (and Lockhart at least was still but an undergraduate in years), is refreshing enough. The dreadful manner in which it fluttered the dovecotes of Edinburgh Whiggism need not be further commented on, till Lockhart's next work (this time an almost though not quite independent one) has been noticed. This was *Peter's Letters to his Kinsfolk*, an elaborate book, half lampoon, half mystification, which appeared in 1819. This book, which derived its title from Scott's account of his journey to Paris, and in its plan followed to some extent *Humphrey Clinker*, is one of the most careful examples of literary hoaxing to be found. It purported to be the work of a certain Dr. Peter Morris, a Welshman, and it

LOCKHART.

is hardly necessary to say that there was no such person. It had a handsome frontispiece depicting this Peter Morris, and displaying not, like the portrait in Southey's *Doctor*, the occiput merely, but the full face and features. This portrait was described, and as far as that went it seems truly described, as "an interesting example of a new style of engraving by Lizars." Mr. Bates, who probably knows, says that there was no first edition, but that it was published with "second edition" on the title-page. My copy has the same date, 1819, but is styled the *third* edition, and has a postscript commenting on the to-do the book made. However all this may be, it is a very handsome book, excellently printed and containing capital portraits and vignettes, while the matter is worthy of the get-up. The descriptions of the Outer-House, of Craigcrook and its high jinks, of Abbotsford, of the finding of "Ambrose's," of the manufacture of Glasgow punch, and of many other things, are admirable; and there is a charming sketch of Oxford undergraduate life, less exaggerated than that in *Reginald Dalton*, probably because the subject was fresher in the author's memory.

Lockhart modestly speaks of this book in his *Life of Scott* as one that "none but a very young and thoughtless person would have written." It may safely be said that no one but a very clever person, whether young or old, could have written it, though it is too long and has occasional faults of a specially youthful kind. But it made, coming as it did upon the heels of the *Chaldee Manuscript*, a terrible commotion in Edinburgh. The impartial observer of men and things may, indeed, have noticed in the records of the ages, that a libelled Liberal is the man in all the world who utters the loudest cries. The examples of the Reformers, and of the eighteenth-century *Philosophes*, are notorious and hackneyed; but I can supply (without, I trust, violating the sanctity of private life) a fresh and pleasing example. Once upon a time, a person whom we shall call A. paid a visit to a person whom we shall call B. "How sad," said A., "are those personal attacks of the —— on Mr. Gladstone."—"Personality," said B., "is always disgusting; and I am very sorry to hear that the —— has followed the bad example of the personal attacks on Lord Beaconsfield."—"Oh! but," quoth A., "that was *quite* a different thing." Now B. went out to dinner that night, and sitting next to a distinguished Liberal member of Parliament, told him this tale, expecting that he would laugh. "Ah! yes," said he with much gravity, "it is *very* different, you know."

LOCKHART.

In the same way the good Whig folk of Edinburgh regarded it as very different that the *Edinburgh Review* should scoff at Tories, and that *Blackwood* and *Peter* should scoff at Whigs. The scorpion which delighted to sting the faces of men, probably at this time founded a reputation which has stuck to him for more than seventy years after Dr. Peter Morris drove his shandrydan through

Scotland. Sir Walter (then Mr.) Scott held wisely aloof from the extremely exuberant Toryism of *Blackwood*, and, indeed, had had some quarrels with its publisher and virtual editor. But he could not fail to be introduced to a man whose tastes and principles were so closely allied to his own. A year after the appearance of *Peter's Letters*, Lockhart married, on 29th April 1820 (a perilous approximation to the unlucky month of May), Sophia Scott, the Duke of Buccleuch's "Little Jacobite," the most like her father of all his children. Every reader of the *Life* knows the delightful pictures, enough for interest and not enough for vulgar obtrusion, given by Lockhart of life at Chiefswood, the cottage near Abbotsford which he and his wife inhabited for nearly six years.

LOCKHART.

They were very busy years for Lockhart. He was still active in contributing to *Blackwood*; he wrote all his four novels, and he published the *Spanish Ballads*. *Valerius* and *Adam Blair* appeared in 1821, *Reginald Dalton* and the *Ballads* in 1823, *Matthew Wald* in 1824.

The novels, though containing much that is very remarkable, are not his strongest work; indeed, any critic who speaks with knowledge must admit that Lockhart had every faculty for writing novels, except the faculty of novel-writing. *Valerius*, a classical story of the visit of a Roman-Briton to Rome, and the persecution of the Christians in the days of Trajan, is, like everything of its author's, admirably written, but, like every classical novel without exception, save only *Hypatia* (which makes its interests and its personages daringly modern), it somehow rings false and faint, though not, perhaps, so faint or so false as most of its fellows. *Adam Blair*, the story of the sudden succumbing to natural temptation of a pious minister of the kirk, is unquestionably Lockhart's masterpiece in this kind. It is full of passion, full of force, and the characters of Charlotte Campbell and Adam Blair himself are perfectly conceived. But the story-gift is still wanting. The reader finds himself outside: wondering why the people do these things, and whether in real life they would have done them, instead of following the story with absorption, and asking himself no questions at all. The same, in a different way, is the case with Lockhart's longest book, *Reginald Dalton*; and this has the additional disadvantage that both hero and heroine are not more than lay-figures, while in *Adam Blair* both are flesh and blood. The Oxford scenes are amusing but exaggerated—the obvious work of a man who supplies the defects of a ten years' memory by deepening the strokes where he does remember. *Matthew Wald*, which is a novel of madness, has excellent passages, but is conventional and wooden as a whole. Nothing was more natural than that Lockhart, with the example of Scott immediately before him, should try novel-writing; not many things are more

LOCKHART.

indicative of his literary ability than that, after a bare three years' practice, he left a field which certainly was not his.

LOCKHART.

In the early autumn of 1825, just before the great collapse of his affairs, Scott went to Ireland with Lockhart in his company. But very early in the following year, before the collapse was decided, Lockhart and his family moved to London, on his appointment as editor of the *Quarterly*, in succession to Gifford. Probably there never was a better appointment of the kind. Lockhart was a born critic: he had both the faculty and the will to work up the papers of his contributors to the proper level; he was firm and decided in his literary and political views, without going to the extreme Giffordian acerbity in both; and his intelligence and erudition were very wide. "He could write," says a phrase in some article I have somewhere seen quoted, "on any subject from poetry to dry-rot;" and there is no doubt that an editor, if he cannot exactly write on any subject from poetry to dry-rot, should be able to take an interest in any subject between and, if necessary, beyond those poles. Otherwise he has the choice of two undesirables; either he frowns unduly on the dry-rot articles, which probably interest large sections of the public (itself very subject to dry-rot), or he lets the dry-rot contributor inflict his hobby, without mercy and unedited, on a reluctant audience. But Lockhart, though he is said (for his contributions are not, as far as I know, anywhere exactly indicated) to have contributed fully a hundred articles to the *Quarterly*, that is to say one to nearly every number during the twenty-eight years of his editorship, by no means confined himself to this work. It was, indeed, during its progress that he composed not merely the *Life of Napoleon*, which was little more than an abridgment, though a very clever abridgment, of Scott's book, but the *Lives* of Burns and of Scott himself. Before, however, dealing with these, his *Spanish Ballads* and other poetical work may be conveniently disposed of.

LOCKHART.

Lockhart's verse is in the same scattered condition as his prose; but it is evident that he had very considerable poetical faculty. The charming piece, "When youthful hope is fled," attributed to him on Mrs. Norton's authority; the well-known "Captain Paton's Lament," which has been republished in the *Tales from Blackwood*; and the monorhymed epitaph on "Bright broken Maginn," in which some wiseacres have seen ill-nature, but which really is a masterpiece of humorous pathos, are all in very different styles, and are all excellent each in its style. But these things are mere waifs, separated from each other in widely different publications; and until they are put together no general impression of the author's poetical talent, except a vaguely favourable one, can be derived from them. The *Spanish Ballads* form something like a substantive work, and one of nearly as great merit as is possible to poetical translations of poetry. I believe opinions differ as to their fidelity to the original. Here and there, it is said, the author has exchanged a vivid and characteristic touch for a conventional and feeble one. Thus, my friend Mr. Hannay points out to me that in the original of "The Lord of Butrago" the reason given by Montanez for not accompanying the King's flight is not the somewhat *fade* one that

LOCKHART.

> Castile's proud dames shall never point the finger of disdain,

but the nobler argument, showing the best side of feudal sentiment, that the widows of his tenants shall never say that he fled and left their husbands to fight and fall. Lockhart's master, Sir Walter, would certainly not have missed this touch, and it is odd that Lockhart himself did. But such things will happen to translators. On the other hand, it is, I believe, admitted (and the same very sufficient authority in Spanish is my warranty) that on the whole the originals have rather gained than lost; and certainly no one can fail to enjoy the *Ballads* as they stand in English. The "Wandering Knight's Song" has always seemed to me a gem without flaw, especially the last stanza. Few men, again, manage the long "fourteener" with middle rhyme better than Lockhart, though he is less happy with the anapæst, and has not fully mastered the very difficult trochaic measure of "The Death of Don Pedro." In "The Count Arnaldos," wherein, indeed, the subject lends itself better to that cadence, the result is more satisfactory. The merits, however, of these *Ballads* are not technical merely, or rather, the technical merits are well subordinated to the production of the general effect. About the nature of that effect much ink has been shed. It is produced equally by Greek hexameters, by old French assonanced *tirades*, by English "eights and sixes," and by not a few other measures. But in itself it is more or less the same—the stirring of the blood as by the sound of a trumpet, or else the melting of the mood into or close to tears. The ballad effect is thus the simplest and most primitive of all poetical effects; it is Lockhart's merit that he seldom fails to produce it. The simplicity and spontaneity of his verse may, to some people, be surprising in a writer so thoroughly and intensely literary; but Lockhart's character was as complex as his verse is simple, and the verse itself is not the least valuable guide to it.

LOCKHART.

It has been said that his removal to London and his responsible office by no means reduced his general literary activity. Whether he continued to contribute to *Blackwood* I am not sure; some phrases in the *Noctes* seem to argue the contrary. But he not only, as has been said, wrote for the *Quarterly* assiduously, but after a short time joined the new venture of *Fraser*, and showed in that rollicking periodical that the sting of the "scorpion" had by no means been extracted. He produced,

LOCKHART.

moreover, in 1828, his *Life of Burns*, and in 1836-37 his *Life of Scott*. These, with the sketch of Theodore Hook written for the *Quarterly* in 1843, and separately published later, make three very remarkable examples of literary biography on very different scales, dealing with very different subjects, and, by comparison of their uniform excellence, showing that the author had an almost unique genius for this kind of composition. The *Life of Scott* fills seven capacious volumes; the *Life of Burns* goes easily into one; the *Life of Hook* does not reach a hundred smallish pages. But they are all equally well-proportioned in themselves and to their subjects; they all exhibit the same complete grasp of the secret of biography; and they all have the peculiarity of being full of facts without presenting an undigested appearance. They thus stand at an equal distance from biography of the fashion of the old academic *Eloge* of the last century, which makes an elegant discourse about a man, but either deliberately or by accident gives precise information about hardly any of the facts of the man's life; and from modern biography, which tumbles upon the devoted reader a cataract of letters, documents, and facts of all sorts, uncombined and undigested by any exercise of narrative or critical skill on the part of the author. Lockhart's biographies, therefore, belong equally (to borrow De Quincey's useful, though, as far as terminology goes, not very happy distinction) to the literature of knowledge and the literature of power. They are storehouses of information; but they are, at the same time, works of art, and of very great art. The earliest of the three, the *Life of Burns*, is to this day by far the best book on the subject; indeed, with its few errors and defects of fact corrected and supplemented as they have been by the late Mr. Douglas, it makes all other Lives quite superfluous. Yet it was much more difficult, especially for a Scotchman, to write a good book about Burns then than now; though I am told that, for a Scotchman, there is still a considerable difficulty in the matter. Lockhart was familiar with Edinburgh society—indeed, he had long formed a part of it—and Edinburgh society was still, when he wrote, very sore at the charge of having by turns patronised and neglected Burns. Lockhart was a decided Tory, and Burns, during the later part of his life at any rate, had permitted himself manifestations of political opinion which Whigs themselves admitted to be imprudent freaks, and which even a good-natured Tory might be excused for regarding as something very much worse. But the biographer's treatment of both these subjects is perfectly tolerant, judicious, and fair, and the same may be said of his whole account of Burns. Indeed, the main characteristic of Lockhart's criticism, a robust and quiet sanity, fitted him admirably for the task of biography. He is never in extremes,

LOCKHART.

and he never avoids extremes by the common expedient of see-sawing between two sides, two parties, or two views of a man's character. He holds aloof equally from *engouement* and from depreciation, and if, as a necessary consequence, he failed, and fails, to please fanatics on either side, he cannot fail to please those who know what criticism really means.

LOCKHART.

These good qualities were shown even to better advantage in a pleasanter but, at the same time, far more difficult task, the famous *Life of Scott*. The extraordinary interest of the subject, and the fashion, no less skilful than modest, in which the biographer keeps himself in the background, and seems constantly to be merely editing Scott's words, have perhaps obscured the literary value of the book to some readers. Of the perpetual comparison with Boswell, it may be said, once for all, that it is a comparison of matter merely; and that from the properly literary point of view, the point of view of workmanship and form, it does not exist. Perhaps the most surprising thing is that, even in moments of personal irritation, any one should have been found to accuse Lockhart of softening Scott's faults. The other charge, of malice to Scott, is indeed more extraordinary still in a certain way; but, being merely imbecile, it need not be taken into account. A delightful document informs us that, in the opinion of the Hon. Charles Sumner, Fenimore Cooper (who,

LOCKHART.

stung by some references to him in the book, attacked it) administered "a proper castigation to the vulgar minds of Scott and Lockhart." This is a jest so pleasing that it almost puts one in good temper with the whole affair. But, in fact, Lockhart, considering his relationship to Scott, and considering Scott's greatness, could hardly have spoken more plainly as to the grave fault of judgment which made a man of letters and a member of a learned profession mix himself up secretly, and almost clandestinely, with commercial speculations. On this point the biographer does not attempt to mince matters; and on no other point was it necessary for him to be equally candid, for this, grave as it is, is almost the only fault to be found with Scott's character. This candour, however, is only one of the merits of the book. The wonderfully skilful arrangement of so vast and heterogeneous a mass of materials, the way in which the writer's own work and his quoted matter dovetail into one another, the completeness of the picture given of Scott's character and life, have never been equalled in any similar book. Not a few minor touches, moreover, which are very apt to escape notice, enhance its merit. Lockhart was a man of all men least given to wear his heart upon his sleeve, yet no one has dealt with such pitiful subjects as his later volumes involve, at once with such total absence of "gush" and with such noble and pathetic appreciation.

For Scott's misfortunes were by no means the only matters which touched him nearly, in and in connection with the chronicle. The constant illness and sufferings of his own child form part of it; his wife died during its composition and publication, and all these things are mentioned with as little parade of stoicism as of sentiment. I do not think that, as an example of absolute and perfect good taste, the account of Scott's death can be surpassed in literature. The same quality exhibits itself in another matter. No biographer can be less anxious to display his own personality than Lockhart; and though for six years he was a constant, and for much longer an occasional, spectator of the events he describes, he never introduces himself except when it is necessary. Yet, on the other hand, when Scott himself makes complimentary references to him (as when he speaks of his party "having Lockhart to say clever things"), he neither omits the passage nor stoops to the missish *minauderie*, too common in such cases, of translating "spare my blushes" into some kind of annotation. Lockhart will not talk about Lockhart; but if others, whom the public likes to hear, talk about him, Lockhart does not put his fan before his face.

This admirable book, however, is both well enough known (if not so well known as it deserves) and large enough to make it both unnecessary and impossible to criticise it at length here. The third work noticed above, the sketch of the life of Theodore Hook, though it has been reprinted more than once, and is still, I believe, kept in print and on sale, is probably less familiar to most readers. It is, however, almost as striking an example, though of course an example in miniature only, of Lockhart's aptitude for the great and difficult art of literary biography as either of the two books just mentioned. Here the difficulty was of a different kind. A great many people liked Theodore Hook, but it was nearly impossible for any one to respect him; yet it was quite impossible for Lockhart, a political sympathiser and a personal friend, to treat him harshly in an obituary notice. There was no danger of his setting down aught in malice; but there might be thought to be a considerable danger of over-extenuation. The danger was the greater, inasmuch as Lockhart himself had certainly not escaped, and had perhaps to some extent deserved, one of Hook's reproaches. No man questioned his integrity; he was not a reckless spendthrift; he was not given to excesses in living, or to hanging about great houses; nor was he careless of moral and social rules. But the scorpion which had delighted to sting the faces of men might have had some awkwardness in dealing with the editor of *John Bull*. The result, however, victoriously surmounts all difficulties without evading one. Nothing that is the truth about Hook is

LOCKHART.

omitted, or even blinked ; and from reading Lockhart alone, any intelligent reader might know the worst that is to be said about him. Neither are any of his faults, in the unfair sense, extenuated. His malicious and vulgar practical jokes ; his carelessness at Mauritius ; the worse than carelessness which allowed him to shirk, when he had ample means of discharging it by degrees, a debt which he acknowledged that he justly owed ; the folly and vanity which led him to waste his time, his wit, and his money in playing the hanger-on at country houses and town dinner-tables ; his hard living, and the laxity which induced him not merely to form irregular connections, but prevented him from taking the only step which could, in some measure, repair his fault, are all fairly put, and blamed frankly. Even in that more delicate matter of the personal journalism, Lockhart's procedure is as ingenuous as it is ingenious ; and the passage of the sketch which deals with "the blazing audacity of invective, the curious delicacy of persiflage, the strong caustic satire" (expressions, by the way, which suit Lockhart himself much better than Hook, though Lockhart had not Hook's broad humour), in fact, admits that the application of these things was not justifiable, nor to be justified. Yet with all this, the impression left by the sketch is distinctly favourable on the whole, which, in the circumstances, must be admitted to be a triumph of advocacy obtained

LOCKHART.

not at the expense of truth, but by the art of the advocate in making the best of it.

LOCKHART.

The facts of Lockhart's life between his removal to London and his death may be rapidly summarised, the purpose of this notice being rather critical than biographical. He had hardly settled in town when, as he himself tells, he had to attempt, fruitlessly enough, the task of mediator in the financial disasters of Constable and Scott; and his own share of domestic troubles began early. His eldest son, after repeated escapes, died in 1831; Scott followed shortly; Miss Anne Scott, after her father's death, came in broken health to Lockhart's house, and died there only a year later; and in the spring of 1837 his wife likewise died. Then Fortune let him alone for a little, to return in no better humour some years later.

It is, however, from the early "thirties" that one of the best known memorials of Lockhart dates; that is to say, the portrait, or rather the two portraits, in the Fraser Gallery. In the general group of the Fraserians he sits between Fraser himself and Theodore Hook, with the diminutive figure of Crofton Croker half intercepted beyond him; and his image forms the third plate in Mr. Bates's republication of the gallery. It is said to be the most faithful of the whole series, and it is certainly the handsomest, giving even a more flattering representation than the full-face portrait by Pickersgill which serves as frontispiece to the modern editions of the *Ballads*. In this latter the curious towzled mop of hair, in which our fathers delighted, rather mars the effect; while in Maclise's sketch (which is in profile) it is less obtrusive. In this latter, too, there is clearly perceivable what the Shepherd in the *Noctes* calls "a sort of laugh aboot the screwed-up mouth of him that fules ca'd no canny, for they couldna thole the meaning o't." There is not much doubt that Lockhart aided and abetted Maginn in much of the mischief that distinguished the early days of *Fraser*, though his fastidious taste is never likely to have stooped to the coarseness which was too natural to Maginn. It is believed that to him is due the wicked wresting of Alaric Watts' second initial into "Attila," which gave the victim so much grief, and he probably did many other things of the same kind. But Lockhart was never vulgar, and *Fraser* in those days very often was.

LOCKHART.

In 1843 Lockhart received his first and last piece of political preferment, being appointed, says one of the authorities before me, Chancellor of the Duchy of Cornwall, and (says another) Chancellor of the Duchy of Lancaster. Such are biographers; but the matter is not of the slightest importance, though I do not myself quite see how it could have been Lancaster. A third and more trustworthy writer gives the post as "Auditorship" of the Duchy of Lancaster, which is possible enough.

LOCKHART.

In 1847, the death of Sir Walter Scott's last surviving son brought the title and estate to Lockhart's son Walter, but he died in 1853. Lockhart's only other child had married Mr. Hope—called, after his brother-in-law's death, Mr. Hope Scott, of whom an elaborate biography has been published. Little in it concerns Lockhart, but the admirable letter which he wrote to Mr. Hope on his conversion to the Roman Church. This step, followed as it was by Mrs. Hope, could not but be, and in this letter is delicately hinted to be, no small grief to Lockhart, who saw Abbotsford fall under influences for which certainly neither he nor its founder had any respect. His repeated domestic losses, and many years of constant work and excitement, appear to have told on him, and very shortly after his son's death in April 1853 he resigned the editorship of the *Quarterly*. He then visited Italy, a visit from which, if he had been a superstitious man, the ominous precedent of Scott might have deterred him. His journey did him no good, and he died at Abbotsford on the 25th of November. December, says another authority, for so it is that history gets written, even in thirty years.

The comparatively brief notices which are all that have been published about Lockhart, uniformly mention the unpopularity (to use a mild word) which pursued him, and which, as I have remarked, does not seem to have exhausted itself even yet. It is not very difficult to account for the origin of this; and the neglect to supply any collection of his work, and any authoritative account of his life and character, will quite explain its continuance. In the first place, Lockhart was well known as a most sarcastic writer; in the second, he was for nearly a lifetime editor of one of the chief organs of party politics and literary criticism in England. He might have survived the *Chaldee Manuscript*, and *Peter's Letters*, and the lampoons in *Fraser*: he might even have got the better of the youthful imprudence which led him to fix upon himself a description which was sure to be used and abused against him by the "fules," if he had not succeeded to the chair of the *Quarterly*. Individual and, to a great extent, anonymous indulgence of the luxury of scorn never gave any man a very bad character, even if he were, as Lockhart was, personally shy and reserved, unable to make up for written sarcasm with verbal flummery, and, in virtue of an incapacity for gushing, deprived of the easiest and, by public personages, most commonly practised means of proving that a man has "a good heart after all." But when he complicated his sins by editing the *Quarterly* at a time when everybody attacked everybody else in exactly such terms as pleased him, the sins of his youth were pretty sure to be visited on him. In the first place, there was the great army of the criticised, who always consider that the editor of the paper which dissects them is really responsible. The luckless Harriet Martineau, who, if I remember rightly, gives in her autobiography a lurid picture of Lockhart "going down at night to the printer's" and inserting dreadful things about her, and who, I believe, took the feminine plan of revenging herself in an obituary article, was only one of a great multitude.

LOCKHART.

Lockhart does not seem to have taken over from Gifford quite such a troublesome crew of helpers as Macvey Napier inherited from Jeffrey, and he was also free from the monitions of his predecessor. But in Croker he had a first lieutenant who could not very well be checked, and who (though he, too, has had rather hard measure) had no equal in the art of making himself offensive. Besides, those were the days when the famous "Scum condensed of Irish bog" lines appeared in a great daily newspaper about O'Connell. Imagine the *Times* addressing Mr. Parnell as "Scum condensed of Irish bog," with the other amenities that follow, in this year of grace!

But Lockhart had not only his authors, he had his contributors. "A' contributors," says the before-quoted Shepherd, in a moment of such

LOCKHART.

preternatural wisdom that he must have been "fou," "are in a manner fierce." They are—it is the nature and essence of the animal to be so. The contributor who is not allowed to contribute is fierce, as a matter of course; but not less fierce is the contributor who thinks himself too much edited, and the contributor who imperatively insists that his article on Chinese metaphysics shall go in at once, and the contributor who, being an excellent hand at articles on the currency, wants to be allowed to write on dancing; and, in short, as the Shepherd says, all contributors. Now it does not appear (for, as I must repeat, I have no kind of private information on the subject) that Lockhart was by any means an easy-going editor, or one of that kind which allows a certain number of privileged writers to send in what they like. We are told in many places that he "greatly improved" his contributors' articles; and I should say that if there is one thing which drives a contributor to the verge of madness, it is to have his articles "greatly improved." A hint in the *Noctes* (and it may be observed that though the references to Lockhart in the *Noctes* are not very numerous, they are valuable, for Wilson's friendship seems to have been mixed with a small grain of jealousy which preserves them from being commonplace) suggests that his friends did not consider him as by any means too ready to accept their papers. All this, added to his early character of scoffer at Whig dignities, and his position as leader *en titre* of Tory journalism, was quite sufficient to create a reputation partly exaggerated, partly quite false, which has endured simply because no trouble has been taken to sift and prove it.

LOCKHART.

The head and front of Lockhart's offending, in a purely literary view, seems to be the famous *Quarterly* article on Lord Tennyson's volume of 1832. That article is sometimes spoken of as Croker's, but there can be no manner of doubt that it is Lockhart's; and, indeed, it is quoted as his by Professor Ferrier, who, through Wilson, must have known the facts. Now I do not think I yield to any man living in admiration of the Laureate, but I am unable to think much the worse, or, indeed, any the worse, of Lockhart because of this article. In the first place, it is extremely clever, being, perhaps, the very best example of politely cruel criticism in existence. In the second, most, if not all, of the criticism is perfectly just. If Lord Tennyson himself, at this safe distance of time, can think of the famous strawberry story and its application without laughing, he must be an extremely sensitive Peer. And nobody, I suppose, would now defend the wondrous stanza which was paralleled from the *Groves of Blarney*. The fact is that criticism of criticism after some time is apt to be doubly unjust. It is wont to assume, or rather to imagine, that the critic must have known what the author was going to do, as well as what he had actually done; and it is wont to forget that the work criticised was very often, as it presented itself to the critic, very different from what it is when it presents itself to the critic's critic. The best justification of Lockhart's verdict on the volume of 1832 is what Lord Tennyson himself has done with the volume of 1832. Far more than half the passages objected to have since been excised or altered. But there are other excuses. In the first place, Mr. Tennyson, as he then was, represented a further development of schools of poetry against which the *Quarterly* had always, rightly or wrongly, set its face, and a certain loyalty to the principles of his paper is, after all, not the worst fault of a critic. In the second, no one can fairly deny that some points in Mr. Tennyson's early, if not in his later, manner must have been highly and rightly disgustful to a critic who, like Lockhart, was above all things masculine and abhorrent of "gush." In the third, it is, unfortunately, not given to all critics to admire all styles alike. Let those to whom it is given thank God therefor; but let them, at the same time, remember that they are as much bound to accept whatever is good in all kinds of critics as whatever is good in all kinds of poets.

LOCKHART.

Now Lockhart, within his own range, and it was for the time a very wide one, was certainly not a narrow critic, just as he certainly was not a feeble one. In the before-mentioned *Peter's Letters* (which, with all its faults, is one of his best, and particularly one of his most spontaneous and characteristic works) the denunciation of the "facetious and rejoicing ignorance" which enabled contemporary critics to pooh-pooh Wordsworth, Charles Lamb, and Coleridge is excellent. And it must be remembered that in 1819, whatever might be the case with Coleridge, Wordsworth and Lamb were by no means taken to the hearts of Tories on their merits, and that in this very passage *Blackwood* is condemned not less severely than the *Edinburgh*. Another point in which Lockhart made a great advance was that he was one of the first (Lamb himself is, in England, his only important forerunner) to unite and combine criticism of different branches of art. He never has the disgusting technical jargon, or the undisciplined fluency, of the mere art critic, any more than he has the gabble of the mere connoisseur. But it is constantly evident that he has a knowledge of and a feeling for the art of line and colour as well as of words. Nothing can be better than the fragments of criticism which are interspersed in the Scott book; and if his estimate of Hook as a novelist seems exaggerated, it must be remembered, as he has himself noted, that Thackeray was, at the time he spoke, nothing more than an amusing contributor of remarkably

LOCKHART.

promising trifles to magazines, and that, from the appearance of *Waverley* to that of *Pickwick*, no novelist of the first class had made an appearance. It is, moreover, characteristic of Lockhart as a critic that he is, as has been noted, always manly and robust. He was never false to his own early protest against "the banishing from the mind of a reverence for feeling, as abstracted from mere questions of immediate and obvious utility." But he never allowed that reverence to get the better of him and drag him into the deplorable excesses of gush into which, from his day to ours, criticism has more and more had a tendency to fall. If he makes no parade of definite æsthetic principles, it is clear that throughout he had such principles, and that they were principles of a very good kind. He had a wide knowledge of foreign literature without any taint of "Xenomania," sufficient scholarship (despite the unlucky false quantity of *Janua*, which he overlooked) in the older languages, and a thorough knowledge and love of English literature. His style is, to me at any rate, peculiarly attractive. Contrasted with the more brightly coloured and fantastically-shaped styles, of which, in his own day, De Quincey, Wilson, Macaulay, and Carlyle set the fashion, it may possibly seem tame to those who are not satisfied with proportion in form and harmony in tint; it will certainly not seem so to those who are more fortunately gifted. Indeed, compared either with Wilson's welter of words, now bombastic, now gushing, now horse-playful, or with the endless and heartbreaking antitheses of what Brougham ill-naturedly but truly called "Tom's snip-snap," it is infinitely preferable. The conclusion of the essay on Theodore Hook is not easily surpassable as an example of solid polished prose, which is prose, and does not attempt to be a hybrid between prose and poetry. The last page of the Tennyson review is perfect for quiet humour.

LOCKHART.

But there is no doubt that though Lockhart was an admirable critic merely as such, a poet, or at least a song-writer, of singular ability and charm within certain limits, and a master of sharp light raillery that never missed its mark and never lumbered on the way, his most unique and highest merit is that of biographer. Carlyle, though treating Lockhart himself with great politeness, does not allow this, and complains that Lockhart's conception of his task was "not very elevated." That is what a great many people said of Boswell, whom Carlyle thought an almost perfect biographer. But, as it happens, the critic here has fallen into the dangerous temptation of giving his reasons. Lockhart's plan was not, it seems, in the case of his *Scott*, very elevated, because it was not "to show Scott as he was by nature, as the world acted on him, as he acted on the world," and so forth. Now, unfortunately, this is exactly what it seems to me that Lockhart, whether he meant to do it or not, has done in the very book which Carlyle was criticising. And it seems to me, further, that he always does this in all his biographical efforts. Sometimes he appears (for here another criticism of Carlyle's on the *Burns*, not the *Scott*, is more to the point) to quote and extract from other and much inferior writers to an extent rather surprising in so excellent a penman, especially when it is remembered that, except to a dunce, the extraction and stringing together of quotations is far more troublesome than original writing. But even then the extracts are always luminous. With ninety-nine out of a hundred biographies the total impression which Carlyle demands, and very properly demands, is, in fact, a total absence of impression. The reader's mind is as dark, though it may be as full, as a cellar when the coals have been shot into it. Now this is never the case with Lockhart's biographies, whether they are books in half a dozen volumes, or essays in half a hundred pages. He subordinates what even Carlyle allowed to be his "clear nervous forcible style" so entirely to the task of representing his subject, he has such a perfect general conception of that subject, that only a very dense reader can fail to perceive the presentment. Whether it is the right or whether it is the wrong presentment may, of course, be a matter of opinion, but, such as it is, it is always there.

LOCKHART.

One other point of interest about Lockhart has

to be mentioned. He was an eminent example, perhaps one of the most eminent, of a "gentleman of the press."

LOCKHART.

He did a great many kinds of literary work, and he did all of them well; novel-writing, perhaps (which, as has been said, he gave up almost immediately), least well. But he does not seem to have felt any very strong or peculiar call to any particular class of original literary work, and his one great and substantive book may be fairly taken to have been much more decided by accident and his relationship to Scott than by deliberate choice. He was, in fact, eminently a journalist, and it is very much to be wished that there were more journalists like him. For from the two great reproaches of the craft to which so many of us belong, and which seems to be gradually swallowing up all other varieties of literary occupation, he was conspicuously free. He never did work slovenly in form, and he never did work that was not in one way or other consistent with a decided set of literary and political principles. There is a great deal of nonsense talked about the unprincipled character of journalism, no doubt; and nobody knows better than those who have some experience of it, that if, as George Warrington says, "too many of us write against our own party," it is the fault simply of those who do so. If a man has a faculty of saying anything, he can generally get an opportunity of saying what he likes, and avoid occasions of saying what he does not like. But the mere journalist Swiss of heaven (or the other place), is certainly not unknown, and by all accounts he was in Lockhart's time rather common. No one ever accused Lockhart himself of being one of the class. A still more important fault, undoubtedly, of journalism is its tendency to slovenly work, and here again Lockhart was conspicuously guiltless. His actual production must have been very considerable, though in the absence of any collection, or even any index, of his contributions to periodicals, it is impossible to say exactly to how much it would extend. But, at a rough guess, the *Scott*, the *Burns*, and the *Napoleon*, the *Ballads*, the novels, and *Peter*, a hundred *Quarterly* articles, and an unknown number in *Blackwood* and *Fraser*, would make at least twenty or five-and-twenty volumes of a pretty closely printed library edition. Yet all this, as far as it can be identified, has the same careful though unostentatious distinction of style, the same admirable faculty of sarcasm, wherever sarcasm is required, the same depth of feeling, wherever feeling is called for, the same refusal to make a parade of feeling even where it is shown. Never trivial, never vulgar, never feeble, never stilted, never diffuse, Lockhart is one of the very best recent specimens of that class of writers of all work, which since Dryden's time has continually increased, is increasing, and does not seem likely to diminish. The growth may or may not be matter for regret;

probably none of the more capable members of LOCKHART. the class itself feels any particular desire to magnify his office. But if the office is to exist, let it at least be the object of those who hold it to perform its duties with that hatred of commonplace and cant and the *popularis aura*, with, as nearly as may be in each case, that conscience and thoroughness of workmanship, which Lockhart's writings uniformly display.

XII

PRAED

IT was not till half a century after his death that Praed, who is loved by those who love him perhaps as sincerely as most greater writers, had his works presented to the public in a form which may be called complete.[1] This is of itself rather a cautious statement in appearance, but I am not sure that it ought not to be made more cautious still. The completeness is not complete, though it is in one respect rather more than complete; and the form is exceedingly informal. Neither in size, nor in print, nor in character of editing and arrangement do the two little fat volumes which were ushered into the world by Derwent Coleridge in 1864, and the one little thin volume which

PRAED.

[1] 1. *The Poems of Winthrop Mackworth Praed, with a Memoir by the Rev. Derwent Coleridge.* In two volumes. London, 1864. 2. *Essays by Winthrop Mackworth Praed, collected and arranged by Sir George Young, Bart.* London, 1887. 3. *The Political and Occasional Poems of Winthrop Mackworth Praed, edited, with Notes, by Sir George Young.* London, 1888.

appeared in 1887 under Sir George Young's name with no notes and not much introduction, and the very creditable edition of the political poems which appeared a year later under the same care but better cared for, agree together. But this, though a nuisance to those who love not a set of odd volumes, would matter comparatively little if the discrepancies were not equally great in a much more important matter than that of mere externals. Only the last of the four volumes and three books just enumerated can be said to have been really edited, and though that is edited very well, it is the least important. Sir George Young, who has thus done a pious work to his uncle's memory, was concerned not merely in the previous cheap issue of the prose, but in the more elaborate issue of the poems in 1864. But either his green unknowing youth did not at that time know what editing meant, or he was under the restraint of some higher powers. Except that the issue of 1864 has that well-known page-look of "Moxon's," which is identified to all lovers of poetry with associations of Shelley, of Lord Tennyson, and of other masters, and that the pieces are duly dated, it is difficult to say any good thing of the book. There are no notes; and Praed is an author who is much in need of annotation. With singular injudiciousness, a great deal of album and other verse is included which was evidently not intended for publication, which does not display

PRAED.

the writer at his best, or even in his characteristic vein at all, while the memoir is meagre in fact and decidedly feeble in criticism. As for the prose, though Sir George Young has prefixed an introduction good as far as it goes, there is no index, no table even of contents, and the separate papers are not dated, nor is any indication given of their origin—a defect which, for reasons to be indicated shortly, is especially troublesome in Praed's case. Accordingly anything like a critical study of the poet is beset with very unusual difficulties, and the mere reading of him, if it were less agreeable in itself, could not be said to be exactly easy. Luckily Praed is a writer so eminently engaging to the mere reader, as well as so interesting in divers ways to the personage whom some one has politely called "the gelid critic," that no sins or shortcomings of his editors can do him much harm, so long as they let him be read at all.

PRAED.

Winthrop Mackworth was the third son of Serjeant Praed, Chairman of the Board of Audit, and, though his family was both by extraction and by actual seat Devonian, he was born in John Street, Bedford Row, on 26th June 1802, the year of the birth of Victor Hugo, who was perhaps about as unlike Praed in every conceivable point, except metrical mastery, as two men possessing poetic faculty can be unlike one another. John Street may not appear as meet a nurse for a poetic child as Besançon, especially now when it has settled down into the usual office-and-chambers state of Bloomsbury. But it is unusually wide for a London street; it has trees — those of the Foundling Hospital and those of Gray's Inn — at either end, and all about it cluster memories of the Bedford Row conspiracy, and of that immortal dinner which was given by the Briefless One and his timid partner to Mr. Goldmore, and of Sydney Smith's sojourn in Doughty Street, and of divers other pleasant things. In connection, however, with Praed himself, we do not hear much more of John Street. It was soon exchanged for the more cheerful locality of Teignmouth, where his father (who was a member of the old western family of Mackworth, Praed being an added surname) had a country house. Serjeant Praed encouraged, if he did not positively teach, the boy to write English verse at a very early age: a practice which I should be rather slow to approve, but which has been credited, perhaps justly, with the very remarkable formal accuracy and metrical ease of Praed's after-work. Winthrop lost his mother early, was sent to a private school at eight years old, and to Eton in the year 1814. Public schools in their effect of allegiance on public schoolboys have counted for much in English history, literary and other, and Eton has counted for more than any of them. But hardly in any case has it counted for so much with the general reader as in Praed's. A friend of mine, who, while entertaining high and

PRAED.

lofty views on principle, takes low ones by a kind of natural attraction, says that the straightforward title of *The Etonian* and Praed's connection with it are enough to account for this. There you have a cardinal fact easy to seize and easy to remember. "Praed? Oh! yes, the man who wrote *The Etonian*; he must have been an Eton man," says the general reader. This is cynicism, and cannot be too strongly reprehended. But unluckily, as in other cases, a kind of critical deduction or reaction from this view has also taken place, and there are persons who maintain that Praed's merit is a kind of coterie-merit, a thing which Eton men are bound, and others are not bound but the reverse, to uphold. This is an old, but apparently still effective trick. I read not long ago a somewhat elaborate attempt to make out that the people who admire Mr. Matthew Arnold's poems admire them because they, the people, are Oxford men. Now this form of "ruling out" is undoubtedly ingenious. "You admire Mr. Arnold's poems?"—"Yes, I do."—"You are an Oxford man?"—"Yes, I am."—"Ah! I see." And it is perfectly useless for the victim to argue that his admiration of the poet and his allegiance to the University have nothing to do with each other. In the present case I, at least, am free from this illogical but damaging disqualification. I do not think that any one living admires Praed more than I do;

PRAED.

and neither Eton nor Cambridge, which may be said to have divided influence on him, claims any allegiance from me.

PRAED.

On Praed himself, however, the influence of Eton was certainly great, if not of the greatest. Here he began in school periodicals ("Apis Matina" a bee buzzing in manuscript only, preceded *The Etonian*) his prose and, to some though a less extent, his verse-exercises in finished literature. Here he made the beginnings of that circle of friends (afterwards slightly enlarged at Cambridge by the addition of non-Etonians and including one or two Oxford men who had been at Eton) which practically formed the staff of *The Etonian* itself and of the subsequent *Knight's Quarterly* and *Brazen Head.* The greatest of them all, Macaulay, belonged to the later Trinity set ; but the Etonians proper included divers men of mark. There has been, I believe, a frequent idea that boys who contribute to school-magazines never do anything else. Praed certainly could not be produced as an instance. He was not a great athlete, partly because his health was always weak, partly because athletics were then in their infancy. But he is said to have been a good player at fives and tennis, an amateur actor of merit, expert at chess and whist, and latterly a debater of promise, while, in the well-known way of his own school and University, he was more than a sufficient scholar. He went to Trinity in October 1821, and in the three following years won the Browne

Medals for Greek verse four times and the Chancellor's Medal for English verse twice. He was third in the Classical Tripos, was elected to a Fellowship at his college in 1827, and in 1830 obtained the Seatonian Prize with a piece, "The Ascent of Elijah," which is remarkable for the extraordinary facility with which it catches the notes of the just published *Christian Year.* He was a great speaker at the Union, and, as has been hinted, he made a fresh circle of literary friends for himself, the chief ornaments whereof were Macaulay and Charles Austin. It was also during his sojourn at Cambridge that the short-lived but brilliant venture of *Knight's Quarterly* was launched. He was about four years resident at Trinity in the first instance; after which, according to a practice then common enough but now, I believe, obsolete, he returned to Eton as private and particular tutor to Lord Ernest Bruce. This employment kept him for two years. He then read law, was called to the Bar in 1829, and in 1830 was elected to Parliament for the moribund borough of St. Germans. He was re-elected next year, contested St. Ives, when St. Germans lost its members, but was beaten, was elected in 1834 for Great Yarmouth, and in 1837 for Aylesbury, which last seat he held to his death. During the whole of this time he sat as a Conservative, becoming a more thorough one as time went on; and as he had been at Cambridge a very decided

PRAED.

Whig, and had before his actual entrance on public life written many pointed and some bitter lampoons against the Tories, the change, in the language of his amiable and partial friend and biographer, "occasioned considerable surprise." Of this also more presently: for it is well to get merely biographical details over with as little digression as possible. Surprise or no surprise, he won good opinions from both sides, acquired considerable reputation as a debater and a man of business, was in the confidence both of the Duke of Wellington and of Sir Robert Peel, was made Secretary of the Board of Control in 1834, married in 1835, was appointed Deputy-High Steward of his University (a mysterious appointment, of the duties of which I have no notion), and died of disease of the lungs on 15th July 1839. Not very much has been published about Praed personally; but in what has been published, and in what I have heard, I cannot remember a single unfriendly sentence.

PRAED.

Notwithstanding his reputation as an "inspired schoolboy," I do not know that sober criticism would call him a really precocious writer, especially in verse. The pieces by which he is best known and which have most individuality, date in no case very early, and in almost all cases after his five-and-twentieth year. What does date very early (and unluckily it has been printed with a copiousness betokening more affection than judgment, considering that the author had more sense than to print it at all) is scarcely distinguishable from any other verses of any other clever boy. It is impossible to augur any future excellence from such stuff as

PRAED.

> Emilia often sheds the tear
> But affectation bids it flow,

or as

> From breasts which feel compassion's glow
> Solicit mild the kind relief;

and, for one's own part, one is inclined to solicit mild the kind relief of not having to read it. Even when Praed had become, at least technically, a man, there is no very great improvement as a whole, though here and there one may see, looking backwards from the finished examples, faint beginnings of his peculiar touches, especially of that pleasant trick of repeating the same word or phrase with a different and slightly altered sense which, as Mr. Austin Dobson has suggested, may have been taken from Burns. The Cambridge prize poems are quite authentic and respectable examples of that style which has received its final criticism in

> Ply battleaxe and hurtling catapult:
> Jerusalem is ours! *Id Deus vult*,—

though they do not contain anything so nice as that, or as its great author's more famous couplet respecting Africa and the men thereof. The longer romances of the same date, "Gog," "Lilian,"

"The Troubadour," are little more than clever reminiscences sometimes of Scott, Byron, Moore, and other contemporaries, sometimes of Prior and the *vers de société* of the eighteenth century. The best passage by far of all this is the close of "How to Rhyme with Love," and this, as it seems to me, is the only passage of even moderate length which, in the poems dating before Praed took his degree, in the least foretells the poet of "The Red Fisherman," "The Vicar," the "Letters from Teignmouth," the "Fourteenth of February" (earliest in date and not least charming fruit of the true vein), "Good-night to the Season," and best and most delightful of all, the peerless "Letter of Advice," which is as much the very best thing of its own kind as the "Divine Comedy."

PRAED.

In prose Praed was a little earlier, but not very much. *The Etonian* itself was, even in its earliest numbers, written at an age when many, perhaps most, men have already left school ; and the earlier numbers are as imitative, of the *Spectator* and its late and now little read followers of the eighteenth century, as is the verse above quoted. The youthful boisterousness of *Blackwood* gave Praed a more congenial because a fresher cue ; and in the style of which Maginn, as Adjutant O'Doherty, had set the example in his Latinisings of popular verse, and which was to be worked to death by Father Prout, there are few things better than the "Musæ O'Connorianæ" which celebrates the great fight of

Mac Nevis and Mac Twolter. But there is here still the distinct following of a model the taint of the school-exercise. Very much more original is "The Knight and the Knave:" indeed I should call this the first original thing, though it be a parody, that Praed did. To say that it reminds one in more than subject of *Rebecca and Rowena*, and that it was written some twenty years earlier, is to say a very great deal. Even here, however, the writer's ground is rented, not freehold. It is very different in such papers as "Old Boots" and "The Country Curate," while in the later prose contributed to *Knight's Quarterly* the improvement in orginality is marked. "The Union Club" is amusing enough all through: but considering that it was written in 1823, two years before Jeffrey asked the author of a certain essay on Milton "where he got that style," one passage of the speech put in the mouth of Macaulay is positively startling. "The Best Bat in the School" is quite delightful, and "My First Folly," though very unequal, contains in the introduction scene, between Vyvian Joyeuse and Margaret Orleans, a specimen of a kind of dialogue nowhere to be found before, so far as I know, and giving proof that, if Praed had set himself to it, he might have started a new kind of novel.

PRAED.

It does not appear, however, that his fancy led him with any decided bent to prose composition, and he very early deserted it for verse; though he is said to have, at a comparatively late period of his short life, worked in harness as a regular leader-writer for the *Morning Post* during more than a year. No examples of this work of his have been reprinted, nor, so far as I know, does any means of identifying them exist, though I personally should like to examine them. He was still at Cambridge when he drifted into another channel, which was still not his own channel, but in which he feathered his oars under two different flags with no small skill and dexterity. Sir George Young has a very high idea of his uncle's political verse, and places him "first among English writers, before Prior, before Canning, before the authors of the 'Rolliad,' and far before Moore or any of the still anonymous contributors to the later London press." I cannot subscribe to this. Neither as Whig nor as Tory, neither as satirist of George the Fourth nor as satirist of the Reform Bill, does Praed seem to me to have been within a hundred miles of that elder schoolfellow of his who wrote

PRAED.

> All creeping creatures, venomous and low,
> Still blasphemous or blackguard, praise Lepaux.

He has nothing for sustained wit and ease equal to the best pieces of the "Fudge Family" and the "Two-penny Postbag"; and (for I do not know why one should not praise a man because he happens to be alive and one's friend) I do not think he has the touch of the true political satirist as Mr. Traill has it in "Professor Baloonatics Craniocracs," or in that admirable satire on democracy which is addressed to the "Philosopher Crazed, from the Island of Crazes."

PRAED.

Indeed, by mentioning Prior, Sir George seems to put himself rather out of court. Praed *is* very nearly if not quite Prior's equal, but the sphere of neither was politics. Prior's political pieces are thin and poor beside his social verse, and with rare exceptions I could not put anything political of Praed's higher than the shoe-string of "Araminta." Neither of these two charming poets seems to have felt seriously enough for political satire. Matthew, we know, played the traitor; and though Mackworth ratted to my own side, I fear it must be confessed that he did rat. I can only discover in his political verse two fixed principles, both of which no doubt did him credit, but which hardly, even when taken together, amount to a sufficient political creed. The one was fidelity to Canning and his memory: the other was impatience of the cant of the reformers. He could make admirable fun of Joseph Hume, and of still smaller fry like Waithman; he could attack Lord Grey's nepotism and doctrinairism fiercely enough. Once or twice, or, to be fair, more than once or twice, he struck out a happy, indeed a brilliant flash. He was admirable at what Sir George Young calls, justly enough, "political patter songs" such as,

Young widowhood shall lose its weeds,
  Old kings shall loathe the Tories,
And monks be tired of telling beads,
  And Blues of telling stories;
And titled suitors shall be crossed,
  And famished poets married,
And Canning's motion shall be lost,
  And Hume's amendment carried;
And Chancery shall cease to doubt,
  And Algebra to prove,
And hoops come in, and gas go out
  Before I cease to love.

He hit off an exceedingly savage and certainly not wholly just "Epitaph on the King of the Sandwich Islands" which puts the conception of George the Fourth that Thackeray afterwards made popular, and contains these felicitous lines:

The people in his happy reign,
  Were blessed beyond all other nations:
Unharmed by foreign axe and chain,
  Unhealed by civic innovations;
They served the usual logs and stones,
  With all the usual rites and terrors,
And swallowed all their fathers' bones,
  And swallowed all their fathers' errors.

When the fierce mob, with clubs and knives,
  All swore that nothing should prevent them,
But that their representatives
  Should actually represent them,
He interposed the proper checks,
  By sending troops, with drums and banners,
To cut their speeches short, and necks,
  And break their heads, to mend their manners.

Occasionally in a sort of middle vein between

politics and society he wrote in the "patter" style just noticed quite admirable things like "Twenty-eight and Twenty-nine." Throughout the great debates on Reform he rallied the reformers with the same complete and apparently useless superiority of wit and sense which has often, if not invariably, been shown at similar crises on the losing side. And once, on an ever-memorable occasion, he broke into those famous and most touching "Stanzas on seeing the Speaker Asleep" which affect one almost to tears by their grace of form and by the perennial and indeed ever-increasing applicability of their matter.

PRAED.

Sleep, Mr. Speaker: it's surely fair,
If you don't in your bed, that you should in your chair:
Longer and longer still they grow,
Tory and Radical, Aye and No;
Talking by night and talking by day;
Sleep, Mr. Speaker; sleep, sleep while you may.

Sleep, Mr. Speaker: slumber lies
Light and brief on a Speaker's eyes—
Fielden or Finn, in a minute or two,
Some disorderly thing will do;
Riot will chase repose away;
Sleep, Mr. Speaker; sleep, sleep while you may.

Sleep, Mr. Speaker; Cobbett will soon
Move to abolish the sun and moon;
Hume, no doubt, will be taking the sense
Of the House on a saving of thirteen-pence;
Grattan will growl or Baldwin bray;
Sleep, Mr. Speaker; sleep, sleep while you may.

Sleep, Mr. Speaker: dream of the time
When loyalty was not quite a crime,
When Grant was a pupil in Canning's school,
And Palmerston fancied Wood a fool.
Lord, how principles pass away!
Sleep, Mr. Speaker; sleep, sleep while you may.

Sleep, Mr. Speaker; sweet to men
Is the sleep that comes but now and then;
Sweet to the sorrowful, sweet to the ill,
Sweet to the children who work in a mill.
You have more need of sleep than they,
Sleep, Mr. Speaker; sleep, sleep while you may.

But the chief merit of Praed's political verse as a whole seems to me to be that it kept his hand in, and enabled him to develop and refine the trick, above referred to, of playing on words so as to give a graceful turn to verse composed in his true vocation.

Of the verse so composed there are more kinds than one; though perhaps only in two kinds is the author absolutely at his best. There is first a certain class of pieces which strongly recall Macaulay's "Lays" and may have had some connexion of origin with them. Of course those who are foolish enough to affect to see nothing good in "The Battle of the Lake Regillus," or "Ivry," or "The Armada," will not like "Cassandra," or "Sir Nicholas at Marston Moor," or the "Covenanter's Lament for Bothwell Brigg," or "Arminius." Nevertheless they are fine in their way. "Arminius" is too long, and it suffers from the obvious comparison with Cowper's far finer "Boadicea." But its best lines, such as the well-known

PRAED.

> I curse him by our country's gods,
> The terrible, the dark,
> The scatterers of the Roman rods,
> The quellers of the bark,

are excellent in the style, and "Sir Nicholas" is charming. But not here either did Apollo seriously wait for Praed. The later romances or tales are far better than the earlier. "The Legend of the Haunted Tree" shows in full swing that happy compound and contrast of sentiment and humour in which the writer excelled. And "The Teufelhaus" is, except "The Red Fisherman" perhaps, the best thing of its kind in English. These lines are good enough for anything:

> But little he cared, that stripling pale,
> For the sinking sun or the rising gale;
> For he, as he rode, was dreaming now,
> Poor youth, of a woman's broken vow,
> Of the cup dashed down, ere the wine was tasted,
> Of eloquent speeches sadly wasted,
> Of a gallant heart all burnt to ashes,
> And the Baron of Katzberg's long moustaches.

And these:

> Swift as the rush of an eagle's wing,
> Or the flight of a shaft from Tartar string,
> Into the wood Sir Rudolph went:
> Not with more joy the schoolboys run
> To the gay green fields when their task is done;
> Not with more haste the members fly,
> When Hume has caught the Speaker's eye.

But in "The Red Fisherman" itself there is nothing that is not good. It is very short, ten small pages only of some five-and-twenty lines each. But there is not a weak place in it from the moment when "the Abbot arose and closed his book" to the account of his lamentable and yet lucky fate and punishment whereof "none but he and the fisherman could tell the reason why." Neither of the two other practitioners who may be called the masters of this style, Hood and Barham, nor Praed himself elsewhere, nor any of his and their imitators has trodden the breadthless line between real terror and mere burlesque with so steady a foot.

PRAED.

Still not here was his "farthest," as the geographers say, nor in the considerable mass of smaller poems which practically defy classification. In them, as so often elsewhere in Praed, one comes across odd notes, stray flashes of genius which he never seems to have cared to combine or follow out, such as the unwontedly solemn "Time's Song," the best wholly serious thing that he has done, and the charming "L'Inconnue." But we find the perfect Praed, and we find him only, in the verses of society proper, the second part of the "Poems of Life and Manners" as they are headed, which began, as far as one can make out, to be written about 1826, and the gift of which Praed never lost, though he practised it little in the very last years of his life. Here, in a hundred pages, with a few to be added from elsewhere, are to be found some of the best-bred and best-natured verses within the English language, some of the most original and remarkable metrical experiments, a profusion of the liveliest fancy, a rush of the gayest rhyme. They begin with "The Vicar," *vir nullâ non donandus lauru.*

PRAED.

[Whose] talk was like a stream, which runs
With rapid change from rocks to roses:
It slipped from politics to puns,
It passed from Mahomet to Moses;
Beginning with the laws which keep
The planets in their radiant courses,
And ending with some precept deep
For dressing eels, or shoeing horses.

Three of the Vicar's companion "Everyday Characters" are good, but I think not so good as he; the fifth piece, however, "The Portrait of a Lady," is quite his equal.

You'll be forgotten—as old debts
By persons who are used to borrow;
Forgotten—as the sun that sets,
When shines a new one on the morrow;
Forgotten—like the luscious peach
That blessed the schoolboy last September;
Forgotten—like a maiden speech,
Which all men praise, but none remember.

Yet ere you sink into the stream
That whelms alike sage, saint, and martyr,
And soldier's sword, and minstrel's theme,
And Canning's wit, and Gatton's charter,
Here, of the fortunes of your youth,
My fancy weaves her dim conjectures,

Which have, perhaps, as much of truth
As passion's vows, or Cobbett's lectures.

Here, and perhaps here first, at least in the order of the published poems, appears that curious mixture of pathos and quizzing, sentiment and satire, which has never been mastered more fully or communicated more happily than by Praed. But not even yet do we meet with it in its happiest form: nor is that form to be found in "Josephine" which is much better in substance than in manner, or in the half-social, half-political patter of "The Brazen Head," or in "Twenty-eight and Twenty-nine." It sounds first in the "Song for the Fourteenth of February." No one, so far as I know, has traced any exact original[1] for the altogether admirable metre which, improved and glorified later in "The Letter of Advice," appears first in lighter matter still like this:

Shall I kneel to a Sylvia or Celia,
Whom no one e'er saw, or may see,
A fancy-drawn Laura Amelia,
An *ad libit* Anna Marie?
Shall I court an initial with stars to it,
Go mad for a G. or a J.,
Get Bishop to put a few bars to it,
And print it on Valentine's Day?

But every competent critic has seen in it the

[1] Since I wrote this I have been reminded by my friend Mr. Mowbray Morris of Byron's

I enter thy garden of roses,
Beloved and fair Haidee.

It is not impossible that this *is* the immediate original But Praed has so improved on it as to deserve a new patent.

origin of the more gorgeous and full-mouthed, if not more accomplished and dexterous, rhythm in which Mr. Swinburne has written "Dolores," and the even more masterly dedication of the first "Poems and Ballads." The shortening of the last line which the later poet has introduced is a touch of genius, but not perhaps greater than Praed's own recognition of the extraordinarily vivid and ringing qualities of the stanza. I profoundly believe that metrical quality is, other things being tolerably equal, the great secret of the enduring attraction of verse: and nowhere, not in the greatest lyrics, is that quality more unmistakable than in the "Letter of Advice." I really do not know how many times I have read it; but I never can read it to this day without being forced to read it out loud like a schoolboy and mark with accompaniment of hand-beat such lines as

PRAED.

Remember the thrilling romances
   We read on the bank in the glen:
Remember the suitors our fancies
   Would picture for both of us then.
They wore the red cross on their shoulder,
   They had vanquished and pardoned their foe—
Sweet friend, are you wiser or colder?
   My own Araminta, say "No!"

. . . . .

He must walk—like a god of old story
   Come down from the home of his rest;
He must smile—like the sun in his glory,
   On the buds he loves ever the best;

And oh! from its ivory portal
  Like music his soft speech must flow!
If he speak, smile, or walk like a mortal,
  My own Araminta, say "No!"

There are, metrically speaking, few finer couplets in English than the first of that second stanza. Looked at from another point of view, the mixture of the comic and the serious in the piece is remarkable enough; but not so remarkable, I think, as its extraordinary metrical accomplishment. There is not a note or a syllable wrong in the whole thing, but every sound and every cadence comes exactly where it ought to come, so as to be, in a delightful phrase of Southey's, "necessary and voluptuous and right."

It is no wonder that when Praed had discovered such a medium he should have worked it freely. But he never impressed on it such a combination of majesty and grace as in this letter of Medora Trevilian. As far as the metre goes I think the eight-lined stanzas of this piece better suited to it than the twelve-lined ones of "Good Night to the Season" and the first "Letter from Teignmouth," but both are very delightful. Perhaps the first is the best known of all Praed's poems, and certainly some things in it, such as

The ice of her ladyship's manners,
The ice of his lordship's champagne,

are among the most quoted. But this antithetical trick, of which Praed was so fond, is repeated a little often in it; and it seems to me to lack the freshness as well as the fire of the "Advice." On the other hand, the "Letter from Teignmouth" is the best thing that even Praed has ever done for combined grace and tenderness.

PRAED.

You once could be pleased with our ballads—
  To-day you have critical ears;
You once could be charmed with our salads—
  Alas! you've been dining with Peers;
You trifled and flirted with many—
  You've forgotten the when and the how;
There was one you liked better than any—
  Perhaps you've forgotten her now.
But of those you remember most newly,
  Of those who delight or enthral,
None love you a quarter so truly
  As some you will find at our Ball.

They tell me you've many who flatter,
  Because of your wit and your song:
They tell me—and what does it matter?—
  You like to be praised by the throng:
They tell me you're shadowed with laurel:
  They tell me you're loved by a Blue:
They tell me you're sadly immoral—
  Dear Clarence, that cannot be true!
But to me, you are still what I found you,
  Before you grew clever and tall;
And you'll think of the spell that once bound you;
  And you'll come—won't you come?—to our Ball!"

Is not that perfectly charming?

It is perhaps a matter of mere taste whether it is or is not more charming than pieces like "School and Schoolfellows" (the best of Praed's purely Eton poems) and "Marriage Chimes," in which, if not Eton, the Etonian set also comes in.

If I like these latter pieces less, it is not so much because of their more personal and less universal subjects as because their style is much less individual. The resemblance to Hood cannot be missed, and though I believe there is some dispute as to which of the two poets actually hit upon the particular style first, there can be little doubt that Hood attained to the greater excellence in it. The real sense and savingness of that doctrine of the "principal and most excellent things," which has sometimes been preached rather corruptly and narrowly, is that the best things that a man does are those that he does best. Now though

PRAED.

> I wondered what they meant by stock,
>   I wrote delightful Sapphics,

and

> With no hard work but Bovney stream,
>   No chill except Long Morning,

are very nice things, I do not think they are so good in their kind as the other things that I have quoted; and this, though the poem contains the following wholly delightful stanza in the style of the "Ode on a Distant Prospect of Clapham Academy":

> Tom Mill was used to blacken eyes
>   Without the fear of sessions;
> Charles Medlar loathed false quantities
>   As much as false professions;
> Now Mill keeps order in the land,
>   A magistrate pedantic;

> And Medlar's feet repose unscanned
> Beneath the wide Atlantic.

The same may even be said of "Utopia," a much-praised, often-quoted, and certainly very amusing poem, of "I'm not a Lover now," and of others, which are also, though less exactly, in Hood's manner. To attempt to distinguish between that manner and the manner which is Praed's own is a rather perilous attempt; and the people who hate all attempts at reducing criticism to principle, and who think that a critic should only say clever things about his subject, will of course dislike me for it. But that I cannot help. I should say then that Hood had the advantage of Praed in purely serious poetry; for Araminta's bard never did anything at all approaching "The Plea of the Midsummer Fairies," "The Haunted House," or a score of other things. He had also the advantage in pure broad humour. But where Praed excelled was in the mixed style, not of sharp contrast as in Hood's "Lay of the Desert Born" and "Demon Ship," where from real pity and real terror the reader suddenly stumbles into pure burlesque, but of wholly blended and tempered humour and pathos. It is this mixed style in which I think his note is to be found as it is to be found in no other poet, and as it could hardly be found in any but one with Praed's peculiar talent and temper combined with his peculiar advantages of education, fortune, and social atmosphere. He never had to "pump out sheets of fun" on a sick-bed for the printer's devil, like his less well-fated but assuredly not less well-gifted rival; and as his scholarship was exactly of the kind to refine, temper, and adjust his literary manner, so his society and circumstances were exactly of the kind to repress, or at least not to encourage, exuberance or boisterousness in his literary matter. There are I believe who call him trivial, even frivolous; and if this be done sincerely by any careful readers of "The Red Fisherman" and the "Letter of Advice" I fear I must peremptorily disable their judgment. But this appearance of levity is in great part due exactly to the perfect modulation and adjustment of his various notes. He never shrieks or guffaws: there is no horse-play in him, just as there is no tearing a passion to tatters. His slight mannerisms, more than once referred to, rarely exceed what is justified by good literary manners. His points are very often so delicate, so little insisted on or underlined, that a careless reader may miss them altogether; his "questionings" are so little "obstinate" that a careless reader may think them empty.

PRAED.

Will it come with a rose or a brier?
  Will it come with a blessing or curse?
Will its bonnets be lower or higher?
  Will its morals be better or worse?

The author of this perhaps seems to some a mere jesting Pilate, and if he does, they are quite right not to even try to like him.

I have seen disdainful remarks on those critics

PRAED.

who, however warily, admire a considerable number of authors, as though they were coarse and omnivorous persons, unfit to rank with the delicates who can only relish one or two things in literature. But this is a foolish mistake. "One to one" is not "cursedly confined" in the relation of book and reader; and a man need not be a Don Juan of letters to have a list of almost *mille e tre* loves in that department. He must indeed love the best or those among the best only, in the almost innumerable kinds, which is not a very severe restriction. And Praed is of this so fortunately numerous company. I do not agree with those who lament his early death on the ground of its depriving literature or politics of his future greatness. In politics he would most probably not have become anything greater than an industrious and respectable official; and in letters his best work was pretty certainly done. For it was a work that could only be done in youth. In his scholarly but not frigidly correct form, in his irregular sallies and flashes of a genius really individual as far as it went but never perhaps likely to go much farther, in the freshness of his imitations, in the imperfection of his originalities, Praed was the most perfect representative we have had or ever are likely to have of what has been called, with a perhaps reprehensible parody on great words, "the eternal undergraduate within us, who rejoices before life." He is thus at the very antipodes of Wertherism and Byronism, a light but gallant champion of cheerfulness and the joy of living. Although there is about him absolutely nothing artificial—the curse of the lighter poetry as a rule—and though he attains to deep pathos now and then, and once or twice (notably in "The Red Fisherman") to a kind of grim earnestness, neither of these things is his real *forte*. Playing with literature and with life, not frivolously or without heart, but with no very deep cares and no very passionate feeling, is Praed's attitude whenever he is at his best. And he does not play at playing as many writers do: it is all perfectly genuine. Even Prior has not excelled such lines as these in one of his early and by no means his best poems (an adaptation too), for mingled jest and earnest—

PRAED.

But Isabel, by accident,
Was wandering by that minute;
She opened that dark monument
And found her slave within it;
The clergy said the Mass in vain,
The College could not save me:
But life, she swears, returned again
With the first kiss she gave me.

Hardly, if at all, could he have kept up this attitude towards life after he had come to forty year; and he might have become either a merely intelligent and respectable person, which is most probable, or an elderly youth, which is of all things

PRAED.

most detestable, or a caterwauler, or a cynic, or a preacher. From all these fates the gods mercifully saved him, and he abides with us (the presentation being but slightly marred by the injudicious prodigality of his editors) only as the poet of Medora's musical despair lest Araminta should derogate, of the Abbot's nightmare sufferings at the hands of the Red Fisherman, of the plaintive appeal after much lively gossip—

> And you'll come—won't you come?—to our Ball,

of all the pleasures, and the jests, and the tastes, and the studies, and the woes, provided only they are healthy and manly, of Twenty-five. Unhappy is the person of whom it can be said that he neither has been, is, nor ever will be in the temper and circumstances of which Praed's verse is the exact and consummate expression; not much less unhappy he for whom that verse does not perform the best perhaps of all the offices of literature, and call up, it may be in happier guise than that in which they once really existed, the many beloved shadows of the past.

XIII

BORROW

IN this paper I do not undertake to throw any new light on the little-known life of the author of *Lavengro*. Among the few people who knew Borrow intimately, surely some one will soon be found who will give to the world an account of his curious life, and perhaps some specimens of those "mountains of manuscript" which, as he regretfully declares, never could find a publisher—an impossibility which, if I may be permitted to offer an opinion, does not reflect any great credit on publishers. For the present purpose it is sufficient to sum up the generally-known facts that Borrow was born in 1803 at East Dereham in Norfolk, his father being a captain in the army, who came of Cornish blood, his mother a lady of Norfolk birth and Huguenot extraction. His youth he has himself described in a fashion which nobody is likely to care to paraphrase. After the years of travel chronicled in *Lavengro*, he seems to have

BORROW.

found scope for his philological and adventurous tendencies in the rather unlikely service of the Bible Society; and he sojourned in Russia and Spain to the great advantage of English literature. This occupied him during the greater part of the years from 1830 to 1840. Then he came back to his native country—or, at any rate, his native district—married a widow of some property at Lowestoft, and spent the last forty years of his life at Oulton Hall, near the piece of water which is thronged in summer by all manner of sportsmen and others. He died but a few years ago; and even since his death he seems to have lacked the due meed of praise which the Lord Chief Justice of the equal foot usually brings, even to persons far less deserving than Borrow.

BORROW.

There is this difficulty in writing about him, that the audience must necessarily consist of fervent devotees on the one hand, and of complete infidels, or at least complete know-nothings, on the other. To any one who, having the faculty to understand either, has read *Lavengro* or *The Bible in Spain*, or even *Wild Wales*, praise bestowed on Borrow is apt to seem impertinence. To anybody else (and unfortunately the anybody else is in a large majority) praise bestowed on Borrow is apt to look like that very dubious kind of praise which is bestowed on somebody of whom no one but the praiser has ever heard. I cannot think of any single writer (Peacock himself is not an exception) who is in quite parallel case.

BORROW.

And, as usual, there is a certain excuse for the general public. Borrow kept himself, during not the least exciting period of English history, quite aloof from English politics, and from the life of great English cities. But he did more than this. He is the only really considerable writer of his time in any modern European nation who seems to have taken absolutely no interest in current events, literary and other. Putting a very few allusions aside, he might have belonged to almost any period. His political idiosyncrasy will be noticed presently; but he, who lived through the whole period from Waterloo to Maiwand, has not, as far as I remember, mentioned a single English writer later than Scott and Byron. He saw the rise, and, in some instances, the death, of Tennyson, Thackeray, Macaulay, Carlyle, Dickens. There is not a reference to any one of them in his works. He saw political changes such as no man for two centuries had seen, and (except the Corn Laws, to which he has some half-ironical allusions, and the Ecclesiastical Titles Bill, which stirred his one active sentiment) he has referred to never a one. He seems in some singular fashion to have stood outside of all these things. His Spanish travels are dated for us by references to Doña Isabel and Don Carlos, to Mr. Villiers and Lord Palmerston. But cut these dates out, and they might be travels of the last century. His Welsh book proclaims itself as written in the full course of the Crimean War; but excise a few passages which bear directly on that event, and the most ingenious critic would be puzzled to "place" the composition. Shakespeare, we know, was for all time, not of one age only; but I think we may say of Borrow, without too severely or conceitedly marking the difference, that he was not of or for any particular age or time at all. If the celebrated query in Longfellow's *Hyperion*, "What is time?" had been addressed to him, his most appropriate answer, and one which he was quite capable of giving, would have been, "I really don't know."

BORROW.

To this singular historical vagueness has to be added a critical vagueness even greater. I am sorry that I am unable to confirm or to gainsay at first hand Borrow's wonderfully high estimate of certain Welsh poets. But if the originals are anything like his translations of them, I do not think that Ab Gwilym and Lewis Glyn Cothi, Gronwy Owen and Huw Morris can have been quite such mighty bards as he makes out. Fortunately, however, a better test presents itself. In one book of his, *Wild Wales*, there are two estimates of Scott's works. Borrow finds in an inn a copy of *Woodstock* (which he calls by its less known title of *The Cavalier*), and decides that it is "trashy": chiefly, it would appear, because the portrait therein contained of Harrison, for whom Borrow seems, on one of his inscrutable principles of prejudice, to have had a liking, is not wholly favourable. He afterwards informs us that Scott's "Norman Horseshoe" (no very exquisite song at the best, and among Scott's somewhat less than exquisite) is "one of the most stirring lyrics of modern times," and that he sang it for a whole evening; evidently because it recounts a defeat of the Normans, whom Borrow, as he elsewhere tells us in sundry places, disliked for reasons more or less similar to those which made him like Harrison, the butcher. In other words, he could not judge a work of literature as literature at all. If it expressed sentiments with which he agreed, or called up associations which were pleasant to him, good luck to it; if it expressed sentiments with which he did not agree, and called up no pleasant associations, bad luck.

BORROW.

In politics and religion this curious and very John Bullish unreason is still more apparent. I suppose Borrow may be called, though he does not call himself, a Tory. He certainly was an unfriend to Whiggery, and a hater of Radicalism. He seems to have given up even the Corn Laws with a certain amount of regret, and his general attitude is quite Eldonian. But he combined with his general Toryism very curious Radicalisms of detail, such as are to be found in Cobbett (who, as appeared at last, and as all reasonable men should have always known, was really a Tory of a peculiar type), and in several other English persons. The

Church, the Monarchy, and the Constitution generally were dear to Borrow, but he hated all the aristocracy (except those whom he knew personally) and most of the gentry. Also, he had the odd Radical sympathy for anybody who, as the vernacular has it, was "kept out of his rights." I do not know, but I should think, that Borrow was a strong Tichbornite. In that curious book *Wild Wales*, where almost more of his real character appears than in any other, he has to do with the Crimean War. It was going on during the whole time of his tour, and he once or twice reports conversations in which, from his knowledge of Russia, he demonstrated beforehand to Welsh inquirers how improbable, not to say impossible, it was that the Russian should be beaten. But the thing that seems really to have interested him most was the case of Lieutenant P—— or Lieutenant Parry, whom he sometimes refers to in the fuller and sometimes in the less explicit manner. My own memories of 1854 are rather indistinct, and I confess that I have not taken the trouble to look up this celebrated case. As far as I can remember, and as far as Borrow's references here and elsewhere go, it was the doubtless lamentable but not uncommon case of a man who is difficult to live with, and who has to live with others. Such cases occur at intervals in every mess, college, and other similar aggregation of humanity. The person difficult to live with gets, to use an Oxford phrase, "drawn." If he is reformable he takes the lesson, and very likely becomes excellent friends with those who "drew" him. If he is not, he loses his temper, and evil results of one kind or another follow. Borrow's Lieutenant P—— seems unluckily to have been of the latter kind, and was, if I mistake not, recommended by the authorities to withdraw from a situation which, to him, was evidently a false and unsuitable one. With this Borrow could not away. He gravely chronicles the fact of his reading an "excellent article in a local paper on the case of Lieutenant P——"; and with no less gravity (though he was, in a certain way, one of the first humorists of our day) he suggests that the complaints of the martyred P—— to the Almighty were probably not unconnected with our Crimean disasters. This curious parochialism pursues him into more purely religious matters. I do not know any other really great man of letters of the last three-quarters of a century of whose attitude Carlyle's famous words, "regarding God's universe as a larger patrimony of Saint Peter, from which it were well and pleasant to hunt the Pope," are so literally true. It was not in Borrow's case a case of *sancta simplicitas*. He has at times flashes of by no means orthodox sentiment, and seems to have fought, and perhaps hardly won, many a battle against the army of the doubters. But when it comes to the Pope, he is as single-minded an enthusiast as John Bunyan

BORROW.

himself, whom, by the way, he resembles in more than one point. The attitude was, of course, common enough among his contemporaries; indeed any man who has reached middle life must remember numerous examples among his own friends and kindred. But in literature, and such literature as Borrow's, it is rare.

Yet again, the curiously piecemeal, and the curiously arbitrary character of Borrow's literary studies in languages other than his own, is noteworthy in so great a linguist. The entire range of French literature, old as well as new, he seems to have ignored altogether—I should imagine out of pure John Bullishness. He has very few references to German, though he was a good German scholar—a fact which I account for by the other fact, that in his earlier literary period German was fashionable, and that he never would have anything to do with anything that fashion favoured. Italian, though he certainly knew it well, is equally slighted. His education, if not his taste for languages, must have made him a tolerable (he never could have been an exact) classical scholar. But it is clear that insolent Greece and haughty Rome possessed no attraction for him. I question whether even Spanish would not have been too common a toy to attract him much, if it had not been for the accidental circumstances which connected him with Spain.

Lastly (for I love to get my devil's advocate

work over), in Borrow's varied and strangely attractive gallery of portraits and characters, most observers must perceive the absence of the note of passion. I have sometimes tried to think that miraculous episode of Isopel Berners and the Armenian verbs, with the whole sojourn of Lavengro in the dingle, a mere wayward piece of irony—a kind of conscious ascetic myth. But I am afraid the interpretation will not do. The subsequent conversation with Ursula Petulengro under the hedge might be only a companion piece; even the more wonderful, though much less interesting, dialogue with the Irish girl in the last chapters of *Wild Wales* might be so rendered by a hardy exegete. But the negative evidence in all the books is too strong. It may be taken as positively certain that Borrow never was "in love," as the phrase is, and that he had hardly the remotest conception of what being in love means. It is possible that he was a most cleanly liver—it is possible that he was quite the reverse: I have not the slightest information either way. But that he never in all his life heard with understanding the refrain of the "Pervigilium,"

BORROW.

> Cras amet qui nunquam amavit, quique amavit cras amet,

I take as certain.

The foregoing remarks have, I think, summed up all Borrow's defects, and it will be observed that even these defects have for the most part the attraction of a certain strangeness and oddity. If

BORROW.

they had not been accompanied by great and peculiar merits, he would not have emerged from the category of the merely bizarre, where he might have been left without further attention. But, as a matter of fact, all, or almost all, of his defects are not only counterbalanced by merits, but are themselves, in a great degree, exaggerations or perversions of what is intrinsically meritorious. With less wilfulness, with more attention to the literature, the events, the personages of his own time, with a more critical and common-sense attitude towards his own crotchets, Borrow could hardly have wrought out for himself (as he has to an extent hardly paralleled by any other prose writer who has not deliberately chosen supernatural or fantastic themes) the region of fantasy, neither too real nor too historical, which Joubert thought proper to the poet. Strong and vivid as Borrow's drawing of places and persons is, he always contrives to throw in touches which somehow give the whole the air of being rather a vision than a fact. Never was such a John-a-Dreams as this solid, pugilistic John Bull. Part of this literary effect of his is due to his quaint habit of avoiding, where he can, the mention of proper names. The description, for instance, of Old Sarum and Salisbury itself in *Lavengro* is sufficient to identify them to the most careless reader, even if the name of Stonehenge had not occurred on the page before; but they are not named. The description of Bettws-y-Coed in *Wild Wales*, though less poetical, is equally vivid. BORROW. Yet here it would be quite possible for a reader, who did not know the place and its relation to other named places, to pass without any idea of the actual spot. It is the same with his frequent references to his beloved city of Norwich, and his less frequent references to his later home at Oulton. A paraphrase, an innuendo, a word to the wise he delights in, but anything perfectly clear and precise he abhors. And by this means and others, which it might be tedious to trace out too closely, he succeeds in throwing the same cloudy vagueness over times as well as places and persons. A famous passage—perhaps the best known, and not far from the best he ever wrote—about Byron's funeral, fixes, of course, the date of the wondrous facts or fictions recorded in *Lavengro* to a nicety. Yet who, as he reads it and its sequel (for the separation of *Lavengro* and *The Romany Rye* is merely arbitrary, though the second book is, as a whole, less interesting than the former), ever thinks of what was actually going on in the very positive and prosaic England of 1824-25? The later chapters of *Lavengro* are the only modern *Roman d'Aventures* that I know. The hero goes "overthwart and endlong," just like the figures whom all readers know in Malory, and some in his originals. I do not know that it would be more surprising if Borrow had found Sir

BORROW.

Ozana dying at the chapel in Lyonesse, or had seen the full function of the Grail, though I fear he would have protested against that as popish. Without any apparent art, certainly without the elaborate apparatus which most prose tellers of fantastic tales use, and generally fail in using, Borrow spirits his readers at once away from mere reality. If his events are frequently as odd as a dream, they are always as perfectly commonplace and real for the moment as the events of a dream are—a little fact which the above-mentioned tellers of the above-mentioned fantastic stories are too apt to forget. It is in this natural romantic gift that Borrow's greatest charm lies. But it is accompanied and nearly equalled, both in quality and in degree, by a faculty for dialogue. Except Defoe and Dumas, I cannot think of any novelists who contrive to tell a story in dialogue and to keep up the ball of conversation so well as Borrow ; while he is considerably the superior of both in pure style and in the literary quality of his talk. Borrow's humour, though it is of the general class of the older English—that is to say, the pre-Addisonian—humorists, is a species quite by itself. It is rather narrow in range, a little garrulous, busied very often about curiously small matters, but wonderfully observant and true, and possessing a quaint dry savour as individual as that of some wines. A characteristic of this kind probably accompanies the romantic *ethos* more commonly than superficial judges both of life and literature are apt to suppose; but

BORROW.

the conjunction is nowhere seen better than in Borrow. Whether humour can or cannot exist without a disposition to satire co-existing, is one of those abstract points of criticism for which the public of the present day has little appetite. It is certain (and that is what chiefly concerns us for the present) that the two were not dissociated in Borrow. His purely satirical faculty was very strong indeed, and probably if he had lived a less retired life it would have found fuller exercise. At present the most remarkable instance of it which exists is the inimitable portrait-caricature of the learned Unitarian, generally known as "Taylor of Norwich." I have somewhere (I think it was in Miss Martineau's *Autobiography*) seen this reflected on as a flagrant instance of ingratitude and ill-nature. The good Harriet, among whose numerous gifts nature had not included any great sense of humour, naturally did not perceive the artistic justification of the sketch, which I do not hesitate to call one of the most masterly things of the kind in literature.

Another Taylor, the well-known French baron of that name, is much more mildly treated, though with little less skill of portraiture. As for "the publisher" of *Lavengro*, the portrait there, though very clever, is spoilt by rather too much evidence of personal animus, and by the absence of redeeming strokes; but it shows the same satiric power as the sketch of the worthy student of German who has had the singular ill-fortune to have his books quizzed by Carlyle, and himself quizzed by Borrow. It is a strong evidence of Borrow's abstraction from general society that with this satiric gift, and evidently with a total freedom from scruple as to its application, he should have left hardly anything else of the kind. It is indeed impossible to ascertain how much of the abundant character-drawing in his four chief books (all of which, be it remembered, are autobiographic and professedly historical) is fact and how much fancy. It is almost impossible to open them anywhere without coming upon personal sketches, more or less elaborate, in which the satiric touch is rarely wanting. The official admirer of "the grand Baintham" at remote Corcubion, the end of all the European world; the treasure-seeker, Benedict Mol; the priest at Cordova, with his revelations about the Holy Office; the Gibraltar Jew; are only a few figures out of the abundant gallery of *The Bible in Spain*. *Lavengro*, besides the capital and full-length portraits above referred to, is crowded with others hardly inferior, among which only one failure, the disguised priest with the mysterious name, is to be found. Not that even he has not good strokes and plenty of them, but that Borrow's prejudices prevented his hand from being free. But Jasper Petulengro, and Mrs. Hearne, and the girl Leonora, and Isopel, that

BORROW.

vigorous and slighted maid, and dozens of minor figures, of whom more presently, atone for him. *The Romany Rye* adds only minor figures to the gallery, because the major figures have appeared before; while the plan and subject of *Wild Wales* also exclude anything more than vignettes. But what admirable vignettes they are, and how constantly bitten in with satiric spirit, all lovers of Borrow know.

BORROW.

It is, however, perhaps time to give some more exact account of the books thus familiarly and curiously referred to; for Borrow most assuredly is not a popular writer. Not long before his death *Lavengro*, *The Romany Rye*, and *Wild Wales* were only in their third edition, though the first was nearly thirty, and the last nearly twenty, years old. *The Bible in Spain* had, at any rate in its earlier days, a wider sale, but I do not think that even that is very generally known. I should doubt whether the total number sold, during some fifty years, of volumes surpassed in interest of incident, style, character and description by few books of the century, has equalled the sale, within any one of the last few years, of a fairly popular book by any fairly popular novelist of to-day. And there is not the obstacle to Borrow's popularity that there is to that of some other writers, notably the already-mentioned author of *Crotchet Castle*. No extensive literary cultivation is necessary to read him. A good deal even of his peculiar charm may be missed by a prosaic or inattentive reader, and yet enough will remain. But he has probably paid the penalty of originality, which allows itself to be mastered by quaintness, and which refuses to meet public taste at least half-way. It is certainly difficult at times to know what to make of Borrow. And the general public, perhaps excusably, is apt not to like things or persons when it does not know what to make of them.

BORROW.

Borrow's literary work, even putting aside the "mountains of manuscript" which he speaks of as unpublished, was not inconsiderable. There were, in the first place, his translations, which, though no doubt not without value, do not much concern us here. There is, secondly, his early hackwork, his *Chaines de l'Esclavage*, which also may be neglected. Thirdly, there are his philological speculations or compilations, the chief of which is, I believe, his *Romano-Lavo-Lil*, the latest published of his works. But Borrow, though an extraordinary linguist, was a somewhat unchastened philologer, and the results of his life-long philological studies appear to much better advantage from the literary than from the scientific point of view. Then there is *The Gypsies in Spain*, a very interesting book of its kind, marked throughout with Borrow's characteristics, but for literary purposes merged to a great extent in *The Bible in Spain*. And, lastly, there are the four original books, as they may be called, which, at great leisure, and writing simply because he chose to write, Borrow produced during the twenty years of his middle age. He was in his fortieth year when, in 1842, he published *The Bible in Spain*. *Lavengro* came nearly ten years later, and coincided with (no doubt it was partially stimulated by) the ferment over the Ecclesiastical Titles Bill. Its second part, *The Romany Rye*, did not appear till six afterwards, that is to say, in 1857, and its resuscitation of quarrels, which the country had quite forgotten (and when it remembered them was rather ashamed of), must be pronounced unfortunate. Last, in 1862, came *Wild Wales*, the characteristically belated record of a tour in the principality during the year of the Crimean War. On these four books Borrow's literary fame rests. His other works are interesting because they were written by the author of these, or because of their subjects, or because of the effect they had on other men of letters, notably Longfellow and Mérimée, on the latter of whom Borrow had an especially remarkable influence. These four are interesting of themselves.

BORROW.

The earliest has been, I believe, and for reasons quite apart from its biblical subject perhaps deserves to be, the greatest general favourite, though its literary value is a good deal below that of *Lavengro*. *The Bible in Spain* records the journeys, which, as an agent of the Bible Society,

Borrow took through the Peninsula at a singularly interesting time, the disturbed years of the early reign of Isabel Segunda. Navarre and Aragon, with Catalonia, Valencia, and Murcia, he seems to have left entirely unvisited; I suppose because of the Carlists. Nor did he attempt the southern part of Portugal; but Castile and Leon, with the north of Portugal and the south of Spain, he quartered in the most interesting manner, riding everywhere with his servant and his saddle-bag of Testaments at, I should suppose, a considerable cost to the subscribers of the Society and at, it may be hoped, some gain to the propagation of evangelical principles in the Peninsula, but certainly with the results of extreme satisfaction to himself and of a very delightful addition to English literature. He was actually imprisoned at Madrid, and was frequently in danger from Carlists, and brigands, and severely orthodox ecclesiastics. It is possible to imagine a more ideally perfect missionary; but it is hardly possible to imagine a more ideally perfect traveller. His early habits of roughing it, his gipsy initiation, his faculties as a linguist, and his other faculties as a born vagrant, certain to fall on his feet anywhere, were all called into operation. But he might have had all these advantages and yet lacked the extraordinary literary talent which the book reveals. In the first chapter there is a certain stiffness; but the passage of the Tagus in the second must have

BORROW.

told every competent reader in 1842 that he had to deal with somebody quite different from the run of common writers, and thenceforward the book never flags till the end. How far the story is rigidly historical I should be very sorry to have to decide. The author makes a kind of apology in his preface for the amount of fact which has been supplied from memory. I daresay the memory was quite trustworthy, and certainly adventures are to the adventurous. We have had daring travellers enough during the last half-century, but I do not know that any one has ever had quite such a romantic experience as Borrow's ride across the Hispano-Portuguese frontier with a gipsy *contrabandista*, who was at the time a very particular object of police inquiry. I daresay the interests of the Bible Society required the adventurous journey to the wilds of Finisterra. But I feel that if that association had been a mere mundane company and Borrow its agent, troublesome shareholders might have asked awkward questions at the annual meeting. Still, this sceptical attitude is only part of the official duty of the critic, just as, of course, Borrow's adventurous journeys into the most remote and interesting parts of Spain were part of the duty of the colporteur. The book is so delightful that, except when duty calls, no one would willingly take any exception to any part or feature of it. The constant change of scene, the romantic episodes of adventure, the

BORROW.

kaleidoscope of characters, the crisp dialogue, the quaint reflection and comment relieve each other without a break. I do not know whether it is really true to Spain and Spanish life, and, to tell the exact truth, I do not in the least care. If it is not Spanish it is remarkably human and remarkably literary, and those are the chief and principal things.

BORROW.

Lavengro, which followed, has all the merits of its predecessor and more. It is a little spoilt in its later chapters by the purpose, the antipapal purpose, which appears still more fully in *The Romany Rye.* But the strong and singular individuality of its flavour as a whole would have been more than sufficient to carry off a greater fault. There are, I should suppose, few books the successive pictures of which leave such an impression on the reader who is prepared to receive that impression. The word picture is here rightly used, for in all Borrow's books more or less, and in this particularly, the narrative is anything but continuous. It is a succession of dissolving views which grow clear and distinct for a time and then fade off into vagueness before once more appearing distinctly; nor has this mode of dealing with a subject ever been more successfully applied than in *Lavengro.* At the same time the mode is one singularly difficult of treatment by any reviewer. To describe *Lavengro* with any chance of distinctness to those who have not read it, it would be necessary to give a series of sketches in words, like those famous ones of the pictures in *Jane Eyre*. East Dereham, the Viper Collector, the French Prisoners at Norman Cross, the Gipsy Encampment, the Sojourn in Edinburgh (with a passing view of Scotch schoolboys only inferior, as everything is, to Sir Walter's history of Green-breeks), the Irish Sojourn (with the horse whispering and the "dog of peace,") the settlement in Norwich (with Borrow's compulsory legal studies and his very uncompulsory excursions into Italian, Hebrew, Welsh, Scandinavian, anything that obviously would not pay), the new meeting with the gipsies in the Castle Field, the fight—only the first of many excellent fights—these are but a few of the memories which rise to every reader of even the early chapters of this extraordinary book, and they do not cover its first hundred pages in the common edition. Then his father dies and the born vagrant is set loose for vagrancy. He goes to London, with a stock of translations which is to make him famous, and a recommendation from Taylor of Norwich to "the publisher." The publisher exacted something more than his pound of flesh in the form of Newgate Lives and review articles, and paid, when he did pay, in bills of uncertain date which were very likely to be protested. But Borrow won through it all, making odd acquaintances with a young man of fashion (his least lifelike sketch); with an apple-seller on London Bridge, who was something of a "fence"

BORROW.

BORROW.

and had erected Moll Flanders (surely the oddest patroness ever so selected) into a kind of patron saint; with a mysterious Armenian merchant of vast wealth, whom the young man, according to his own account, finally put on a kind of filibustering expedition against both the Sublime Porte and the White Czar, for the restoration of Armenian independence. At last, out of health with perpetual work and low living, out of employ, his friends beyond call, he sees destruction before him, writes *The Life and Adventures of Joseph Sell* (name of fortunate omen!) almost at a heat and on a capital, fixed and floating, of eighteen-pence, and disposes of it for twenty pounds by the special providence of the Muses. With this twenty pounds his journey into the blue distance begins. He travels, partly by coach, to somewhere near Salisbury, and gives the first of the curiously unfavourable portraits of stage coachmen, which remain to check Dickens's rose-coloured representations of Mr. Weller and his brethren. I incline to think that Borrow's was likely to be the truer picture. According to him, the average stage coachman was anything but an amiable character, greedy, insolent to all but persons of wealth and rank, a hanger-on of those who might claim either; bruiser enough to be a bully but not enough to be anything more; in short, one of the worst products of civilisation. From civilisation itself, however, Borrow soon disappears, as far as any traceable signs go. He journeys, not farther west but northwards, into the West Midlands and the marches of Wales. He buys a tinker's beat and fit-out from a feeble vessel of the craft, who has been expelled by "the Flaming Tinman," a half-gipsy of robustious behaviour. He is met by old Mrs. Hearne, the mother-in-law of his gipsy friend Jasper Petulengro, who resents a Gorgio's initiation in gipsy ways, and very nearly poisons him by the wily aid of her grand-daughter Leonora. He recovers, thanks to a Welsh travelling preacher and to castor oil. And then, when the Welshman has left him, comes the climax and turning-point of the whole story, the great fight with Jem Bosvile, "the Flaming Tinman." The much-abused adjective Homeric belongs in sober strictness to this immortal battle, which has the additional interest not thought of by Homer (for goddesses do not count) that Borrow's second and guardian angel is a young woman of great attractions and severe morality, Miss Isopel (or Belle) Berners, whose extraction, allowing for the bar sinister, is honourable, and who, her hands being fully able to keep her head, has sojourned without ill fortune in the Flaming Tinman's very disreputable company. Bosvile, vanquished by pluck and good fortune rather than strength, flees the place with his wife. Isopel remains behind and the couple take up their joint residence, a residence of perfect propriety, in this dingle, the exact locality of which I

BORROW.

have always longed to know, that I might make an autumnal pilgrimage to it. Isopel, Brynhild as she is, would apparently have had no objection to be honourably wooed. But her eccentric companion confines himself to teaching her "I love" in Armenian, which she finds unsatisfactory; and she at last departs, leaving a letter which tells Mr. Borrow some home truths. And, even before this catastrophe has been reached, *Lavengro* itself ends with a more startling abruptness than perhaps any nominally complete book before or since.

It would be a little interesting to know whether the continuation, *The Romany Rye*, which opens as if there had been no break whatever, was written continuously or with a break. At any rate its opening chapters contain the finish of the lamentable history of Belle Berners, which must induce every reader of sensibility to trust that Borrow, in writing it, was only indulging in his very considerable faculty of perverse romancing. The chief argument to the contrary is, that surely no man, however imbued with romantic perversity, would have made himself cut so poor a figure as Borrow here does without cause. The gipsies reappear to save the situation, and a kind of minor Belle Berners drama is played out with Ursula, Jasper's sister. Then the story takes another of its abrupt turns. Jasper, half in generosity it would appear, half in waywardness, insists on Borrow purchasing a thorough-bred horse which is for sale, advances the money, and despatches him across England to Horncastle Fair to sell it. The usual Lesage-like adventures occur, the oddest of them being the hero's residence for some considerable time as clerk and store-keeper at a great roadside inn. At last he reaches Horncastle, and sells the horse to advantage. Then the story closes as abruptly and mysteriously almost as that of *Lavengro*, with a long and in parts, it must be confessed, rather dull conversation between the hero, the Hungarian who has bought the horse, and the dealer who has acted as go-between. This dealer, in honour of Borrow, of whom he has heard through the gipsies, executes the wasteful and very meaningless ceremony of throwing two bottles of old rose champagne, at a guinea apiece, through the window. Even this is too dramatic a finale for Borrow's unconquerable singularity, and he adds a short dialogue between himself and a recruiting sergeant. And after this again there comes an appendix containing an *apologia* for *Lavengro*, a great deal more polemic against Romanism, some historical views of more originality than exactness, and a diatribe against gentility, Scotchmen, Scott, and other black beasts of Borrow's. This appendix has received from some professed admirers of the author a great deal more attention than it deserves. In the first place, it was evidently written in a fit of personal pique; in the second, it is chiefly argumentative, and Borrow had absolutely no argu-

BORROW.

mentative faculty. To say that it contains a great deal of quaint and piquant writing is only to say that its writer wrote it, and though the description of "Charlie-over-the-waterism" probably does not apply to any being who ever lived, except to a few school-girls of both sexes, it has a strong infusion of Borrow's satiric gift. As for the diatribes against gentility, Borrow has only done very clumsily what Thackeray had done long before without clumsiness. It can escape nobody who has read his books with a seeing eye that he was himself exceedingly proud, not merely of being a gentleman in the ethical sense, but of being one in the sense of station and extraction—as, by the way, the decriers of British snobbishness usually are, so that no special blame attaches to Borrow for the inconsistency. Only let it be understood, once for all, that to describe him as "the apostle of the ungenteel" is either to speak in riddles or quite to misunderstand his real merits and abilities.

BORROW.

I believe that some of the small but fierce tribe of Borrovians are inclined to resent the putting of the last of this remarkable series, *Wild Wales*, on a level with the other three. With such I can by no means agree. *Wild Wales* has not, of course, the charm of unfamiliar scenery and the freshness of youthful impression which distinguish *The Bible in Spain*; it does not attempt anything like the novel-interest of *Lavengro* and

The Romany Rye; and though, as has been pointed out above, something of Borrow's secret and mysterious way of indicating places survives, it is a pretty distinct itinerary over great part of the actual principality. I have followed most of its tracks on foot myself, and nobody who wants a Welsh guide-book can take a pleasanter one, though he might easily find one much less erratic. It may thus have, to superficial observers, a positive and prosaic flavour as compared with the romantic character of the other three. But this distinction is not real. The tones are a little subdued, as was likely to be the case with an elderly gentleman of fifty, travelling with his wife and stepdaughter, and not publishing the record of his travels till he was nearly ten years older. The localities are traceable on the map and in Murray, instead of being the enchanted dingles and the half-mythical woods of *Lavengro*. The personages of the former books return no more, though, with one of his most excellent touches of art, the author has suggested the contrast of youth and age by a single gipsy interview in one of the later chapters. Borrow, like all sensible men, was at no time indifferent to good food and drink, especially good ale; but the trencher plays in *Wild Wales* a part, the importance of which may perhaps have shocked some of our latter-day delicates, to whom strong beer is a word of loathing, and who wonder how on earth our grandfathers and fathers used to

BORROW.

dispose of "black strap." A very different set of readers may be repelled by the strong literary colour of the book, which is almost a Welsh anthology in parts. But those few who can boast themselves to find the whole of a book, not merely its parts, and to judge that whole when found, will be not least fond of *Wild Wales*. If they have, as every reader of Borrow should have, the spirit of the roads upon them, and are never more happy than when journeying on "Shanks his mare," they will, of course, have in addition a peculiar and personal love for it. It is, despite the interludes of literary history, as full of Borrow's peculiar conversational gift as any of its predecessors. Its thumbnail sketches, if somewhat more subdued and less elaborate, are not less full of character. John Jones, the Dissenting weaver, who served Borrow at once as a guide and a whetstone of Welsh in the neighbourhood of Llangollen; the "kenfigenous" Welshwoman who first, but by no means last, exhibited the curious local jealousy of a Welsh-speaking Englishman; the doctor and the Italian barometer-seller at Cerrig-y-Druidion; the "best Pridydd of the world" in Anglesey, with his unlucky addiction to beer and flattery; the waiter at Bala; the "ecclesiastical cat" (a cat worthy to rank with those of Southey and Gautier); the characters of the walk across the hills from Machynlleth to the Devil's Bridge; the scene at the public-house on the Glamorgan Border, where the above-mentioned jealousy comes out so strongly; the mad Irishwoman, Johanna Colgan (a masterpiece by herself); and the Irish girl, with her hardly inferior history of the faction-fights of Scotland Road (which Borrow, by a mistake, has put in Manchester instead of in Liverpool); these make a list which I have written down merely as they occurred to me, without opening the book, and without prejudice to another list, nearly as long, which might be added. *Wild Wales*, too, because of its easy and direct opportunity of comparing its description with the originals, is particularly valuable as showing how sober, and yet how forcible, Borrow's descriptions are. As to incident, one often, as before, suspects him of romancing, and it stands to reason that his dialogue, written long after the event, must be full of the "cocked-hat-and-cane" style of narrative. But his description, while it has all the vividness, has also all the faithfulness and sobriety of the best landscape-painting. See a place which Kingsley or Mr. Ruskin, or some other master of our decorative school, has described—much more one which has fallen into the hands of the small fry of their imitators—and you are almost sure to find that it has been overdone. This is never, or hardly ever, the case with Borrow, and it is so rare a merit, when it is found in a man who does not shirk description where necessary, that it deserves to be counted to him at no grudging rate.

BORROW.

But there is no doubt that the distinguishing feature of the book is its survey of Welsh poetical literature. I have already confessed that I am not qualified to judge the accuracy of Borrow's translations, and by no means disposed to over-value them. But any one who takes an interest in literature at all, must, I think, feel that interest not a little excited by the curious Old-Mortality-like peregrinations which the author of *Wild Wales* made to the birth-place, or the burial-place as it might be, of bard after bard, and by the short but masterly accounts which he gives of the objects of his search. Of none of the numerous subjects of his linguistic rovings does Borrow seem to have been fonder, putting Romany aside, than of Welsh. He learnt it in a peculiarly contraband manner originally, which, no doubt, endeared it to him; it was little known to and often ridiculed by most Englishmen, which was another attraction; and it was extremely unlikely to "pay" in any way, which was a third. Perhaps he was not such an adept in it as he would have us believe—the respected Cymmrodorion Society or Professor Rhys must settle that. But it needs no knowledge of Welsh whatever to perceive the genuine enthusiasm, and the genuine range of his acquaintance with the language from the purely literary side. When he tells us that Ab Gwilym was a greater poet than Ovid or Chaucer I feel considerable doubts whether he was quite competent to understand

BORROW.

Ovid and little or no doubt that he has done wrong to Chaucer. But when, leaving these idle comparisons, he luxuriates in details about Ab Gwilym himself, and his poems, and his lady loves, and so forth, I have no doubt about Borrow's appreciation (casual prejudices always excepted) of literature. Nor is it easy to exaggerate the charm which he has added to Welsh scenery by this constant identification of it with the men, and the deeds, and the words of the past.

BORROW.

Little has been said hitherto of Borrow's more purely literary characteristics from the point of view of formal criticism. They are sufficiently interesting. He unites with a general plainness of speech and writing, not unworthy of Defoe or Cobbett, a very odd and complicated mannerism, which, as he had the wisdom to make it the seasoning and not the main substance of his literary fare, is never disgusting. The secret of this may be, no doubt, in part sought in his early familiarity with a great many foreign languages, some of whose idioms he transplanted into English : but this is by no means the whole of the receipt. Perhaps it is useless to examine analytically that receipt's details, or rather (for the analysis may be said to be compulsory on any one who calls himself a critic), useless to offer its results to the reader. One point which can escape no one who reads with his eyes open is the frequent, yet not too abundant, repetition of the same or very similar words—a point wherein much of the secret of persons so dissimilar as Carlyle, Borrow, and Thackeray consists. This is a well-known fact—so well known indeed that when a person who desires to acquire style hears of it, he often goes and does likewise, with what result all reviewers know. The peculiarity of Borrow, as far as I can mark it, is that, despite his strong mannerism, he never relies on it as too many others, great and small, are wont to do. The character sketches, of which, as I have said, he is so abundant a master, are always put in the plainest and simplest English. So are his flashes of ethical reflection, which, though like all ethical reflections often one-sided, are of the first order of insight. I really do not know that, in the mint-and-anise-and-cummin order of criticism, I have more than one charge to make against Borrow. That is that he, like other persons of his own and the immediately preceding time, is wont to make a most absurd misuse of the word individual. With Borrow "individual" means simply "person": a piece of literary gentility of which he, of all others, ought to have been ashamed.

BORROW.

But such criticism has but very little propriety in the case of a writer, whose attraction is neither mainly nor in any very great degree one of pure form. His early critics compared him to Lesage, and the comparison is natural. But if it is natural, it is not extraordinarily critical. Both men wrote of vagabonds, and to some extent of picaroons; both neglected the conventionalities of their own language and literature; both had a singular knowledge of human nature. But Lesage is one of the most impersonal of all great writers, and Borrow is one of the most personal. And it is undoubtedly in the revelation of his personality that great part of his charm lies. It is, as has been fully acknowledged, a one-sided, wrong-headed, not always quite right-hearted personality. But it is intensely English, possessing at the same time a certain strain of romance which the other John Bulls of literature mostly lack, and which John Bunyan, the king of them all, only reached within the limits, still more limited than Borrow's, of purely religious, if not purely ecclesiastical, interests. A born grumbler; a person with an intense appetite for the good things of this life; profoundly impressed with, and at the same time sceptically critical of, the bad or good things of another life; apt, as he somewhere says himself, "to hit people when he is not pleased"; illogical; constantly right in general, despite his extremely roundabout ways of reaching his conclusion; sometimes absurd, and yet full of humour; alternately prosaic and capable of the highest poetry; George Borrow, Cornishman on the father's side and Huguenot on the mother's, managed to display in perfection most of the characteristics of what once was, and let us hope has not quite ceased to be, the English

BORROW.

BORROW.

type. If he had a slight overdose of Celtic blood and Celtic peculiarity, it was more than made up by the readiness of literary expression which it gave him. He, if any one, bore an English heart, though, as therc often has been in Englishmen, there was something perhaps more as well as something less than English in his fashion of expression.

To conclude, Borrow has—what after all is the chief mark of a great writer—distinction. "Try to be like somebody," said the unlucky critic-bookseller to Lamartine; and he has been gibbeted for it, very justly, for the best part of a century. It must be admitted that "try not to be like other people," though a much more fashionable, is likely to be quite as disastrous a recommendation. But the great writers, whether they try to be like other people or try not to be like them (and sometimes in the first case most of all), succeed only in being themselves, and that is what Borrow does. His attraction is rather complex, and different parts of it may, and no doubt do, apply with differing force to this and that reader. One may be fascinated by his pictures of an unconventional and open-air life, the very possibilities of which are to a great extent lost in our days, though patches of ground here and there in England (notably the tracts of open ground between Cromer and Wells in Borrow's own county) still recall them. To others he may be attractive for his sturdy patriotism, or his adventurous and wayward spirit, or his glimpses of superstition and romance. The racy downrightness of his talk; the axioms, such as that to the Welsh alewife, "The goodness of ale depends less upon who brews it than upon what it is brewed of"; or the sarcastic touches as that of the dapper shopkeeper, who, regarding the funeral of Byron, observed, "I, too, am frequently unhappy," may each and all have their votaries. His literary devotion to literature would, perhaps, of itself attract few; for, as has been hinted, it partook very much of the character of will-worship, and there are few people who like any will-worship in letters except their own; but it adds to his general attraction, no doubt, in the case of many. That neither it, nor any other of his claims, has yet forced itself as it should on the general public is an undoubted fact; a fact not difficult to understand, though rather difficult fully to explain, at least without some air of superior knowingness and taste. Yet he has, as has been said, his devotees, and I think they are likely rather to increase than to decrease. He wants editing, for his allusive fashion of writing probably makes a great part of him nearly unintelligible to those who have not from their youth up devoted themselves to the acquisition of useless knowledge. There ought to be a good life of him. The great mass of his translations, published and unpublished, and the smaller mass of his early hackwork, no

BORROW.

doubt deserve judicious excerption. If professed philologers were not even more ready than most other specialists each to excommunicate all the others except himself and his own particular Johnny Dods of Farthing's Acre, it would be rather interesting to hear what some modern men of many languages have to say to Borrow's linguistic achievements. But all these things are only desirable embellishments and assistances. His real claims and his real attractions are comprised in four small volumes, the purchase of which, under modern arrangements of booksellers, leaves some change out of a sovereign, and which will about half fill the ordinary bag used for briefs and dynamite. It is not a large literary baggage, and it does not attempt any very varied literary kinds. If not exactly a novelist in any one of his books, Borrow is a romancer, in the true and not the ironic sense of the word, in all of them. He has not been approached in merit by any romancer who has published books in our days, except Charles Kingsley; and his work, if less varied in range and charm than Kingsley's, has a much stronger and more concentrated flavour. Moreover, he is the one English writer of our time, and perhaps of times still farther back, who seems never to have tried to be anything but himself; who went his own way all his life long with complete indifference to what the public or the publishers liked, as well as to what canons of

BORROW.

literary form and standards of literary perfection seemed to indicate as best worth aiming at. A most self-sufficient person was Borrow, in the good and ancient sense, as well as, to some extent, in the sense which is bad and modern. And what is more, he was not only a self-sufficient person, but is very sufficient also to the tastes of all those who love good English and good literature.

BORROW.

APPENDIX A

DE QUINCEY

A SHORT time after the publication of my essay on De Quincey I learnt, to my great concern, that it had given offence to his daughter Florence, the widow of one of the heroes of the Indian Mutiny, Colonel Baird Smith. Mrs. Baird Smith complained, in a letter to the newspapers, that I had accused her father of untruthfulness, and requested the public to suspend their judgment until the publication of certain new documents, in the form of letters, which had been discovered. I might have replied, if my intent had been hostile, that little fault could be justly found with a critic of the existing evidence if new evidence were required to confute him. But as the very last intention that I had in writing the paper was to impute anything that can be properly called untruthfulness to De Quincey, I thought it better to say so and to wait for the further documents. In a subsequent private correspondence with Mrs. Baird Smith, I found that what had offended her (her complaints being at first quite general) was certain remarks on De Quincey's aristocratic acquaintances as appearing in the *Autobiography* and "not heard of afterwards," certain comments on the Malay incident and others like it, some on the mystery of her father's money affairs, and the passage on his general "impenetrability." The matter

DE QUINCEY.

is an instance of the difficulty of dealing with recent reputations, when the commentator gives his name. Some really unkind things have been said of De Quincey; my intention was not to say anything unkind at all, but simply to give an account of the thing "as it strikes" if not "a contemporary" yet a well-willing junior. Take for instance the Malay incident. We know from De Quincey himself that, within a few years, the truth of this famous story was questioned, and that he was accused of having borrowed it from something of Hogg's. He disclaimed this, no doubt truly. He protested that it was a faithfully recorded incident: but though the events were then fresh, he did not produce a single witness to prove that any Malay had been near Grasmere at the time. And so elsewhere. As I have remarked about Borrow, there are some people who have a knack of recounting truth so that it looks as if it never had been true. I have been informed by Mr. James Runciman that he himself once made considerable inquiries on the track of *Lavengro*, and found that that remarkable book is, to some extent at any rate, apparently historic. On the other hand I have been told by another Borrovian who knew Borrow (which I never did) that the *Life of Joseph Sell* never existed. In such cases a critic can only go on internal evidence, and I am sure that the vast majority of critics would decide against most of De Quincey's stories on that. I do not suppose that he ever, like Lamb, deliberately begat "lie-children": but opium-eating is not absolutely repugnant to delusion, and literary mystification was not so much the exception as the rule in his earlier time. As to his "impenetrability," I can only throw myself on the readers

DE QUINCEY.

of such memoirs and reminiscences as have been published respecting him. The almost unanimous verdict of his acquaintances and critics has been that he was in a way mysterious, and though no doubt this mystery did not extend to his children, it seems to have extended to almost every one else. I gather from Mrs. Baird Smith's own remarks that from first to last all who were concerned with him treated him as a person unfit to be trusted with money, and while his habit of solitary lodging is doubtless capable of a certain amount of explanation, it cannot be described as other than curious. I had never intended to throw doubt on his actual acquaintance with Lord Westport or Lady Carbery. These persons or their representatives were alive when the *Autobiography* was published, and would no doubt have protested if De Quincey had not spoken truly. But I must still hold that their total disappearance from his subsequent life is peculiar. Some other points, such as his mentioning Wilson as his "only intimate male friend" are textually cited from himself, and if I seem to have spoken harshly of his early treatment by his family I may surely shelter myself behind the touching incident, recorded in the biographies, of his crying on his deathbed, "My dear mother! then I was greatly mistaken." If this does not prove that he himself had entertained on the subject ideas which, whether false or true, were unfavourable, then it is purely meaningless.

DE QUINCEY.

In conclusion, I have only to repeat my regret that I should, by a perhaps thoughtless forgetfulness of the feelings of survivors, have hurt those feelings. But I think I am entitled to say that the view of De Quincey's character and cast of thought given in the text, while imputing nothing discreditable in intention, is founded on the whole published work and all the biographical evidence then accessible to me, and will not be materially altered by anything since published or likely to be so in future. The world, though often not quite right, is never quite wrong about a man, and it would be almost impossible that it should be wrong in face of such autobiographic details as are furnished, not merely by the *Autobiography* itself, but by a mass of notes spread over seven years in composition and full of personal idiosyncrasy. I not only acquit De Quincey of all serious moral delinquency,—I declare distinctly that no imputation of it was ever intended. It is quite possible that some of his biographers and of those who knew him may have exaggerated his peculiarities, less possible I think that those peculiarities should not have existed. But the matter, except for my own regret at having offended De Quincey's daughter, will have been a happy one if it results in a systematic publication of his letters, which, from the specimens already printed, must be very characteristic and very interesting. In almost all cases a considerable collection of letters is the most effective, and especially the most truth-telling, of all possible "lives." No letters indeed are likely to increase the literary repute of the author of the *Confessions* and of the *Cæsars*; but they may very well clear up and fill in the hitherto rather fragmentary and conjectural notion of his character, and they may, on the other hand, confirm that idea of both which, however false it may seem to his children, and others who were united to him by ties of affection, has commended itself to careful students of his published works.

DE QUINCEY.

APPENDIX B

LOCKHART

LOCKHART.

THE most singular instance of the floating dislike to Lockhart's memory, to which I have more than once referred in the text, occurred subsequently to the original publication of my essay, and not very long ago, when my friend Mr. Louis Stevenson thought proper to call Lockhart a "cad." This extraordinary *obiter dictum* provoked, as might have been expected, not a few protests, but I do not remember that Mr. Stevenson rejoined, and I have not myself had any opportunity of learning from him what he meant. I can only suppose that the ebullition must have been prompted by one of two things, the old scandal about the duel in which John Scott the editor of the *London* was shot, and a newer one, which was first bruited abroad, I think, in Mr. Sidney Colvin's book on Keats. Both of these, and especially the first, may be worth a little discussion.

I do not think that any one who examines Mr. Colvin's allegation, will think it very damaging. It comes to this, that Keats's friend Bailey met Lockhart in the house of Bishop Greig at Stirling, told him some particulars about Keats, extracted from him a promise that he would not use them against the poet, and afterwards thought he recognised some of the details in the *Blackwood* attack which ranks next to the famous *Quarterly* article. Here it is to be observed, first, that there is no sufficient evidence that Lockhart wrote this *Blackwood* article; secondly, that it is by no means certain that if he did, he was making, or considered himself to be making, any improper use of what he had heard; thirdly, that for the actual interview and its tenor we have only a vague *ex parte* statement made long after date.

LOCKHART.

The other matter is much more important, and as the duel itself has been mentioned more than once or twice in the foregoing pages, and as it is to this day being frequently referred to in what seems to me an entirely erroneous manner, with occasional implications that Lockhart showed the white feather, it may be well to give a sketch of what actually happened, as far as can be made out from the most trustworthy accounts, published and unpublished.

One of Lockhart's signatures in *Blackwood*—a signature which, however, like others, was not, I believe, peculiar to him—was "Zeta," and this Zeta assailed the Cockney school in a sufficiently scorpion-like manner. Thereupon Scott's magazine, the *London*, retorted, attacking Lockhart by name. On this Lockhart set out for London and, with a certain young Scotch barrister named Christie as his second, challenged Scott. But Scott refused to fight, unless Lockhart would deny that he was editor of *Blackwood*. Lockhart declared that Scott had no right to ask this, and stigmatised him as a coward. He then published a statement, sending at the same time a copy to Scott. In the published form the denial of editorship was made, in the one sent to Scott it was omitted. Thereupon Scott called Lockhart a liar. Of this Lockhart took no notice, but Christie his second did, and, an altercation taking place between them, Scott challenged Christie and they went out, Scott's second being Mr. P. G. Patmore, Christie's Mr. Traill, afterwards well known as a London police magistrate. Christie fired in the air, Scott fired at Christie and missed. Thereupon Mr. Patmore demanded a second shot, which, I am informed, could and should, by all laws of the duello, have been refused. Both principal and second on the other side were, however, inexperienced and probably unwilling to baulk their adversaries. Shots were again exchanged, Christie this time (as he can hardly be blamed for doing) taking aim at his adversary and wounding him mortally. Patmore fled the country, Christie and Traill took their trial and were acquitted.

LOCKHART.

I have elsewhere remarked that this deplorable result is said to have been brought on by errors of judgment on the part of more than one person. Hazlitt, himself no duellist and even accused of personal timidity, is said to have egged on Scott, and to have stung him by some remark of his bitter tongue into challenging Christie, and there is no doubt that Patmore's conduct was most reprehensible. But we are here concerned with Lockhart, not with them. As far as I understand the imputations made on him, he is charged either with want of straightforwardness in omitting part of his explanation in the copy sent to Scott, or with cowardice in taking no notice of Scott's subsequent lie direct, or with both. Let us examine this.

LOCKHART.

At first sight the incident of what, from the most notorious action of Lord Clive, we may call the "red and white treaties" seems odd. But it is to be observed, first, that Lockhart could not be said to conceal from Scott what he published to all the world; secondly, that his conduct was perfectly consistent throughout. He had challenged Scott, who had declined to go out. Having offered his adversary satisfaction, he was not bound to let him take it with a proviso, or to satisfy his private inquisitiveness. But if not under menace, but considering Scott after his refusal as unworthy the notice of a gentleman, and not further to be taken into account, he chose to inform the public of the truth, he had a perfect right to do so. And it is hardly necessary to say that it was the truth that he was not editor of *Blackwood.*

This consideration will also account for his conduct in not renewing his challenge after Scott's offensive words. He had offered the man satisfaction and had been refused. No one is bound to go on challenging a reluctant adversary. At all times Lockhart seems to have been perfectly ready to back his opinion, as may be seen from a long affair which had happened earlier, in connection with the "Baron Lauerwinkel" matter. There he had promptly come forward and in his own name challenged the anonymous author of a pamphlet bearing the title of "Hypocrisy Unveiled." The anonym had, like Scott, shirked, and had maintained his anonymity. (Lord Cockburn says it was an open secret, but I do not know who he was.) Thereupon Lockhart took no further notice, just as he did in the later matter, and I do not believe that a court of honour in any country would find fault with him. At any rate, I think that we are entitled to know, much more definitely than I have ever seen it stated, what the charge against him is. We may indeed blame him in both these matters, and perhaps in others, for neglecting the sound rule that anonymous writing should never be personal. If he did this, however, he is in the same box with almost every writer for the press in his own generation, and with too many in this. I maintain that in each case he promptly gave the guarantee which the honour of his time required, and which is perhaps the only possible guarantee, that of being ready to answer in person for what he had written impersonally. This was all he could do, and he did it.

LOCKHART.

INDEX

THE END